The Tahltan Indians

George Thornton Emmons

UNIVERSITY OF PENNSYLVANIA

THE UNIVERSITY MUSEUM

ANTHROPOLOGICAL PUBLICATIONS

VOLUME IV

PHILADELPHIA
THE UNIVERSITY MUSEUM
1911–1914

CONTENTS.

UNIVERSITY OF PENNSYLVANIA
THE MUSEUM
ANTHROPOLOGICAL PUBLICATIONS
VOL. IV   NO. I

THE TAHLTAN INDIANS

BY

G. T. EMMONS

ILLUSTRATED BY SPECIMENS IN THE
GEORGE G. HEYE COLLECTION

PHILADELPHIA
PUBLISHED BY THE UNIVERSITY MUSEUM
1911

CONTENTS

INTRODUCTION

The Tahltan form the southwesternmost division of the Nahane, a branch of that great interior aboriginal family, variously known as Déné, Tinneh, and Athapascan, that ranges across the breadth of the North American continent almost from ocean to ocean, and is found under many varied conditions of territory and climate from Mexico to beyond the Arctic circle.

The Nahane, "People of the West," constitute an outpost of the Déné culture. They occupy, or rather roam over, that considerable area of northern British Columbia and the adjacent Northwest Territories stretching from the headwaters of Nass river to the uplands of the Mackenzie, and included between the Rocky mountains and the Coast range — a broad, broken plateau the drainage of which is distributed by three great river systems to the Pacific, Bering sea, and the Arctic. This great and almost inaccessible stretch is eroded by glacial action and rent by the convulsions of nature, and in parts is little known even to the resident native. The four divisions which constitute the Nahane are separate and distinct tribes, independent in government and in geographic distribution, but with only dialectic differences in their speech. In their mode of living they are similar to one another except where they have been influenced by their neighbors.

The Taku (who are to be distinguished from the Tlingit Taku), one of the divisions of the Nahane, occupy the basin of Taku river and its tributaries, and the lake region about Atlin, together with the southern sources of Lewis river; but within the past few years, particularly since the gold excitement of the Klondike, they have deserted their old villages and have scattered, some seeking work in the mining camps, others settling among the Tlingit Taku of the coast at Takuan, near the head of Stevens Passage in Alaska, while a few have joined the

Tahltan. The two eastern and northern divisions are known generally as Kaska, a corruption of the native name of McDane creek, a small affluent of Dease river, where these people assemble in summer to fish and trade. They are a primitive, nomadic people, hunters of big game, who wander in search of their food supply as changes of season demand. Their territory extends from Dease lake and Liard river to the Mackenzie mountains.

The Tahltan constitute the fourth division of the Nahane; they are centered about the upper reaches of the Stikine, and as far back as their traditions extend their dwelling places always have been thereabout. Their hunting grounds, however, cover an extended area, including the drainage basin of the Stikine and its tributaries as far down as the mouth of the Iskoot, the interlocking sources of the Nass, the lower half of Dease lake, and some of the southern branches of the Taku. The Nass region as a hunting ground was always in dispute with the Nishka, and was the cause of bitter feuds and disastrous wars that ever kept these two peoples apart. As an old Tahltan expressed the situation, "the upper Nass land is ours, and when we find a Nishka hunting there, we kill him." Rightfully the upper half of Dease lake was Kaska territory, but these more simple and primitive people, with little or no tribal organization, were dominated by the Tahltan, on whom in later years they were dependent for the products of civilization, particularly arms and ammunition, and so in time they have been compelled to share their half of the lake, and even their land beyond, along the river, with their more powerful neighbors. Their northern hunting grounds, bordering on the Sheslay and the Nahlin, were always in dispute with the Taku much as was the Nass region, and the right of might was the principal factor in determining the boundary at different periods. But to-day, with the decrease in population, the establishment of trading posts and the administration of law, peace reigns supreme, past differences are forgotten and the two peoples are as one. A strange overlapping of Tahltan and Stikine Tlingit territory occurred on the river from just below Glenora to Telegraph creek, a distance of some fifteen miles. Here the Tlingit claimed the exclusive fishing rights of all the salmon streams along the northern shore, and the ownership of the contiguous berry fields, leaving the main river, as well as all hunting rights, out of account. The value of these privileges to the coast people was of more than seeming importance, for while salmon which was their staple food supply, was even more abundant on the coast, yet the humid climate rendered the curing uncertain, whereas the dry atmosphere and continuous sunshine of the interior promised certainty; and the abundance of berries, particularly the soapberry and the cranberry, so esteemed for winter use, are not indigenous to the coast.

How or when this territorial claim originated or was established is wholly missing from the history of both peoples. Certain of the Stikine families of the Tlingit appropriated the interior trade and at prearranged times they ascended the river to or beyond Telegraph creek, where they met the Tahltan and exchanged the products of the coast, and later those of civilization for furs and caribou skins. This barter was mutually advantageous, and was a factor in the promotion of peace; but the better armed and more savage Tlingit was master of the situation and never permitted the Déné to penetrate to the coast country.

During the Hudson's Bay Company's lease of the Alaska littoral, a Tahltan chief wished to see a ship that was anchored off the mouth of the Stikine river. But permission to descend to salt water, and a safe conduct, were granted to him by a Stikine chief, only upon the payment of five hundred beaver skins. Some time after the establishment of Dominion authority at Glenora on the Stikine, the Tahltan protested against this encroachment of the coast people, and the waters were declared open to all. This would show that at heart the Tahltan never acknowledged the right of this occupancy, but through necessity accepted a condition that they were unable to combat.

The account of the Tahltan here presented was obtained during the summers of 1904 and 1906.

To the patient and kindly investigations of Doctor Frederick Ingles, resident physician and missionary among the Tahltan, and to Warburton Pike, Esq., of Victoria, B. C., I am under deep obligations, for much valuable information.

The illustrations are after photographs made by the author and from photographs and drawings of objects in the George G. Heye collection now in the University Museum.

THE TAHLTAN COUNTRY

The country of the Tahltan may be divided into two distinct physiographical and climatic areas each with its characteristic flora and fauna. The lower valley of the Stikine from just below Glenora to the coast, a direct distance of about eighty miles, is included within the coastal range and constitutes a region of great humidity, with leaden skies and an annual precipitation equalling if not exceeding that of the coast which reaches a mean of eighty-six inches. The snowfall thereabouts is excessive, and accounts for the extensive glaciers that fill the valleys; and long after spring has opened in the colder interior the lower river flats are covered with their burden of snow and ice. The general trend of the mountains is parallel with the coast, but the ridges present so little uniformity in direction, that the impression is given of mountains piled one upon another, a chaotic, rugged mass of rock with peaks reaching an altitude of eight thousand to ten thousand feet. The more equable climate and the constant rain induce a luxuriant vegetation. Forests of spruce, fir, cedar and hemlock cover the mountain slopes to the limit of tree growth, while in the river valleys cottonwoods grow to considerable size, and groves of alder and willow, with the devil's club and berry bushes, form an almost impenetrable barrier. Animal life is greatly wanting here. The mountain goat, the marmot, and bears of the brown and black species live in the mountains, while otter, beaver, marten, mink, ermine, porcupine, wolves, and foxes are found in limited numbers in the lower lands. Grouse, ptarmigan, eagles, ravens, and crows are the most numerous of the permanent feathered residents, while spring and fall are marked by extensive migrations of wild fowl about the water courses. It may be pertinent

9

to remark here, that this region which may be characterized as the wet belt has never been inhabited by either Tahltan or Tlingit in the sense that they have permanently occupied it and it is scarcely more popular as a hunting ground owing to its poverty and inaccessibility.

Beyond Glenora, which is at the inland limit of the coastal mountains, a wholly different character of country is found: one that approximates the more southerly dry belt of British Columbia. The land is rolling and much broken. The effect of glacial action is everywhere evident in the well rounded hills and the level valley floors of silt and clay through which the rivers have cut deep cañons. At many points the basaltic flow speaks of volcanic energies antedating the ice period. Here climatic conditions are localized by proximity to greater altitudes, for while about the Tahltan river there is scarcely any rainfall and the depth of snow hardly exceeds eighteen inches, beyond in the vicinity of the Cassiar mountains, the precipitation greatly increases. The extremes of temperature are very marked. The heat of summer, often reaching almost 100° F., is followed by excessive cold in winter when the mercury falls to −60° F. Spring opens in May, and ice commences to run in the streams in October. The rivers flow through narrow cañons so far below the land level that they do not water it and with scarcely any rainfall the soil becomes so parched that the possibility of raising the commonest garden produce becomes a question of irrigation. The tree growth is small and white spruce is the only available building timber. The black pine, spruce, aspen, white birch, alder, and willow commonly abound, while thickets of rose, service berry, and cranberry frequently occur. Much of the country presents the appearance of having been burnt over, and when open and not timbered the arid soil sustains but a sparse growth of grass and vines. This is a country of big game, and animal life is most abundant. Caribou and moose abound. The former has always constituted the principal food supply of the native, as well as his chief dependence for clothing and household and hunting implements. The mountain goat, the mountain sheep and the marmot are found on the higher lands. The beaver, fisher, mink, marten, and ermine are found about the rivers and lakes, and the grizzly bear and black bear, the wolf, the red fox with its varieties the cross, silver and black fox, the wolverene, lynx, porcupine, rabbit, several species of tree and ground squirrel, rats and mice are found everywhere. Of birds, grouse and ptarmigan are the most important from an economic point of view. This interior region is the home of the Tahltan, for while his permanent habitations may be few, he travels and hunts over the entire area and looks to it for his maintenance.

Salmon and trout are abundant in the rivers during summer and early fall, while whitefish are taken in considerable numbers from Dease lake.

HISTORY AND TRIBAL DIVISIONS

Historical data relating to the Tahltan are meagre. Prior to the Cassiar gold excitement of 1874, when the country was invaded by a horde of prospectors, the difference between them and the many other nomads of the great interior Northwest had not been recognized. As early as 1799 trading vessels visited the waters about the mouth of the Stikine, attracted by the furs from the interior. In 1834 the Hudson's Bay Company, keenly alive to the wealth of this section, made two ineffectual attempts to plant trading posts on the river for the purpose of controlling this trade. In that year John M. McLeod, a chief trader of the Company, following up the Liard river, discovered Dease lake, which he named, and crossing to the headwaters of the Stikine, reached the mouth of the Tuya. In 1836 a party was sent out from Fort Halkett to establish a post thereabouts, but returned without accomplishing any results through fear of the hostility of a reported party of natives. In 1838, Robert Campbell, acting for the Company, spent the winter at Dease lake, but was so harassed by the coast Tlingit, who claimed the sole right to trade in this region, that the project was abandoned and no further attempt was made to reach the Tahltan directly until 1867, when a small store was established on the lower river by a French Canadian, in the interest of the Hudson's Bay Company.

At the time these earlier efforts were being made to cross the mountains from the eastward, the Company fitted out the ship *Driard* for the purpose of establishing a factory and a colony on the lower Stikine, but this attempt was frustrated by the Russian authorities at Sitka, who dispatched two armed vessels and hastily constructed a rude fort, which they named Fort Dionysius, on Etolin Island, where Wrangel now stands. The controversy that ensued was adjusted in 1837 by the lease of the Alaska littoral, which in 1840 was turned over to the Hudson's Bay Company, and the coast Indians continued in control of the interior fur trade. In 1861, ".Buck" Choquette, a French Canadian, discovered placer gold in the river bottom below Glenora, which brought some white men into the country, and resulted in desultory prospecting until 1874, when the Cassiar excitement occurred, since which time the natives have been in constant contact with the whites, greatly to their disadvantage, as smallpox was introduced from the coast in 1864, and again in 1868.

In writing the term *Tahltan* I have conformed to the semi-official and generally accepted spelling, although Father A. G. Morice, in his "Notes on the Western Déné," says that it should be "*Thalhthan*, a contraction of *Thasaelhthan*, from *tha* or *thu*, water, and *saelhthan*, a verb that refers to some heavy object lying thereon."[1]   I found widely divergent opinions regarding

---

[1] A similar explanation of its meaning was given to me by one of the older men of the tribe in relating the story of the origin of his family. The discoverers of the land were two

the origin and derivation of the tribal name. The older people generally agree that it is from some foreign tongue, while others ascribe it to *thalla-a*, 'point,' from the first living place on the rocky tongue of land between Stikine and Tahltan rivers; and still others claim that it originated from the exhibition or giving away of a piece of steel, *thal*, by a chief at a great feast given at this point in early days, in celebration of the bringing out of his daughter. But the local name of this people was taken from the first settlement at the mouth of the Tahltan river. *Tutcher anne*, 'where the fish (salmon) jump up the little water' (Tahltan river), or, 'when the fish leave the water for the land,' referring to the stranding of the salmon as they work their way over the shallows in the smaller river. This term, contracted to *Tchaane*, was, I believe, used only among themselves, while *Tahltan* was a later designation from a foreign source that has become fastened upon them since the advent of Europeans. The coast Tlingit included them in the general designation *Giv-na-na*, 'stranger people,' just as the Tahltan call them *To-tee-heen*, 'people of the water.'

The eastern divisions of the Nahane are said to be patriarchal in government, with but a loosely organized social system. It is probable that the Tahltan were originally the same; but at some later period they borrowed the social organization of their Tlingit neighbors of the coast, which is founded on matriarchy and is dependent on the existence of two exogamous phratries which marry one with the other and which supplement each other on all occasions of ceremony. These phratries are known as *Cheskea da*, 'one family raven,' and *Cheona da*, 'one family wolf,' and from their principal totemic emblems may be thus distinguished as *Cheskea*, Raven, and *Cheona*, Wolf. Of the former there is but one family, the Kartch-ottee; of the latter there are

women who met on opposite banks of Tahltan river near its junction with the Stikine. It was the summer season when the salmon were running in from the sea. After the first greeting, one asked the other what it was that she saw on the surface of the water, and the other replied, "something heavy going up the little water," referring to the fish working their way up through the rapids of the smaller stream.

three families, the Tuck-clar-way-tee, the Tal-ar-ko-tin, and the Nan-yi-ee. Besides the phratral crest which is the birthright of every individual, the subdivisions or families assume other emblems, which may be displayed to the exclusion of the former. In explanation of this subdivision among the Tlingit I believe that originally the phratries consisted of two families and that with the increase in numbers, parties went forth to seek new homes and in time took upon themselves the functions of independent families and assumed new crests while always retaining that of the phratry. Strange people coming among them took their places as separate families within the group.

(1). The Tuckclarwaytee claim to be the progenitors of the Tahltan people, and this is generally conceded by the other families. Their early home is placed in the interior country, about the head waters of the Nass, and after the flood—an epoch in the history of all the coast peoples—a branch of those who survived migrated northward and settled in the lake region where the Yukon has its source.

In after years two women, one from the sources of the Nass and the other from Tagish lake, wandered from their homes and met on the banks of Tahltan river at its mouth. The woman from the south said she had journeyed over a great sand country and that she was worn and tired, and now that she had met her sister of the north they would stop here and make their home, and that they would call themselves, from the region of travels, *Tuck-clar-way-tee*, 'back-sand family.' But the accepted meaning of this name by the several branches of this people that have settled among the Tlingit of the coast is 'the company from back (the interior), and in numbers like the grains of sand on the shore.' The Tagish woman walked with a copper staff, which she planted in the ground to mark their living place on the site of the present fishing village of *Tutcha n ne*, 'fish go up little stream,' for it was summer when the salmon were running in from the sea for spawning.

That these women found husbands in the land is a fact, but who the men were, and of what people, tradition does not tell and it matters not, as the offspring was of the mother and perpetuated her family only.

With the increase of population internal dissension arose, or the question of food became a problem, when separation was brought about by a party which went forth to seek a new home. They travelled down the Stikine until they reached a great glacier that spanned the river valley and blocked their progress. Here they encamped, and during a council that ensued, Koo-os-sick and Orn-os-tay, two very old women of high caste, together with two equally old men, arose and said that their lives were of the past and that they were of little use either to themselves or to others, and as it was a question of turning back or of following the flow of the waters under the ice bridge, they would attempt the passage and if successful all could follow. After being dressed as for an important ceremony, and sprinkled with the down of the eagle, the four embarked in a small canoe and drifted from the shore, chanting their death song which was taken up by those assembled on the bank, and their tiny craft caught in the swirl of the swift current was soon lost to view. The barrier was climbed, and as the canoe with its occupants was seen to shoot out from under the wall of ice a mighty shout was carried from man to man until those in camp knew that all was well, whereupon the canoes were quickly loaded and passed through in safety, and they continued their way to the coast. It is reasonable to suppose that from time to time other parties followed, and, on reaching salt water, pursued different routes; as this family is found among the Tongass people of Portland Canal, the Hootzahtarqwan of Admiralty Island, and the Chilkat at the head of Lynn Canal, the traditions of all of whom speak of a migration from the Stikine river.

How many generations or centuries ago this migration occurred is not known, and can be approximated only by the recession of the glacier that crossed the valley then and is now so far separated from the opposite mountains.   But to-day these offshoots are Tlingit in every respect, although among the Chilkat they seem to intermarry more frequently with the interior people of the Yukon basin than do any of the other families.   This return to the parent stock is evident in the more characteristic Déné features, and while exceeding in numbers any other of the Chilkat families, they are held in low esteem, much as are all of the interior people by those of the coast.   They are of *Cheona*, the Wolf phratry, and they hold this emblem in highest esteem, although they claim also the brown bear, the eagle, and the killer whale.   I think it very probable that all three of these crests have been borrowed from the Tlingit branch of the family.   It is certain that the killer whale must have been unknown to the early life of these interior people, who were never permitted to reach salt water, and it could have come to them only through intercourse with the coast tribes.

To-day the Tuckclarwaytee constitute the second most numerous family, and they possibly take the first place in point of wealth.   They occupy eight houses in the village of Tahltan.

(2).   The Kartchottee were the second people to reach the Tahltan country.   They came first and collectively from the interior, and later and individually from the coast.   The family traditions tell of a migration from the headwaters of the Taku, where they crossed overland from Narlin and settled on Tahltan river twelve miles above its mouth, where it receives a small tributary.   They named this village *Thlu-dlin*, 'waters meet.' Living such a short distance away, they unquestionably at this period came in contact with the Tuckclarwaytee, and the union of these two branches was the foundation of the Tahltan people.   One winter when a number of the men of the village were getting firewood on the mountain side, they were overwhelmed by a snowslide, which caused such consternation that the remaining inhabitants gathered their belongings and trailed overland to Six Mile creek, reaching the Stikine midway between the present Telegraph and Glenora, where they built rafts and dugouts and followed the river to its mouth. Thence they continued westward until they reached the southern shore of Admiralty Island, where they established themselves and took their name, 'Belonging to Kartch,' from a fresh water stream that enters a bay at that point. The name is also said to be derived from *kartch*, 'bark,' from their primitive bark shelters. Later they crossed Frederick Sound to Kuprianof Island where they affiliated with the Kehkqwan, among whom they are still found in considerable numbers. In the course of time, through family dissension, a party retraced their steps eastward and joined the Stikine people about the mouth of the river, and of this body individuals have ascended the river from time to time and returned to the parent stock. A story told me by an old Stikine man says that in early days this family, to their great shame, were in the habit of enslaving the poor and orphans of their own blood, and that a chief so held a widow in bondage. He was then drying fish at Shek's creek, up the Stikine. The woman's duty was to care for the large travelling canoe, to keep it wet and covered with bark and brush, as these great dugouts quickly check when exposed to the sun. One day she neglected this, and her master made her kneel at the water's edge, fill her mouth with water, and squirt it over the canoe until it was well saturated. That night she escaped and wandered up the river until she reached a camp of the Tahltan. Here she married, and from the union came this later division of the family, and to-day when the Tlingit Kartchottee are angry with their brothers of the interior, they speak of them as the descendents of a slave.

Another version of the tradition of the return of the Kartchottee from the coast inland, tells of a chief of the Nanyiee of Wrangel, who had married a Kartchottee woman and with her daughter was fishing on the Stikine. The chief of the Tuckclarwaytee of the Tahltan stole her and took her to wife, from which marriage the other Kartchottee have sprung.

A branch of this family living on the Narlin, a southern

tributary of the Taku was called Narlotin; and in the early days possibly more Taku than Tahltan were spoken of as half Kartchottee, and they recognized the same totemic emblems. They have no existence as a separate family at Tahltan. Another division, purely local in character, that made its home on a great flat called Klabba, beyond the Tahltan river, took the name Klabbahnotin, but to-day no house name of this branch is recognized.

The Kartchottee belong to Cheskea, the Raven phratry, and recognize the raven and the frog as their emblems, one of which seems to be as much in evidence as the other, but I believe that the former is the older and possibly the more honored. The Kartchottee form the most numerous and influential family of the Tahltan tribe, a fact readily understood when it is remembered that they constitute the Raven phratry, while the other three families all belong to the Wolf phratry and intermarriage within the tribe can take place only between themselves and members of the other three families. They occupy eleven houses in the village. While in the past each family recognized only the authority of its own chief, in later years, with the decreased population, through mutual consent they have agreed on one chief to represent all, and the selection has fallen to the lot of the hereditary head of this family, known as Nan-nook. The same name or title was given by the Tlingit of Sitka to the early Russian ruler Baranof. It is said to be of Tlingit origin, meaning chief.

The Talarkotin are of interior origin, and while some say that they came from the Liard river country by way of the Dease, other accounts give them a still more easterly home in the Peace river valley. Their journey ended at the mouth of the second north fork, or Tuya river. This was in early days, when the land was young, and they, a mere handful of people, believed themselves alone. One day a Kartchottee hunter in following a game trail looked down from the high river bank and saw a tiny curl of smoke rising from the point of land at the mouth of the cañon. Crawling down the steep slope, he concealed himself, and soon saw a young girl come out of a brush hut prepared for berrying. He followed her into the woods, and, overtaking her, either persuaded her to accompany him or carried her off to his village as his wife; and this third family was added to those already comprising the tribe. The name is said to be derived from *Tahlar*, the designation of a precipitous rocky point between the two waters, where they first settled, and hence they are known as 'the point people.' They are called also Karkarkwan, variously translated as point people, cañon people, and rabbit people; but this term is of indefinite meaning and is likely of Tlingit origin. They are of the Cheona, or Wolf phratry, and take the wolf as their crest. They are almost extinct, occupying but two houses in the village. Their pronounced Déné features seem to mark them from the other families as of purer stock, less influenced by mixture with the coast people.

(3). The Nanyiee constitute the latest addition to the tribal circle. Their coming has been rather a gradual drifting in of individuals, through intermarriage and trade relations from two entirely different sources—the Stikine and the Taku. This people originated in the interior, and travelling westward, reached the sources of Taku river which they descended to the coast. Their separation from the parent stock was the result of a family quarrel involving the young wife of a chief, the offending branch being forced to leave. On reaching salt water at Stevens Passage, they started south in two bands, which became separated, and later, on meeting, each inquired of the other as to its camping place. One answered, "Sick-nuh," while the other replied "Nan-yuh," whereupon they respectively took the names of *Sick-nar-hut-tee*, 'belonging to Sick-nuh,' and *Nan-yi-ee*, 'the people of Nan-yuh.' On the other hand it is claimed that the latter name antedates this incident and means 'those from up the River,' and this meaning is more generally accepted. The Nanyiee continued southward through Frederick Sound and the Dry Passage, and settled on the mainland just below the mouth of the Stikine river, back of Etolin Island, by a waterfall, from which they named their village *Chu-Khass-an*, 'Waterfall Town.' They married with the neighboring peoples and became Tlingit, and in time reached the leading position in the Stikine tribe. In their hunting and fishing trips they ascended the Stikine until they reached Glenora, and finding an abundance of salmon and a favorable climate for the curing of their winter supply they pre-empted the streams thereabouts. The name of the hereditary chief, Sheks, was given to this camp, to which they returned annually. Whether or not the Nanyiee came in contact with the Tahltan before or after they had discovered the streams mentioned is not known, but trade relations existed between the two peoples before the advent of the whites, although it was greatly stimulated by the increased demand for furs after European trading vessels appeared on the coast. The advantage of controlling the valuable fur trade of the interior was readily appreciated, and the Tahltan were met for trade above Telegraph creek. This annual coming together resulted in intermarriage, and so the Nanyiee became established. They are also found among the Taku; and during the intervals of peace, when the two tribes met in friendly intercourse, individuals went from one to the other and by this means became members of the Tahltan people.

The Nanyiee belong to the Cheona, or Wolf division, and I believe this was their original crest, but those of the Stikine people assume the emblems of the brown bear, the shark, and the killer whale, which are accepted by the interior branch. They occupy four houses at Tahltan and number only a few families, but with the arrogance of their Tlingit blood they hold themselves superior to their neighbors.

Reviewing the events set forth in these family narratives, which, taken together, constitute all that there is of tribal history, it appears that at some early period a general westward movement prevailed among the interior people. It was not a wave of migration, as of a vanquished people fleeing before an enemy, but rather a restless wandering of bands or families seeking new homes. The routes followed were naturally along the rivers and lakes until the headwaters of the Taku and the Stikine were reached. Here favorable conditions seem to have been found and permanent camps were made. No mention is made of any previous dwellers in the land, which seems to have been a wilderness, for of a certainty such small bands could not have prevailed against a resident population, and had they done so their songs and stories would be frought with the hero worship of these early days, whereas of this they contain nothing. With natural increase and the accession of new parties the westward movement was resumed down the rivers to the coast. Here they met the Tlingit, a more aggressive and virile people, among whom, through intermarriage and environment, they forgot the ways of the trail and the woods and became sea hunters and fishermen. Then in generations following when the coast and the interior peoples had come in contact, individuals drifted back to the homes of their forefathers, strangers to the mother tongue and the simple life of the Déné, bringing with them the superstitions and the traditions of the coast, together with the social organization and the elaborate cere-monials, that have for their end the glorification of family in the display of the totemic emblems. Intercourse through trade relations was likewise responsible for these changes, but in a lesser degree.

The Portland Canal People

Portland Canal is a narrow, deep arm of the sea, reaching inland almost a hundred miles. The shores are rocky and precipitous, rising to an average height of three thousand feet and exceeding this altitude in many places. Where there is sufficient soil to sustain life, coniferous trees cover the mountains from the water's edge to a height of two thousand feet. The melting snows supply numerous mountain torrents and small streams, and in summer a fair run of salmon seek these waters. During most of the year, however, it is a wind-swept, inhos-pitable shore, offering few advantages of life.

On the authority of James W. McKay, the former inhabitants of Portland Canal were an offshoot of the Tahltan who, toward the middle of the last century, wandered across the Coast range and thereabouts reached salt water. Now, the people referred to were clearly not of the coast, but from their roving habits and their language were of interior origin; yet the Tahltan of to-day claim relationship with them only through the Kaska, from whom they say they are descended, and they call them *Tseco to tinneh*. The writer visited this people in the summer of 1907, when the following information respecting them was gathered.

They are known to the Nishka as *Tsits Zaons*, but call themselves *Wetalth*. They claim that they originally comprised three totemic families, having for their crests the raven, the eagle, and the wolf. The first two families have become practically extinct, and of the other, called *Nahta*, there remain but four men, two old women, and one grown girl. Should the last not have issue, with the death of these the tribe will cease to exist.

The people of Portland Canal were dominated by the Nishka and the Tsimshian of the coast, and were harassed by the Tlingit of Cape Fox. By these tribes they were confined to the inlet, and even after the establishment of Fort Simpson they were not permitted to trade with Europeans. The Nishka claimed the trade of the Wetalth, meeting them at stated seasons and taking their furs in trade at their own valuation and giving them what they pleased of foreign products in exchange. In this way they were kept very poor, and little better than slaves; but this was the treatment accorded to all the interior people by those of the coast. They seem to have been nomadic within their restricted range, but this may have been an inherited tendency, undoubtedly increased by fear of their more powerful neighbors, and by their limited food supply. They sought the shelter of caves, many of which are found along the rocky shores, and in summer gathered about the salmon streams. Their principal camping ground was about midway of the northern shore of the canal, and was known as Keneanokh. They claim to have been much reduced by the Tlingit of Cape Fox, with whom they were at constant enmity.

In 1885 the pitiful remnant of the tribe, twelve men with their women and children, weary of the struggle for existence, presented themselves at the then recently established Nishka mission village of Kincolith, where, through the influence and kind offices of Archdeacon W. H. Collison, they were allowed to settle and were practically received into the Nishka tribe; but the old prejudice against them as an inferior people has never been entirely overcome.

PHYSICAL CHARACTERISTICS

The Tahltan cannot be said to represent a strictly homogeneous people. The infusion of Tlingit blood from the Stikine tribe of the coast is responsible for a type that is readily recognizable in the heavier build, the abnormally large head, and fuller, grosser features. As these characteristics, however, are not of frequent occurrence, they may be regarded as individual, and they seem to disappear in the descendants of mixed unions after two or more generations of return to the parent stock. The dominant type is Nahane. In stature they are below the average height, are symmetrical in form, and well proportioned; they are never fat, seldom stout, sinewy rather than muscular, with well developed straight limbs, small wrists and ankles, and correspondingly small hands and feet. The head is small and well rounded, and the face inclined to length, which is rather accentuated by the high cheek bones and less prominent though pointed chin. The forehead is moderately broad, rather low, projecting in a ridge over the eyes and receding upward. The hair is black and coarse, and in age gray, but never white. The eyes are small, black, and rather deep set. The nose is straight, or, in the purest type, aquiline, with a good bridge and expanded nostrils. The mouth is full, with thin lips and perfect teeth. The complexion varies with mode of life: with exposure it takes on a dark brown, which is more noticeable in the men. The women, whose occupations are more indoors, are almost as fair as the European. In age the face becomes much wrinkled. While it was the custom formerly to remove hair growing on the face with pincers of metal or of bone, worn suspended around the neck, to-day a number of the older men have mustaches and straggling beards.

The senses are naturally well developed among a people whose hunter's life depends on their acuteness. The sense of sight, the most important of the senses to a hunting people, is among the Tahltan almost abnormally keen, not that the vision itself is of a higher order (indeed I think our eyes are stronger, and they unquestionably last longer, than those of the natives), for with the constant strain of sun and snow, and the effect of the smoke of the open fire, few reach middle age without some local affection of the eyes, and the older people usually suffer from some form of ophthalmia. But, to express the matter simply, they distinguish every object within the field of vision. Their eyes comprehend more, and are better trained and quicker to detect than are those of the white man. Hearing is developed to a high degree of sensitiveness owing to their habit of following the trails of animals. Living in the quiet of nature, they are conscious of the slightest sound. The sense of smell of the Tahltan is possibly no more acute than our own, but as they depend on it to tell them many of the secrets of the woods, they cultivate it to a higher degree. Their power of endurance is great, and their vitality is surprising even in these latter days of their decline, when their constitutions have been weakened through disease and liquor. They are a fairly prolific race, and under reasonable sanitary conditions should survive. Two women were pointed out to me each of whom had borne ten or twelve children, and families of three to five children are commonly met with. Their principal ailment at the present time is pulmonary trouble, induced by the changed condition of life within houses, and less nourishing food, aggravated by an undermining of the system through syphilis derived from the whites. After spending the winter in the field, living in rude shelters, they return to the village and shut themselves in their log houses, heated beyond the point of endurance and without ventilation. From the activities of the hunt and the strong diet of meat, they completely relax and gorge themselves with bread, sweets, and canned goods, which results in colds and indigestions that lay the foundation for organic diseases.

MORAL AND MENTAL CHARACTERISTICS

Honesty is so characteristic of the nature of the Tahltan that they do not look upon it as a virtue. They hold the cache inviolate, and when employed as hunters or packers by white men, they hold themselves responsible for the safe carriage and preservation of everything entrusted to their care. In disposition they are mild and peaceful, but when aroused by jealousy or offended pride they become taciturn and sullen. That they have been dominated to a certain degree by the more arrogant coast people seems natural when it is remembered that they were few in numbers and that they were wholly dependent on the tribes of the coast for arms and ammunition. Constant feuds with the Nishka and the Taku bespeak their courage, and in the hunting field their fearlessness has often been proven. Their ignorance of natural phenomena rendered them superstitious and engendered a childlike fear of the unknown. Affection for their children is very marked, and the older people are cared for when unable to provide for themselves. The peculiar totemic relations that divide the family so sharply and separate the children when grown from the father are unnatural and cultivate an apparent indifference that is difficult to reconcile with parental affection, but this in a sense is compensated by their total renunciation of self whenever the weal of the totemic family is concerned. They are hospitable, and, while individually generous and grateful, their ethics require a return for every favor, even to assisting one another in time of need, and a present given requires a return of even greater value in order to preserve one's standing with the donor. The accusation that native people are always grasping and lacking in gratitude probably arises from our ignorance of their laws and customs, together with a misconception on their part of our business methods and means of existence, and their failure to understand why, from our apparent plenty, we should not give freely, believing that the white man's store is inexhaustible. Once in selling me a piece of native work an old woman asked me several times its value, and when I demurred, another woman said, "why do you not give her what she wants? You can get all the money you wish." When asked, "how do you suppose I get money?" she replied, "you write on paper and the money comes!" Hence the feeling of the more primitive people when they see the white man performing little manual labor, living in apparent luxury and possessing what appears to them unlimited means. An incident of small moment but illustrative of a generous impulse occurred when I was staying at Tahltan. It was in early summer, and the people were assembled at the fishing camps, only a few older people remaining in the village. The spring salmon were late in arriving but when the first one was speared it was brought to the village and was divided among the few older people. Native dignity marks their intercourse with one another, and with strangers an evident reserve. They are, however, sociably inclined, conversational after acquaintance, and, if kindly treated, very friendly. Few white men who hunt with them leave them without the kindest feelings and a full appreciation of their many excellent traits of character. Mentally they may be classed as fair; their rather isolated hunter's life during the greater portion of the year is not calculated to stimulate the faculties. Their occupation in the pursuit of game makes them quick to see and to act, and they are sufficiently ingenious in contriving hunting and trapping appliances to insure the necessities of life. They are particularly receptive and adaptable, and they have so changed in the last thirty years that the present generation is not only ignorant of the life of the past but seems rather to scorn the old customs in its desire to be considered as the white man. They have little artistic sense or it is but slightly developed as is evident in their houses and belongings. Their implements are generally devoid of any attempt at ornamentation, and show no elegance of form. Rude etchings on bone in geometric lines filled in with red ochre characterize their highest idea of decorative art, except the beadwork of the women, which is attractive both in design and in the selection and placing of colors, and the pipes of the men, which are carved in animal figures and elaborately inlaid with haliotis shell, showing that there is at least some appreciation of the beautiful dormant in their nature.

GOVERNMENT AND SLAVERY.

While the recognized social organization of the Nahane was originally patriarchal in form, and remains so among the more primitive eastern branches, the Tahltan through intermarriage and association with the coast Tlingit, have adopted the matriarchal system whereby succession and inheritance follow directly in the line of the mother and remain always in the totemic family. Hence it would seem that substitution could never take place. The brother, the maternal nephew and cousin are successively eligible; but within these limits the chief is elected by the entire family, and the next in line may be passed over for one more eligible, though farther removed. Wealth and personal character are the principal factors. Women can not succeed to chieftainship. The custom both in the household and in the family is that the nephew on the sister's side should succeed the uncle and take the widow, his aunt, to wife, which gives her a home and provides for her personal needs, for being of the opposite branch she can inherit nothing from her husband. To this end the nephew is given to the uncle in boyhood to be brought up by him. For the same reason children can receive nothing from the estate of the father. Hunting rights are the most important inheritance. The whole country is divided among the families, and subdivided among households and individuals; and while in travelling through another's territory one might kill an animal for food, the pelt would be given to the landowner. Boys have the privilege of the father's hunting ground while they are recognized members of his household, that is, before reaching manhood; but after that period they exercise the rights of their mother's family. After marriage a man is permitted to hunt in the country of his wife's direct family as well as in his own country, and on this account plural wives are taken for the advantages they may bring.

The chieftainship even of old was more a position of honor than of power. In time of peace a chief represented the family, within which he arbitrated all disputes, and took precedence on all occasions of ceremony. He was accorded the place of honor at feasts, and received proportionately the greater number of presents. Generally of larger means than his fellows, his following was thereby increased, and he was the recipient of service and presents from his household, but he hunted and worked as did others. His obligations to the poorer and dependent members of the family were recognized. In case of war his counsel was sought and, age permitting, he was the logical leader. Each family was a distinct organization, controlling its internal affairs, recognizing only the authority of its own chief, and meeting the other families on common ground.

Councils, either tribal or family, were attended by the chiefs and the older men, although the family councils were more general in their character and attendance. Few happenings were regarded as personal where they occurred between members of different clan divisions, as the social organization was such that the act of the individual involved the whole family. In the discussion of such disputes after the family had met and considered a line of action, the chief of the aggrieved party would go outside and announce his position in a loud voice, as if speaking to the air, addressing no one in particular, and when he had concluded he would enter the lodge again and remain silent. Then the chief of the other family would act in the same manner, stating his side of the contention. In this manner the case was argued to a settlement.

With the decrease in numbers after their removal to their present village, the Tahltan met as a community and elected one chief to represent all. He is the hereditary chief of the most numerous family—the Kartchottee—and is addressed as *Nannook*. His office is recognized by the Department of Indian Affairs and on his decease his successor will be appointed by that department.

There are two recognized classes among the Tahltan, the aristocracy and the common people; but the line of demarcation is not very distinct, and while the accumulation of wealth, the giving of an elaborate feast, and the distribution of much property may elevate the one, continued poverty through several generations will not wholly reduce the other. There is no warrior class, nor do any secret societies exist. The shamans are wholly individual: they neither come from nor form any particular class.

Slavery existed in the past. Captives taken in war with the Nishka and the Taku were held in bondage, but could be redeemed at any time. Tlingit and Kaska were never enslaved, probably by reason of the mutually advantageous trade relations existing, and the more or less frequent intermarriage. Slaves were purchased from the Tlingit, who procured them from the Haida; they were generally Salish, Kwakiutl, or Vancouver Island natives taken by those island pirates in their forays along the coast. The value of a male slave was one hundred beaver skins; of a female, fifty beaver skins. Slaves could marry among themselves, but the children were slaves. If the head of a household should die or if a child should be seriously hurt, a slave might be freed in honor of the dead or in propitiation for the weak. On the death of a chief, one or more of these unfortunates might be killed in order that their spirits might attend the spirit of the departed in the future life. This was accomplished by laying the victim on the ground with his neck resting on a log; a small tree trunk was then placed over his neck, which was broken by several men jumping on the log. The body was usually thrown in the river, but if the slave should have been an especial favorite, his remains were cremated. Slaves worked and hunted for their masters. As an institution I believe that slavery was borrowed from the Tlingit, but the Tahltan did not own many slaves. Their continual hunting in small bands, their poverty, and their mild disposition all militated against extensive slavery.

VILLAGES

From a purely nomadic people the Tahltan might in theory now be termed settled, inasmuch as they have built a permanent village of substantial log houses after the manner of the whites. But it must not be inferred that they are to be found resident there during any extended period of the year; indeed their comfortable houses seem to be but an expression of their desire to be considered civilized, while at heart they are wanderers as were their forefathers.

Of necessity their hunter's life keeps them in camp from September until April; then with the first warm days of spring they become restless and go forth from the confinement of the house to the freedom of tent life, and in June, when the first salmon run in from the sea, they seek the fishing villages where they remain throughout the summer. So in truth their houses are little more than storage depots, marks of social standing, and meeting places for feasts and ceremonies. Shortly after the Cassiar gold excitement in 1874, the Tahltan built a modern village, on a slightly elevated plateau, a mile and a half to the northward and westward of the mouth of the Tahltan river. The older settlements were deserted, and the entire

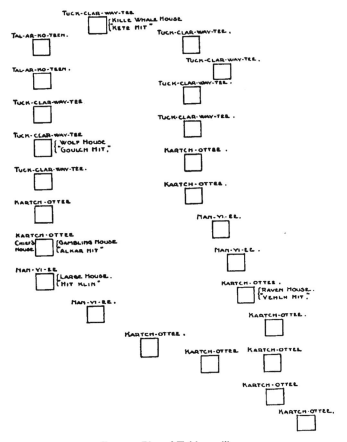

FIG. 1.—Plan of Tahltan village.

tribe, now much reduced in numbers, assembled there. To-day this is their only living place, although many of the younger men and those who are employed by the trading companies at Telegraph creek are building small log houses there, while they still retain an interest in the tribal village.

The earlier villages, some of which are still remembered by the older people while others are known only by name, centered about the upper reaches of the Stikine and its two northern tributaries, the Tahltan and the Tuya, and beyond on the Shesley and the Narlin, southern branches of the Taku; but these last named waters in early days were properly within the territory of the Taku people. The lower valley of the Stikine, while hunted over, was never inhabited. The village sites were selected wholly on account of their proximity to favorable fishing sites, as the swift streams rushing through narrow cañons offered few points where fishing could be carried on advantageously. To-day little remains to mark these places save a decayed grave post or a more luxuriant growth of berry bushes and grass.

Possibly the first settlement was *Teetch ar-an-ee*, 'fish go up little water,' on the southern bank of the Tahltan near its mouth, where the present fishing village stands. On the bluff above, some old grave posts are still visible. Several miles beyond on the rock ridge that separates the two rivers, was what is believed to have been the most important village, *Tsa-qu-dartsee*, 'rocks move,' so-called from the friable character of the cliff, the face of which was constantly crumbling and falling off. In the constantly recurring wars with the Nishka of the upper Nass this village was destroyed.

Another very old settlement was situated a few miles above the last, on the southern bank of the Stikine at the mouth of a small stream; but this is only a memory.

Thlu-dlin, 'waters meet,' was the first living place of the Kartchottee family. It was on the Tahltan river, some twelve miles above its mouth, and was deserted, as related in the family traditions, after many of its men had been overwhelmed by a snowslide.

The Tahlarkotin first settled at the mouth of the Tuya, but all knowledge of any settlement there is lost to the present generation.

There were several villages at different periods up the Tahltan. The earliest belonged to the Tuckclarwaytee family, but sickness came to the inhabitants about six generations ago, when, with the death of the men, the remaining women married Kartchottee, hence to-day this latter people have become the possessors of these fishing grounds.

Fig. 2.—Skin-dressing frame.

At Nine Mile flat, on the Stikine river, the Tahltan assembled in summer to fish, and here they met the Stikine Tlingit to trade. A peculiar separation of the rock from the shore forms a shallow channel through which the salmon came up stream and were easily taken, whence the name *Tra-tuck-ka*, 'rock crack,' was given to the camp. This was also destroyed by the Nishka.

Across the Stikine, on the southern bank, was another fishing village, where the use of the long weir was permitted. This was called *Gi-kah-ne-gah*, from *ge-de* the name of the fish basket.

At Ten Mile creek, on the southern bank of the Stikine, was a later meeting place for trade with the Tlingit.

3

The villages on the Narlin and the Shesley were more Taku than otherwise in early days, but in 1840 the Taku Tlingit of the coast came up the river and destroyed Kahgitzah near the head of the Shesley, when the remaining inhabitants crossed the stream and joined the Tahltan.

Smallpox was introduced from the coast to the interior people several times during the last century, and the Cassiar mining rush that swept the country in 1874 proved most disastrous, reducing the population to such an extent that to preserve their identity they found it necessary to unite in a single community. This is their present village, commonly called Tahltan, but by themselves known as *Goon-tdar-shage*, 'where

FIG. 3.—Grave house.

the spring water stops,' or, 'at the mouth of the spring,' on account of a small spring, at the upper end of the village, that bubbles out of the ground, flows a few rods, and is lost. It is this spring that affords the villagers their supply of drinking water. The ground plan of the village is a parallelogram, the houses surrounding an open space where public meetings and ceremonies are held; but this has been slightly interfered with toward the upper end, where the ground rises more abruptly, causing the houses to straggle somewhat (Fig. 1). The dwellings are of spruce logs, neatly laid, dovetailed or notched at the corners, the joints between chinked and plastered with mud. The roof consists of a frame of fore-and-aft beams resting on the gable ends, and a ridge pole, which support saplings following the pitch and placed close together, over which are laid slabs of spruce bark covered with two or three inches of mud. The poorer houses have only a hard earth floor, but in the better structures hewn planks are laid a foot or two above the ground with small cellars for the preservation of food during the winter. Originally there was a central fireplace, and a corresponding smoke hole in the roof, but to-day large cooking stoves are in universal use. A central doorway and a window or two in the front or the sides complete the house. The interior is without partitions; the sleeping places of the several families in the larger houses are separated from each other by boxes or trunks containing their personal effects. While of late years tables,

FIG. 4.—Grave house.

chairs, and even bedsteads have been introduced by the more progressive element, yet the simple furnishings of more primitive times are found among the older people. These consist of skins and furs for bedding and covering, boxes and chests procured in trade from the coast people for the storage of blankets and clothing, and rugs of many small pieces of skin of the leg of the caribou and the moose, sewn together. About the walls hang snowshoes, clothing, guns and other articles of the chase. In the rear of each house is a small storehouse of logs for various objects not in immediate use, as furs, traps and the like. Permanent dressing frames (Fig. 2) for caribou and moose skins are set up in convenient places back of the dwellings, also light frames for smoking the dressed skins. Winter kennels for the dogs consist of low log structures approximating eight feet square, earthed over and having the appearance of caves with only the front logs showing (Pl. VI, C). The grave houses (Figs. 3, 4, 5), in the character of family vaults in which are deposited the chests or trunks containing the charred bones of those cremated, consist of small box-like structures with one or more windows, and in several instances ornamented with painted or carved fronts representing the totemic emblems of the family. These grave houses at Tahltan are on the hillside in rear of the houses, but at Telegraph creek they rest on the high bank of the cañon. The latter type is clearly Tlingit, both in architecture and in ornamentation. Older and more characteristic graves are to be seen on the bluffs overlooking Tahltan river; these are marked by rude mortuary columns, and cribs of logs on top of which are placed the chests containing the cremated remains.

FIG. 5.—Grave houses.

In summer temporary brush shelters are erected in the rear of the houses by those who remain in the village; here the fish are cured, the cooking is done, and the daily work is carried on, for instead of being a necessity, the house is still a luxury, and heredity asserts itself in the love of the open, which has been the Déné mode of living through all time.

HABITATIONS

The primitive habitations of the Tahltan (Pl. VI, D) were lean-to shelters and oblong tent-like structures, framed of poles and covered with slabs of spruce bark and willow branches weighted down with a few heavier poles. Generally two lean-tos stood a few feet apart, opening toward each other. The passageway between remained open in summer, but in winter it was closed with brush at one end, while the other served as the entrance. The fire was built in the middle under the opening; the ground within was strewn with pine branches. The pack bags, bundles of food, furs, and personal effects were piled around the interior, forming protective walls. Caribou, moose, and sheep skins in the hair, simply scraped clean on the under side, served as beds; and robes of marmot, lynx, fox, and squirrel were used as blankets. Snowshoes, snares, and implements of the chase were suspended from the pole supports out of reach of the dogs. Lean-tos such as hose described are in general use to-day in the field, except that cotton drilling (Pl. VI, B) has superseded he primitive roofing of bark and boughs.

The earliest type of house, according to the testimony of the older people, was similar to that still found in the fishing villages. This is in the form of a parallelogram, the framework consisting of four corner posts with two central higher ones between at either end. The posts are rudely hewn tree trunks, about a foot in diameter, grooved at the top to receive the rounded beams that extend lengthwise and support the roof. The walls are of saplings, from three inches to five inches in diameter, driven into the ground and fastened along the top to a pole by a twining of willow bark and twigs, and secured also at intervals to the roof beam resting on the corner posts. The roof frame rests on the ridgepole and the two side beams, and is crossed at every foot or two by poles placed lengthwise and lashed to them with withes of willow bark; and over all are laid spruce bark and brush which is held in place with small tree trunks.

The doorway consists of a narrow opening at one end of the structure, and a movable gate keeps the dogs out. The earthen floor is sometimes covered with hewn planks, but more generally it is strewn with pine branches, on which the skin bedding is laid. There is a central fireplace with a hearth of gravel, and a smoke hole in the roof. As such structures are very open a lean-to is often set up within on either side of the fire. These houses serve the double purpose of shelter and smokehouse. Additional interior posts support beams across which rods are laid as a rack for split fish; while from the roof are hung other poles and cross-pieces in several tiers which the fish successively occupy in the process of curing, those freshly caught being placed over the fire, while those the most cured form the highest tier directly under the roof.

Caches for storing food (Pl. VII, A) for winter use and for containing household belongings have always been a necessity for protection against the ravages of wild animals and the dogs. These are substantial log cribs built on posts well above the ground, and are entered by means of notched tree trunks which are removed when not in use. On old village sites, and sometimes at a distance away in the woods, one may still see square excavations that resemble cellars. These were the salmon caches, in which the fish were stored in the late fall for winter and early spring, for both people and dogs. They were covered with logs, boughs, and earth, so that if the village should be sacked by an enemy there would still remain this hidden source of supply. In the present village of Tahltan, in the rear of each house, is a smaller substantial log building containing odds and ends and all material not in immediate use.

The sweat bath (Pl. VI, A) is a common necessity. The sweat house is a temporary affair, erected at a few moments' notice, consisting of a dome-shaped frame of small branches cut green, stuck in the ground, bent over, and lashed with bark. In use a fire is kindled within or near by, thoroughly heated boulders are introduced, and the fire having died down, skins or blankets are thrown over the frame and steam is produced by throwing water on the heated stone. Urine is used as a solvent in cleansing the body after long journeys or hunting trips.

DIVISION OF TIME

Time is reckoned by moons corresponding to our months, which are characteristically named from the weather conditions or from the habits of animals. The calendar year commences with October. The Tahltan names for the months or moons are as follow:

October,	*Men ten tchet ly,*	Little cold. (Little ponds get ice.)
November,	*Men ten tche,*	Big cold. (Big lakes and rivers freeze.)
December,	*Ghar u wue sa,*	Rabbit eats quickly. (Meaning the days are getting short.)
January,	*Sartses lar,*	Bad (weather) moon. Also Middle (of year) moon.
February,	*Den o tenna,*	Little crust comes on snow.
March,	*Iht si sa,*	Wind moon. South wind comes.
April,	*Khlee ten narsa,*	Dog runs over crust on snow. Dog barks.
May,	*Ih a zee e sa,*	Running moon. (Animals come out of winter houses and travel on loose snow.)
June,	*A ya ze sa,*	Young (born) moon.
July,	*A chi zee sa,*	Molting (birds) moon. Geese molt.
August,	*Da deah e sa,*	Groundhog gets white hair. Animals fatten.
September,	*Hos talh e sa,*	Groundhog in prime condition. She animals getting fat.

LIFE THROUGHOUT THE YEAR

The routine of life is carried on from year to year with little variation. Commencing with the fall, when the fishing season has come to an end and the animals have fattened and have taken on their winter coats, the hunting season begins. The natives return first to the village, the dried fish that is not required for use is cached, traps and snares are gathered together, winter clothing is stored in the pack bags, and when all is in readiness they set out for the hunting grounds by families, generally two together, with all the dogs. Men, women, and children, to the extent of their ability, carry back packs, and the dogs saddlebags. Having selected a favorable locality, they make camp and hunt and trap thereabouts until the game has become scarce, when they shift their camp, and so continue throughout the winter; but it is now the custom to return to the village about Christmas, and to go out again later for the early spring hunting, after which they come in with their stock of furs, and the trading commences. This is the time of sickness and excesses, for after months of hard work and of healthful living in the open, they shut themselves in their badly ventilated, overheated houses, and with immoderate eating and complete relaxation they become susceptible to colds and to digestive troubles that weaken their constitutions and often sow the seed of chronic diseases. With the first warm days of spring they become restless and prepare for tent life, and by the middle of June, with the coming of the salmon, they are settled in the summer fishing villages, where they remain until September This is the season of ease and enjoyment, for fishing is a mere pastime after the winter hunting. The weather is delightful and fish, together with many varieties of berries and roots, prove a healthful change from a continuous diet of meat. This being the only period when the members of the tribe are brought together, social functions are in order, but to celebrate them they return to their permanent village for the while. The close of the fishing season is generally selected for such events.

HOUSE LIFE

The division of labor by the sexes is clearly defined, although men and women do not appear unwilling to help one another whenever circumstances require. The man is the provider. He hunts, traps, fishes, brings in the game, removes the skin, builds the house, constructs the camp, erects the skin-dressing frame, fashions the household utensils and his hunting and fishing implements, working tools, and the snowshoe frame, and in travelling carries a pack. The woman cares for the children, prepares and cooks the food, tans the skins and makes them into clothing, including the carrying bags of skin and netting, cuts the babiche for nets and snowshoes, and fills in the latter. She cares for the house and the tent, keeps the bedding dry and in order, provides the water, and usually furnishes the firewood. The children render cheerful assistance to the parents, those too young to hunt or to do laborious work, care for the smaller children. The older boys hunt with their fathers and look after the snares and traps, while the girls assist their mothers in multifarious domestic duties. No attempt is made to teach the children; they learn by observation and through contact from the earliest age, and they play and work with equal cheerfulness.

The position of the woman is perfectly assured, and while her work is arduous and never ceasing, her influence in the household is unmistakable. This is especially evident with the older women, whose advice is sought on all occasions involving an exchange or a sale. The woman usually acts as the family treasurer and holds the purse strings. The relations existing between husband and wife are particularly happy as a rule, they appear to be affectionate, and reasonable in their treatment of each other, although they are not demonstrative. The devotion of the parents to the children is most noticeable, and they certainly merit it. Corporal punishment is uncommon; indeed, even in the quarrels of adults, they never come to blows: they may talk or they may kill, but they regard a blow as an unworthy act.

CLOTHING

Primitive clothing passed out of use with the Cassiar invasion, but even before that period the Hudson's Bay blanket was the staple of trade with the coast natives. In neither of my visits to Tahltan, although I ransacked every house, could I find a single piece of aboriginal wearing apparel, aside from fur blankets, moccasins, and mittens, which are still in common use. From the testimony of the older people, the dress of the men was of tanned skins of the caribou, the moose, and the mountain sheep, and consisted of a shirt reaching just below the thighs, trousers either reaching to the ankles or having feet attached, moccasins, mittens, and a cap of fur.

The shirt for general wear was ornamented usually with fringe along the seams of the body and the sleeves. The trousers sometimes were similarly ornamented and were confined below the knee with a garter. In cold weather fur shirts were worn.

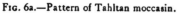
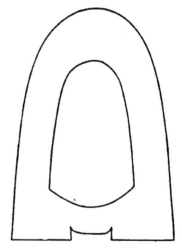

Fig. 6a.—Pattern of Tahltan moccasin.   Fig. 6b.—Pattern of moccasin used by the Tahltan but borrowed from the Kaska.

The moccasin is the one article of clothing that has survived the period of change and is in general use to-day (Fig. 6). It is made of moose or caribou skin, with a high flap to protect the ankle, and is provided with tie strings which are passed around several times. In winter marmot skins with the fur side inward are used. Two styles of moccasins are worn, distinguished from each other by the form of the toe. The square-toed moccasin is essentially Tahltan, while that with the pointed toe was borrowed from the Kaska. The trailer is rectangular and is much the same in each kind. The ornamental feature consists of a tongue of cloth, generally red, worked in beads or in colored thread. In earlier days the decoration was in colored quillwork.

Mittens of caribou skin, ornamented around the wrist-piece in quill embroidery or with colored cloth worked in thread or beads, are attached to each other by a band worn over the shoulders to prevent loss. Gloves and gauntlets are much used to-day, but these articles are not aboriginal and have been borrowed from the whites.

In old times the cap was of the fur of the fox, marten, marmot, or one of the smaller animals, and was tight fitting. The more decorative clothing worn on ceremonial occasions and by the chiefs was ornamented with a yoke of porcupine quill embroidery on the shirt in front and similar bands down the trousers, and garters of embroidery or of wrapped quillwork. The fringe of such shirts about the border and seams was very fine and was wrapped with colored quill at the base. Red ochre was much used to color the fringe, and for marking a line around the border, but it was superseded by vermilion, and in like manner beads took the place of quill embroidery.

The clothing of the women was of material similar to that of the men and differed from it only in length, the principal garment assuming more the proportions of a dress. In severe weather every woman was provided also with a skin blanket of fox, lynx, marten, ground squirrel, or marmot fastened about the neck with tie strings and around the waist with a belt. The finer blankets were bordered in front with a strip of caribou skin, often ornamented in quill or bead embroidery. The pads of the fox and the lynx were made into blankets for wear and as covers. Rabbit skins were used for the dress of the children.

FIG. 7.—Cartridge belt worn in the winter dances.

Blankets of marmot and other furs were universally worn around the shoulders by both sexes and all ages in camp when the weather required, and are still used by the older people.

· A girl on reaching the age of puberty went into confinement and could appear in public only when dressed in a skin robe worn over the head and reaching to the ground, thus concealing her from view.

The principal ceremonial apparel found among the Tahltan had been procured from the Tlingit, and includes Chilkat blankets, the distinctive chief's headdress consisting of a carved wooden mask surmounted by sea lion whiskers and a train of ermine skins pendent behind, the carved raven rattle of the coast, and the Hudson's Bay Company's blue blanket bordered with red cloth and trimmed with pearl buttons. But these articles were found only among the wealthy who ascribed to them a fictitious value. Articles of their own design and workmanship are confined almost entirely to embroidered cartridge belts (Fig. 7), knife sheaths, and bags for suspending from the neck. These are of caribou skin or of colored cloth ornamented with colored beads. In addition they wear crowns of grizzly bear claws, the skins of the heads of animals (Fig. 8), ornamented fur caps, and eagle feathers. I saw but one cloth shirt ornamented in colored beadwork, one blanket shirt decorated with lynx teeth, and another shirt made of the pads of the black fox trimmed with colored silk. Eagle tails, often colored red, are carried in the hand. I found one very beautiful belt, worked in colored quill with a fine fringe wrapped with quill, which was a piece of dance apparel, and might have been procured from the Kaska or the Liard people, who excel in such work (Fig. 9).

FIG. 8.—Dancing headdress made of the skin of the head of a young caribou.

Necklaces of bone and glass beads, dentalium, beaver claws, and lynx teeth were formerly worn by the women but to-day they are rarely found in use. Bracelets of silver procured from the Tlingit have superseded the older ones of horn, brass, and beads. Finger rings of silver from the same source are still worn by the women. In the case of both sexes, on the day of birth or shortly afterwards the lobe of the ear and the septum of the nose are pierced—formerly with a sharpened claw or bone awl, later with an iron point—and a cord of sinew is inserted to keep the aperture open. Later in life the helix of the ear of the man may be perforated at one, two, or three points, according to his social position. On ceremonial occasions an ornament of bone, or of dentalium or haliotis shell, or a silver ring, is worn through the nose. Pendent from the lobe and from the holes in the helix of the ear, dentalium and haliotis shell and silver rings are likewise worn on dance occasions, although that through the lobe may be of every day use. I saw no evidence of the use of the labret among this people, and they assured me that this custom did not exist among them in early days, and that if a woman were found with the lip pierced, it was because she was of the coast people or related to them.

FIG. 9.—Quill embroidered ceremonial belt.

For personal decoration the face was daubed with red ochre or with charcoal, and vermilion procured from traders was used later for the same purpose. No figures, totemic or otherwise, were known. To protect the skin from bites of insects and from the reflection of the sunlight on the snow, to prevent sun blindness from the glare, and t indicate grief or anger the face is smeared with a thin coating of suet from the goat, sheep, or caribou, and then blackened by puffing over it the finely charred powder of a fungus growth of the hemlock. Rudely improvised snow goggles of birch bark, with narrow slits to admit the light, are also used while travelling over the snow in bright sunshine.

The men formerly wore the hair cut straight around, hanging to or almost to the shoulders, and banged across the forehead. For dances and other ceremonies it was covered with swansdown. The hair of the women was plaited in one braid that hung down the back. Those of the higher class wore, fastened around this braid, near the head and hanging down over it, a strip of hide covered with dentalium in parallel rows, each row separated from the other by lines of colored beads (Pl. VIII,

D). Attached to this pendant there was sometimes a copper, iron, or silver ornament of peculiar shape.

Tattooing was common in the past, but I found no good examples of this form of personal ornamentation, only insignificant geometric figures on the backs of the hands. Formerly it was shown in lines and dots on the forearm, the ankles, the chin, and the face. It was accomplished by means of a fine needle and a thread of sinew rubbed in powdered charcoal.

The drum is so intimately associated with the dress, its

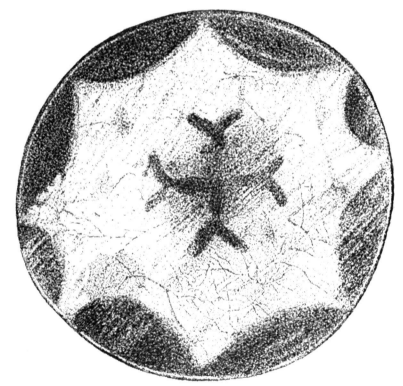

Fig. 10.—Drum consisting of a piece of goat skin stretched on a wooden frame and decorated with red ochre.

use being for dance occasions only, that it may not be amiss to mention it here (Fig. 10). It is made of the tanned hide of the mountain goat, stretched, when wet, over a circular wooden frame, and secured on the under side by cutting the skin into four strips, tapering from the circumference to the centre, where they are knotted, and so serve as a handle. At the present time tacks are often used around the lower edge of the frame to bring all parts taut. The head is often painted in totemic design. The drums are much smaller than those used by the Tlingit and some of them are very small. The instrument may be beaten with the fist, but generally an improvised drumstick is employed. No regular drumstick was seen.

Etched or carved implements and utensils were further ornamented with red ochre.

Porcupine quills were dyed black by boiling in water with a powdered black stone. Red was likewise obtained from a red mineral powder. Articles were dyed yellow by boiling tree moss and steeping the objects in the decoction and boiling. Green was obtained from decayed wood.

The primitive ornamentation of clothing was in colored quill embroidery, but with the acquisition of trade beads this was abandoned. The oldest beadwork was made by stringing the beads on sinew; the whole piece of work was then attached to the body material. With the introduction of steel needles the cloth ground was embroidered and then sewed on the skin.

HOUSEHOLD IMPLEMENTS AND UTENSILS

As previously stated, in household utensils the Tahltan were particularly poor, judging from their own accounts, and indeed little has survived their transformation, for to-day they depend entirely on what they obtain from trading stores. The aboriginal water vessels and cooking utensils were of birch bark similar to those found among the neighboring Déné people, and in their trade with the Tlingit they obtained wooden food dishes, boxes, and woven spruce root baskets which were used for like purposes. I failed to find any evidence of the bark vessel among them, although I saw some boxes and baskets from the coast on which they set great value, and also a single dish made from mountain sheep horn used to hold oil. Spoons of the horn of the mountain sheep, mountain goat, and caribou, and also of wood, were rudely fashioned and were ornamented in geometric figures filled in with red ochre or with brass tacks. Some artistically carved goat horn spoons inlaid with haliotis shell, and several painted wooden spoons in possession of the chief, had been procured from the coast. The soapberry spoon was of wood or of caribou horn and was without ornamentation. The only visible stone implements used in the preparation of food were a couple of woman's hand hammers, or mashers which were clearly procured in trade from the coast. Trinket boxes were made by scraping very thin a section of caribou horn, which was softened in boiling water, then bent around a circular bottom of wood, and the end overlapped and sewed. The cover was similarly made.

Root diggers are simply sharpened sticks. Snow shovels are used for making paths from the house or camp. Hooks of horn of or wood, secured to the house walls or to camp poles, serve for hanging hunting implements.

Fire was formerly produced by means of a drill stick manipulated between the palms pressed against a bed-piece of wood, but it is said that a bow drill was used by the women as more easy of manipulation. In later years flint and steel and light tree-punk were employed.

BAGS AND NETTING

Bags of skin and net, varying in size and shape for the sexes and to meet the requirements for which they are intended form an all important feature in the economic life of the Tahltan. These people are indifferent workers in wood, and make no attempt to fashion boxes and chests; neither are they basket weavers. The bag takes the place of such articles, and its lightness and compactness make it indispensable to a travelling people whose only means of transportation is the pack. The

4

dry climate in which they live permits its use in all seasons.   All
the varieties of bags are made by the woman.

The largest size is that used as a trunk for the storage of
clothing (Pl. IX, C).   It is of a single piece of tanned caribou skin,
sewed up the sides, the extension of the back piece forming a flap
that can be buttoned or tied down over the opening.   Not being
designed for transportation, it is not fitted with carrying loops.
This bag is fringed around the sides and bottom, and ornamented
with colored cloth and beadwork within the border and over the
flap.   It is wholly the property of the woman, and much taste
is displayed in its ornamentation.

Second in size, but first in importance, is the pack bag, which
differs according to the sex for which it is designed (Pl. VII, B).
As has been seen, the Tahltan are trail men and land travellers.
Their rivers are swift and treacherous, flowing through rock cañons,
and are dangerous or impossible to navigate, hence they have
little knowledge of the water, and seldom trust themselves upon
it except to cross a lake or a stream on rude, improvised rafts.
When travelling they pack their belongings on their backs.
Formerly, in winter, they used a bag-like sledge of skin, but this
has been superseded by the conventional wooden sledge drawn
by large dogs.

The woman's bag is of tanned caribou skin, about two feet
long by eighteen inches deep, made in one piece.   The sides
are sewn together, leaving a double border of about three inches
outside the seam, which is cut in fringe; a corresponding fringe
is sewn along the bottom, and the outside is ornamented with a
band of colored cloth, edged with beads or bead embroidery
extending around the sides.   This form of ornamentation has
superseded the more primitive embroidery in porcupine quills.
A line of skin is inserted and half-hitched at short intervals
around the mouth.   Through this a lacing is passed to secure
the contents; and at each end is sewn a stout loop to which
the pack straps are made fast.

A bag similar in character, but larger and heavier, was

formerly carried by the men, but it is seldom seen to-day. The back was of tanned caribou skin, the front of strips of the leg skin of the moose or caribou with the hair remaining and showing on the outside. It was generally plain, but sometimes was ornamented with fringe.

The bag used by the man is of babiche, netted to a band of caribou skin, from an inch to three inches wide, sometimes embroidered in porcupine quill or beads, and extending around the mouth (Pl. IX, D). It is about two feet long and fourteen inches deep, with quarter-inch to half-inch meshes. The band around the mouth is slit at short intervals, and through these slits the double tie string, made fast in the middle, is laced, to secure the contents in carriage. Two stout loops are sewn to the band at each corner to receive the pack straps. This bag serves for carrying food for a day's travel, or for transporting game, snares, utensils, and other belongings of the man.

Another pack bag of net is used for carrying fresh fish. It is made of a coarse, two-strand, twisted cord of the wool of the mountain goat (Pl. IX, E). The meshes are from three quarters of an inch to an inch, and the cord is an eighth of an inch in diameter. The network is half-hitched around a four-strand plaited rope at the mouth, and is held secure by a single line wound around each half-hitch and the rope. The rope is knotted into loops at each end, and continues beyond one end for three feet or more in two lines that serve as breast cords for packing. The advantage of using the goat's wool cord in these bags for carrying fresh fish is that

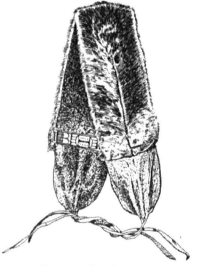

Fig. 11.—Carrying strap.

it remains soft and pliable with the constant wetting and the slime of the fish, which would soon ruin a bag of skin or babiche. This bag is seldom seen to-day; I saw but one woman who still used it.

In using the pack bag, two carrying straps are employed, the breast cord and the headband. The former is always used, but the latter is brought into service only on long journeys and when the weight of the load is great. The breast cord is of four-strand plaited strips of well tanned caribou hide from fifteen to twenty-five feet long; it is generally doubled and secured to a leg bone of the marten, mink, or other small animal. In use it is secured near the end to the loop of the pack bag, carried over the shoulders and chest, run through the other loop, brought back again and carried around the bone, and secured to its own part; or, if the bone is wanting, the two ends are tied together in front. The advantage of the bone attachment is in the easy adjustment of the cord by using the bone as a pulley, and the readiness with which the pack can be slipped. Generally, in packing, a piece of old blanket or clothing is thrown over the shoulders and brought across the chest to relieve the pressure of the cord. The headband (Fig. 11), which is used when heavy burdens are borne, or on long journeys, consists of a strip of the leg-skin of the moose or caribou, slightly tanned and with the hair remaining, about two feet long by four to five and one-half inches in breadth. It is lengthened about six inches at each end by the addition of a heavy, rounded piece of hard, tanned leather, to which is sewn a double tie string of caribou hide from a foot to eighteen inches in length. Just within the junction of the band and the leather ends a bone stretcher is seized to keep the band flattened out, thus distributing the weight over a greater surface of the head. This band passes above the forehead. It is the first to be adjusted, then the tie strings are made fast to the loops of the pack bag. With few exceptions the stretching bones are ornamentally etched or cut in geometric figures, which are filled in with red ochre or vermilion (Fig. 12).

The skin sledge, above alluded to, is a capacious oblong pack bag that is drawn over the snow in winter, and is aboriginal in both design and construction. It consists of strips of the

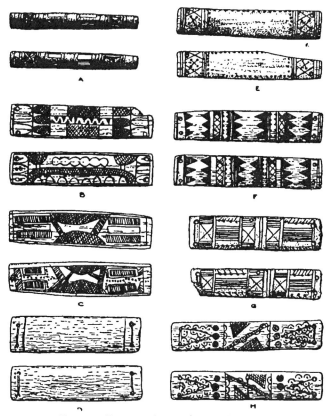

FIG. 12.—Bone attachments for carrying straps.

leg skin of moose or caribou, untanned, and sewed together in such manner that the hair lies lengthwise. The sewn strips are drawn together at the fore end, and along the border are cut slits through which a cross-lashing is carried when the bag is packed, so that the sides are brought well over the contents. Two heavy loops of hide are sewed near the head, one on each

side, to which the span is made fast, and to this the hauling line
is secured. This sledge is drawn by hand, and when moving
in the direction of the hair it offers but little resistance. If, when
going down steep inclines, over a frozen surface, the sledge
acquires too great momentum, by a dexterous turn of the drag
rope it can be quickly slued and its progress checked through
the resistance of the short, stiff hairs against the ground.
Wooden sleds of the conventional type drawn by dogs have superseded this older type.

To-day the Tahltan possess many dogs of all breeds and
sizes, a mongrel lot, but very useful for packing and for hauling
sledges. Prior to the Cassiar gold excitement they had only
very small fox-like dogs, of a breed I have never seen elsewhere,
intelligent, keen of scent, and excellent hunters, but too
tiny to be of any service in transportation. Dog packing,
therefore, is a borrowed industry, and consequently the pack
saddle is not original with the Tahltan. The saddle is sometimes
of skin, but more often of canvas, and is provided with a pocket
on each side. The pack line passes over the bags, then comes
beneath and around outside, around the dog in the rear of the
pack, and about the neck. A dog carries from twenty-five to
fifty pounds, according to its size and strength.

Every adult is provided with a work or repair bag of conventional form but differing according to the sex of the owner,
in which the implements and other articles of every day use
are kept. Whether in the house or in the camp this bag is
always at hand, and in travel it is placed at the top of the pack,
convenient of access. The man's bag of tanned caribou skin
is rectangular in form, with an average length of fourteen inches
and a depth of eight inches. It is generally of two pieces,
sewn together along the sides and bottom, leaving outside a
margin of an inch or more which is fringed for ornamentation.
Within the outside seam a strip of colored cloth is attached all
the way around, and is edged with beads. Around the opening

a cording of hide extends, or narrow slits are cut, through which a tie string serves as a lacing to protect the contents (Pl. X).

Certain tools and accessories are found in every sack, the most important being the following.

(1) The knife is of two varieties: one with a straight, the other with a curved steel blade, fitted and secured by means of a hide seizing to a handle of wood, bone, or horn. Both of these have their uses in the manufacture of household, hunting, and fishing implements.

(2) The snowshoe chisel, of steel, has a thick blade, but a narrow cutting edge, and is used principally for perforating the frame of the snowshoe to receive the lacing. It is set in and lashed with hide to a short, thick handle of wood or of bone, larger at the head, and cut out so that considerable pressure may be brought to bear upon it without danger of slipping. This form of blade and handle is universal among the interior tribes as far as the Alsech valley, and is also found among the Chilkat.

(3) The awl, consisting of a steel point inserted in a handle of horn or of wood, serves a variety of purposes in addition to its original use as a sewing instrument. The point is sometimes protected by a wooden case. Before the introduction of iron the awl was a sharpened bone.

(4) A piece of fine-grained sandstone of convenient size and shape to sharpen the steel tools.

(5) A beaver jawbone with the teeth intact, or a bear's incisor, across which the knife blade is drawn after it has been ground on the stone to give it a keen edge.

(6) A strip of caribou sinew for thread or seizing.

(7) A lancet for surgical purposes, consisting of a steel blade inserted in a wooden handle, or wrapped with bark, root, or sinew, and extending well down the blade so that it can penetrate only so far in the flesh. The Tahltan puncture swellings and inflammation to produce irritation and to bleed the parts, and dress the wounds with bird's down. This, so far as I could learn, is the only surgical operation they perform. When not in

use, the lancet is wrapped in a small piece of skin to protect the blade. The same practice and a similar instrument are common among the Tlingit and may have been borrowed from them.

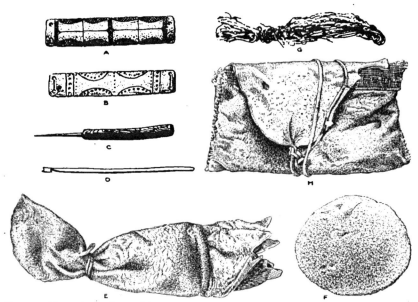

FIG. 13.—Woman's workbag with contents. A and B: bone attachments for carrying strap C: sewing awl. D: netting needle for netting mocassins. E: paint bag. F: stone scraper for dressing skins. G: sinew thread. H: workbag.

(8) A long, narrow, skin bag containing pulverized red ochre or vermilion for facial decoration, as well as for filling the incisions and etched figures on bone implements, and for coloring skin clothing.

Besides the articles enumerated above, there are numerous spare articles for repairing, together with odds and ends more individual in character, that may be found in one or another bag, as bone gambling toggles, pack strap stretchers, bone skinning knife, medicinal roots, snowshoe friction brakes of goat horn, gaff hooks, fishhooks, beaver spears, and sometimes such old pieces as have been used in the past and have possibly been found and are kept for no particular reason, as cutting chips of obsidian, and arrow and bow heads.

The woman's workbag is smaller than that of the man, more square in shape, and made with a long flap beyond the pocket (Pl. XI). When not in use it is rolled up and secured with a single tie string wrapped around. This bag is generally ornamented with a strip of colored cloth around the border, beaded but never fringed (Figs. 13, 14, 15). It usually contains the following articles.

(1) A knife, with a straight blade similar to that of the man's knife but very much smaller. This is used in cutting babiche, and skins for clothing, and in netting snowshoes, bags, and lines. In early days obsidian splinters served as knives for such purposes.

(2) An awl, consisting of an iron point set in a handle of horn, bone, or wood. It serves the purpose of a needle when sinew thread is used in making skin clothing, and is the most personal article in the woman's life; indeed a favorite awl is seldom parted with. It is made by the man, and, inartistic as these people are, this particular implement exhibits in both the

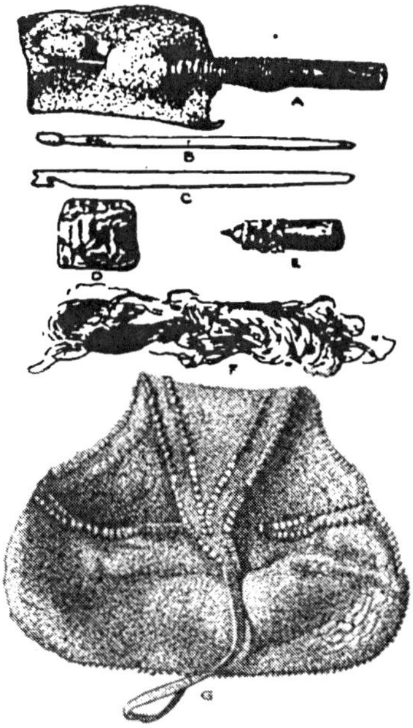

FIG. 14.—Woman's workbag with contents. *A*: sewing awl. *B* and *C*: netting needles. *D*: earring of abalone shell. *E*: lancet. *F*: sinew thread. *G*: workbag.

selection of the material and its construction a desire to produce something more ornate than the ordinary working tool.

(3) Caribou sinew for thread, made by separating the tendonous tissue with the finger nail and stripping off very fine fibres. These are rolled on the leg, and two of them may be rolled together to produce longer thread. In connection with the awl

and the sinew thread may here be mentioned the thread holders, which, though not kept in the bag, on account of their size, form a part of the sewing outfit. Only three of these were found among the Tahltan, two of wood and one of bone, all ornamentally shaped and incised. They are no longer used.

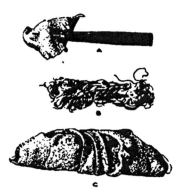

FIG. 15.—Woman's workbag and contents. *A*: sewing awl. *B*: sinew thread. *C*: workbag rolled up and fastened with attached thong.

They are in the form of a small stake sharpened at the lower end. Near the head they are cut halfway through, and then split down one-third the length. When in use the sharpened end was stuck in the ground, within easy reach of the sewer. The threads were middled, passed through the horizontal opening, and arranged in the vertical slit one above the other with the shorter projecting end toward the operator, who, as she needed a new thread, drew out the uppermost one.

(4) A small whetstone and a beaver tooth or a bear tooth for sharpening the knife and the awl may often be found in the woman's workbag.

(5) A net needle of bone, used in netting the babiche filling of snowshoes.

(6) A hand skin dresser of stone, and sometimes a short one of bone.

(7) Such articles as fungus for blackening the face, a bag of red ochre for personal adornment, a lancet, and such odds and ends as may have been found or have been dropped into the bag for safe keeping.

A small bag of tanned moose or caribou skin, carried by the man, suspended by a strap over the shoulders, used originally as a fire sack, later to hold ammunition for the muzzle loader, has, with the introduction of the breech loader, degenerated into a ceremonial appendage, and as such bids fair to survive every other type of bag (Pl. IX, A). In every household these were found in great abundance, as many as ten or twelve in the possession of an individual. Indeed these bags from their number and ornamentation seem to mark the measure of the wife's affection for her husband, for in no other product of the Tahltan (save the knife case, which forms a companion piece) is so fully expressed a sense of the æsthetic both in elegance of design and in harmony of color, which is in marked contrast with the general inartistic work of this people. While a few square and oblong bags are met with, the characteristic form is rounded at the bottom. The pocket is in depth about two-thirds of that of the bag; to the back piece, which is the longer, a broad neckband is attached. The primitive embroidery was in colored porcupine quill, and dentalium shells were often added; but of late years red and blue cloth, and trade beads, have formed their chief media of decoration.

Another type of bag, wholly ornamental, in which the bottom is divided into strips, elaborately beaded, is worn on dance occasions; but it is not confined to the Tahltan, as it is found as far north as the Yukon basin and is equally popular among the Tlingit of the coast.

Improvised bags consisting of the whole skins of smaller animals, as the marmot, the rabbit, the young of the mountain goat, and the beaver, with the fur intact, are used for storing small articles of various kinds.

SNOWSHOES

Snowshoes form an indispensable adjunct to the life of this entire region, and its native inhabitants are very expert in their manufacture. The men furnish the frame complete, and the women provide and net the filling. The frame is fashioned of willow, spruce, or birch. The willow is the lightest wood, but is not very durable; the spruce is somewhat heavy, and to a degree brittle; the birch is best in dry snow, but absorbs moisture readily, when it becomes heavy.

The frames are made in three distinct shapes, each depending on the service for which the shoe is to be used, and on the fancy of the individual. For travel over lakes, rivers, and open country the raised oval toe is preferred; for hunting in the small wood and over brush lands the raised pointed toe is best (known as the Kaska type after the people from whom it was borrowed). Children use the flat rounded toe which is of simpler construction. The toe of the shoe is raised to keep it from digging in the snow. The frame of all the types is of two equal pieces, spliced and wound at the toe, and brought together and secured at the heel. The bending of the toe to produce the upward and rounding curve is done gradually by successive wetting, steaming over the fire, and lashing. The oval flattened cross-pieces, of which there are three in the rounded toe form and two in that with the pointed toe, are let into horizontal mortises in the frame; and the perforation for the selvage thong on which the netting is woven is made with the special awl described among the implements to be found in the repair bag of every man. When finished the frame is turned over to the woman to be netted.

The filling of the front and rear spaces on the hexagonal netting is of fine babiche of caribou skin, but it is said that the skin of the mountain sheep is sometimes substituted. It is passed around the cross-bars and through the loops of the selvage thong, which is woven in two different ways: (1) by looping through the perforation and around a small peg on the outside, and drawing the peg and loop into the V-shaped hole and countersink; or (2) the thong is doubled around each alternate pair of perforations and countersunk on the outside of the frame in horizontal grooves, giving a continuous series of loops along the inside. In the wake of the permanent toe wrapping, the thong passes inside and over alternate pairs of the seizings.

The netting of the central foot space of moose or caribou rawhide, in a coarse hexagonal weave, passes over both cross-bars and frame. The rest for the ball of the foot is simply a double cross-line. Beaver skin was sometimes used as an extra strong foot filling in the shoes of the leader who broke the trail in heavy snow.

For ornamental purposes tufts of red and blue worsted are gathered into the knots or loops of the netting thong around the outside of the front and rear spaces. The foot loops are of coarse hide. The usual proportion of the adult's shoe is in length about four and one-half times the maximum breadth.

A brake attachment to the snowshoe, to prevent slipping on hard or crusted snow, particularly when travelling over a hilly country, consists of the tip of a horn of the mountain goat, which, lashed to the frame and projecting beneath the margin, inclining inward and backward, prevents slipping. Such a brake is secured to each side of the frame, abreast the main front crossbar, and the hide seizing passes around the frame and over the notched head of the horn to resist the upward pressure from crusted snow. This attachment is employed by the people of the interior, back of the Chilkat mountains. It has been adopted by the Chilkat, and is in use also by the Nishka on the upper waters of Nass river.

The snowshoe staff, an accompaniment of the shoe often necessary when the travel is over soft and deep snow, consists of a staff of the thickness of a walking stick, and about five feet long, the lower end terminating in a dull point. A few inches above the point is cut a shallow groove, around which is lashed a small, circular, netted shoe about six inches in diameter. The frame of this shoe consists of a flat section of birch or of willow, cut green, bent round and seized to its own part. The netting is of coarse babiche made from caribou skin and woven over a thong which is run through the perforations of the frame.

FOOD

The Tahltan, being hunters, are essentially meat eaters, and while they enjoy fresh fish in the summer season, and cure a certain amount, they care little for the dried product as a winter diet, using it more for dog food, when other sources of supply fail.

They cook all fresh meat and fish, and while to-day they are supplied with kettles and pans, in primitive times they had very few utensils, so that fresh food was prepared in the simplest manner by roasting on a spit before the open fire. In boiling food they used watertight vessels of birch bark, rude wooden dugouts, and boxes and baskets, which latter were procured in trade from the coast people. The operation of cooking was accomplished by means of heated stones dropped into the water.

The nomadic life of the Tahltan, which necessitates the carrying of all burdens on the back compels them to dispense with everything superfluous, hence the lack of utensils.

Caribou and moose meat constitute the main food supply, although the Tahltan say that before they were supplied with firearms they depended largely on the smaller animals which were more easily taken, particularly the ground hog, which they snared in great numbers in the fall and dried for winter use. The fat of the marmot was removed and packed away in bags made of the stomach of the animal, or of the whole skin, which was removed by drawing back over the carcass through an incision made at the mouth. The fat is sometimes melted, poured into the bladder and the latter tied at the opening. Rabbits being abundant, and easily snared, become a very important adjunct when naught else can be obtained. Bears of the black, grizzly, and brown species, the mountain sheep and mountain goat, beaver, porcupine, grouse, ptarmigan, and all migratory water fowl likewise serve as food. The soapberry is dried in the form of cakes for winter use. Certain roots, as well as the inner bark of the black pine, are also eaten.

Whitefish are procured from Dease lake, but in such a limited quantity that, although greatly esteemed, they are hardly worthy of mention.

It is probable that in early days fish, both dried and frozen, was a much more important item of food than it is to-day, when, with improved arms, the Tahltan can procure all the game they require, not to mention the products of civilization which are becoming necessary to their changed condition.

The cultivation of potatoes has met with little success on account of the lack of rain and the extreme dryness of the soil.

SMOKING AND ITS SUBSTITUTES

Tobacco was unknown to the Tahltan and their neighbors until the beginning of the nineteenth century, when it was introduced from the coast by the Tlingit who had procured it in trade from visiting European vessels. Prior to that time smoking was not practised by either people. A substitute for tobacco, likewise brought from the coast, consisted of a mixture of powdered burnt clam shell, charred tree bark and a species of nicotine plant dried; these were reduced to the form of a paste and rolled into little pellets the size of a pea. One of the pellets was placed between the lower lip and the gum and sucked, necessitating constant expectoration. The nicotine plant, which was cultivated among the Tlingit, is said to have been brought up the Stikine river and planted in small garden patches at the old village of Tutchararone, near the mouth of the Tahltan river.

Of pipes two varieties are found, the one designed for ordinary use, and the other for ceremonial occasions (Pls. XV–XVII). The former, although the plainer, and in shape evidently copied from the pipe of commerce, is the more characteristic. When made of stone it is rather small and of a red homogeneous volcanic rock found in pockets in the cliffs overlooking the Stikine near the Tahltan. I have seen no stone pipes that were ornamentally carved, but on account of the material of which they are made they are highly prized. The everyday pipe of wood is of very different shape, having an extended main stem in one piece with the bowl. It often has a reclining grotesque figure resting on top of the stem near the bowl, but in most cases this form of pipe is without ornamentation. The bowl of every wooden pipe is lined with metal, often a section of musket barrel extending slightly above the bowl. The stem or mouthpiece is of any suitable wood, rudely cut and often consisting of the section of a branch of pith wood.

The feast pipes, used at the death feast and on family ceremonial occasions, are always carved, and in almost every instance represent the family crest. They are inlaid with haliotis shell and often ornamented with copper and brass, and daubed with red ochre. These pipes are the most ornamental specimens of handiwork of the Tahltan men, but they are few in number, and, although cruder both in conception and in workmanship, they exhibit a striking similarity to the feast pipes of the Tlingit.

There is no indication that the Tahltan ever possessed any intoxicant. The introduction of liquor by both the whites and the coast natives has proved a great curse to them, and is largely accountable for their bodily ills and decrease in numbers.

HUNTING AND HUNTING IMPLEMENTS

From environment and through necessity the Tahltan have always been trappers and hunters. Food, clothing, implements, and household utensils were formerly made almost entirely from animal products. Before the acquisition of firearms they depended more on the snare and the deadfall than on the bow and the spear. To-day they depend on the rifle to supply the larder and on the trap to furnish the valuable peltries of the smaller fur bearing animals.

In September the permanent villages are rapidly deserted, and by families and parties the people set out for the hunting grounds, where camps are established and shifted as occasion demands. Of late years it has become a custom with many to return about Christmas for a short season of meeting and feasting, then again to go out for the late winter hunting. But in more primitive times they claim to have followed the game until spring. Of course little can now be learned of the life of this people before the fur trade was established by Europeans in the latter half of the eighteenth century. Up to that period hunting was conducted solely for the purpose of providing food and clothing. There was no inducement to accumulate beyond their actual needs except for the limited trade with their neighbors. It seems very likely that with an abundance of salmon for winter consumption the Tahltan in former times were more sedentary than they are known to have been after the great demand for furs made itself felt, when the incentive to hunt was stimulated by the desire for European products.

The implements of the chase were few in number and simple in construction, consisting of bow and arrow, spear, and knife. As elsewhere the bow was discarded as soon as the musket made its appearance, while blades of iron superseded those of stone and bone. I failed to find a single bow or arrow of aboriginal make, although barbs and blades of stone are of common occurrence. The following descriptions are from the testimony of older people and from models made by them.

The oldest and best bow was made of balsam, although spruce and birch were also used. It was five feet or more in length, and was not backed or otherwise artificially strengthened except in its manufacture when it was heated and rubbed with

5

the castorium to toughen the wood. It was stout in body, rectangular in cross section, tapering slightly toward each end, and rather clumsy in its proportions owing to the fact that it was used also as a spear at close quarters for dispatching the wounded. An obsidian blade was attached to one end. This blade differed from the arrowhead only in its greater length and the proportionately narrow base and shallow notches. Horn and latterly iron blades were also used. The bowstring was of caribou sinew, which was twisted when wet until perfectly round; it was sometimes permanently attached to the bow by weaving it through a tiny hole in the arm beyond the notch, drawing it up to a knot in the end, and then half-hitching it around the notch.

The following sketch and description of another type of bow and its manner of construction was written by the first accredited missionary to the Tahltan, the Reverend Mr. Palgrove, and sent to me by Dr. Ingles of Telegraph creek (see cut p. 67).

1. Wooden bow.
2. Caribou horn.
3. Sinew, fastening caribou horn to bow.
4. Ends of bow wound around with split porcupine quills, securing ends of the thick moose skin, which is also attached to the bow by quills.
5. numerous porcupine quills used in the fashion of tintacks.
6. Part of bow grasped by the hand, where consequently the skin is not tacked on, but glued on with spruce gum.

Bows were first made without the moose skin covering (which covered only the convex outside of the bow), but one day an Indian's bow broke while he had it fully drawn, and the horn flew off, together with the broken wood, striking him just below the neck and piercing him to the backbone, so that he fell dead. After this tragedy the Tahltan always safeguarded their horn knives by having the bow covered with skin, so that if any part of the bow should break it could not fly off and do damage.

The caribou horn was fixed to the top end of the bow, and when an animal which had been shot was overtaken, the hunter killed it by prodding it with the horn knife, holding his bow like a spear.

The arrow shaft was of black pine; foreshafts were never

used. The feathering was double, of hawk or owl feathers laid flat on opposite sides of the shaft and secured at each end with a wrapping of sinew. It is said that points of bone, horn, and ivory were used, but the only ones found were of obsidian, and these were dug from old village sites or found in the vicinity of springs that had been frequented by animals. The obsidian was obtained from the country between upper Stikine and Iskoot rivers, where it abounds The point was fitted into the split shaft head, secured with a seizing of sinew, and the whole smoothed over with a dressing of spruce gum applied when semi-liquified by heating. For big game, especially caribou, the barb was fitted but not seized to the shaft, so that when it penetrated the animal it detached itself and worked its way into the flesh, finally causing death. For grouse, ptarmigan, water fowl, rabbits and other small game the wooden shaft was expanded to a rounded head which served its purpose well.

The quiver was of caribou skin, almost cylindrical in form, ornamentally fringed, and painted in lines or smeared with red ochre or vermilion. It was carried over the back.

The bow was held vertically in the left hand, the thumb extended along the inner side and the index finger over the arrow, which was steadied in place between the index and middle fingers. The notch of the arrow was grasped with the straightened thumb and the bent forefinger, assisted by the middle finger to draw the string back.

The spear, used both as an implement of the chase and in warfare, consisted of an obsidian blade much like the bow point, but of greater length, carefully fitted in a corresponding cleft in the end of a stout wooden handle about six feet long, and securely lashed with hide. Iron blades were substituted as soon as this metal was introduced by the whites. A type of the latter, procured in trade from the fur companies, was very broad, double edged, with two notches at the base around which the lashing passed holding it firmly in place. Cases for protecting the blades were of wood, split in halves, hollowed out to conform to the shape of the blade, and grooved horizontally outside for the purpose of accommodating the seizing of hide.

The primitive knife used equally for hunting and in war was of obsidian, differing little from the spear blade. It was hafted in a short wooden handle split into halves and wrapped with sinew or hide, and was carried suspended around the neck or attached to the belt in a wooden case similar to the spear case. The obsidian knife was superseded by the iron blade which was fitted in a handle of horn, bone, or wood. The iron hunting knife was much shorter and ruder in workmanship than the war knife, and was carried in a case of wood or skin.

The flintlock musket of the Hudson's Bay Company was procured by the Tahltan from the coast people, in exchange for furs, early in the nineteenth century. The percussion cap musket was introduced later, but this in turn gave place to the rifle, and to-day no people have more approved arms than the Tahltan.

The accompaniment of the muzzle loader was the powder

Fig. 16.—Powder flask.

horn or a bag (Fig. 16) made of intestine tied about a hollow bone nozzle, a shot pouch of similar shape, and an open mouthed oblong bag for bullets, all of which, with shredded bark for wadding, were carried hanging under the left arm, in a small skin pouch generally ornamented in beadwork, still retained as an adjunct of the ceremonial dress. The powder charger, a hollow section of mountain goat or caribou horn or bone, was attached to the string of the powder horn or it served as the stopper of the shot pouch. Percussion caps were carried in small bone tubes, but for convenience circular or oblong pieces of leather were often cut on one edge to take the caps, and then were hung to the powder horn or to the trigger guard. A small wire pick for cleaning the vent or nipple was similarly carried. With the introduction of breech loaders, cartridge belts came into use.

Each animal had its peculiar economic value in the life of the people. The skins of all were utilized, and the flesh of all was eaten save that of the wolf, fox, wolverene, otter, fisher, marten, mink, muskrat, and ermine, and even these were used as food when necessity required. But the caribou has always had first place in the economic life of the Tahltan. Its flesh, together with that of the moose and the mountain sheep, was the most highly esteemed. Its skin was the most valued for clothing and for sleeping mats, and it furnished sinew for thread, nets, bowstrings, and seizings. From the horns and bones, skin dressing implements, knives, spoons, hooks, awls, and other tools as well as ornaments were fashioned. Indeed the caribou was to the Tahltan what the buffalo was to the tribes of the plains and the seal to the Eskimo. It is still abundant, and attracts sportsmen from many parts of the world. Its habitat is the uplands to the north and east of Dease lake, where moss is most plentiful.

The great value of the caribou made its hunting a matter of the first importance, and several different methods were employed for its capture. The bow and arrow were not very effectual in the open country, hence driving and snaring were resorted to in the late fall and winter when the caribou travelled in herds.

Frozen lakes, and particularly Dease lake, which is long and narrow, were obstructed at favorite points of crossing with brush barriers connected with wide mouthed corrals on each shore. These obstructions were built of stakes driven in the ground, interlaced with branches, and terminating in long narrow passages into which the frightened animals crowded, with no room to turn, thus falling easy prey to the thrusts of the spear and the knife in the hands of the hunters concealed on each side. Caribou are fond of the open, and the wall of brush on the ice was sufficient to turn them when pursued by shouting men and barking dogs.

A similar form of game barrier consisted of fences of stakes and boughs built across low divides or well travelled trails, with frequent narrow openings in which simple noose snares of twisted rawhide were set and which caught the branching antlers as the animals attempted to pass. When a herd was located nearby, it was partly surrounded and driven toward the ambuscade, behind which the hunters with bows and spears were concealed. Many caribou were killed by this means.

When snow covered the ground to a depth of two feet or more caribou were hunted systematically. The natives, having found a herd of the animals, made arrangements to drive them to some point at a distance, generally a valley or a pocket, where the snow was of sufficient depth to impede their movements, and where the swiftest runners secreted themselves. Others were stationed on each side. The old men and the boys with the dogs served as drivers, and with their cries and the beating of drums started the herd and kept it moving. When travelling in the snow the caribou follow in line, the leader breaking the trail and when the leader tires he steps aside, gives place to the next in succession, and falls in at the rear. When the animals reached the deeper snow the concealed hunters rose on all sides, and the frightened animals broke into confusion and were easily run down and speared by the swift-footed runners on snowshoes.

With the uniform cold of winter, meat kept indefinitely. The portion not needed for immediate use was cut in thin strips, notched, and sundried or smoked for future consumption, and particularly for use while travelling. In early days the dressed caribou skin was the most valuable article of exchange with the coast people.

The primitive methods of hunting were abandoned on the acquisition of the rifle.

The history of the occurrence of the moose in this section can not well be accounted for. It is believed to have been a habitant of all this region in early days, but for some unexplained reason the animal entirely disappeared early in 1800, to make its appearance again in 1877, when several were killed in the Dease country. Since then they have steadily increased in numbers, and have extended their range along the Stikine to below Telegraph creek. They are most abundant in the willow country toward Teslin, along the headwaters of the Tuya, and the tributaries of the Taku. The belief prevails among the natives that the return of the moose was due to the coming of white men, as this occurred soon after the Cassiar gold excitement. Its flesh is esteemed equally with that of the caribou. It is believed to exceed the Cook's Inlet moose in size, although the spread of its horns is not so great.

The mountain sheep, the most graceful of the species, is still found in abundance on the mountains across from Telegraph creek along the upper reaches of the Iskoot, and about the Narlin, Sheslay, and Teslin. From its inaccessibility and wariness it could never have proved a great source of supply with such primitive arms as the Tahltan possessed. Its flesh is the most delicate of all the animals of the continent. Its skin makes the most elastic of sleeping mats, and the horns after being softened by boiling, are cut, shaped, and pressed into dishes, spoons, knife handles, and tools, and have always been greatly in demand by the coast tribes, as the sheep does not approach salt water except at Cook Inlet, Alaska. The mountain sheep was hunted formerly with bow and arrow, as it is to-day with the rifle, by stalking. In spring and summer it is often found about the streams. The writer remembers a sheep being shot just above the river bank at the junction of the Tahl-tan with the Stikine in the latter part of June, 1906.

The mountain goat is another habitant of the mountains; it is found everywhere in this region and is common also on the coast. It is hunted in the early fall, when it has taken on an abundance of leaf fat between the skin and the flesh, which is removed in mass, melted and run into cakes. The skins serve as mats and rugs, and the wool is rolled and twisted into cord that is netted into carrying bags. It has been claimed that the Tahltan formerly wore blankets of mountain goat wool, but I could not corroborate this by the testimony of any living member of the tribe, and there is no evidence of such use in any surviving fabric. Formerly the horns, boiled in water until softened, were cut, shaped, and modeled into spoons; they were used also for snowshoe breaks, for knife, awl, and other tool handles, for powder chargers, and the like. Goats were hunted in the same manner as were the sheep.

The black bear and the grizzly are both abundant throughout the mountainous districts. They are hunted both for the flesh and the pelt; the claws are worn as headdresses and as necklaces, and the teeth are used as knife sharpeners and worn as charms. Bears are speared or shot in their hibernating holes, which are scented by the dogs, and during the salmon season they are killed about the streams. But deadfalls and snares are more effectual. The former are constructed of heavy tree trunks weighted with others and baited with fish or meat; the latter are set in the trails and attached to a tossing pole, as shown in the illustrations.

The clothing, implements, utensils, and ornaments of every primitive hunting or fishing people, by reason of their constant and intimate contact with mammals or fish, are distinguished by an unmistakable odor. For instance, the coast people, together with their houses and all they possess, are impregnated with the smoke of curing fish; everything pertaining to the life of the Esquimo is redolent of seal, walrus, and whale oil, while everything associated with the Tahltan gives out the pungent odor of the castoreum.

The beaver was formerly very abundant along the lower Stikine, in the country of sluggish streams and about the smaller lakes; but with the advent of European trading vessels and the establishment of posts by the Husdon's Bay Company along the northwest coast, the demand for beaver fur so increased that it was pursued unremittingly until the extinction of the animal seemed imminent. Besides the marketable value of the fur and the delicacy of the flesh, the castoreum was used for baiting traps, as it seemed to attract all animals equally. It was carried by the hunter in a horn, bone, or wooden box (Fig. 17), toggled to the belt, and was smeared over the bait or diluted and scattered over the adjacent ground. The cylindrical box was more often of caribou horn, plugged with wood at the bottom, and fitted with a wooden stopper attached with a slack hide string to the toggle so that it was not subjected to strain as the box hung from the belt. I found one very remarkable specimen of a castoreum case, made of a section of bamboo that must

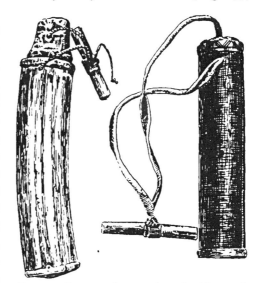

FIG. 17.—Castoreum boxes. *A*: made of horn. *B*: made of bamboo.

have been procured from the coast early in trade. Drifts of cocoanut, bamboo, and other Oriental woods are not infrequently found on the seaward shores of the Queen Charlotte Islands, brought thither by the Japan current.

The beaver was hunted with arrow and spear, and trapped with the deadfall in the milder seasons, but was not pursued during the summer months. When the lakes were well frozen, netting was resorted to with great success. The beaver net is of babiche, about twelve feet in length, stretching to half of that in depth, with six-inch meshes. It is square at one end and pointed at the other. A draw string passes around through the outer meshes, which, when pulled, bring the net together at the apex.

The net is set through a hole in the ice across the accustomed path of the animal from his lodge. The pointed end with its bone attachment is made fast to a stake driven in the ground, and the draw string is attached to a bent sapling to which is hung a rattle consisting of three or four sections of caribou or moose hoof, which sounds upon the slightest disturbance of the net (Fig. 18). The hunter now breaks into the beaver's house, and

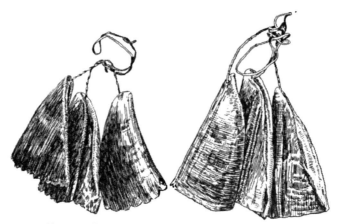

FIG. 18.—Rattles for beaver net made of animal hoofs.

the fleeing animal becomes entangled in the meshes of the net, causing the rattle to sound. The draw strings are quickly hauled in and the game dispatched with a short handled, iron barbed

spear.   The primitive barb was made of caribou horn or of bone.
Sometimes the net, rubbed with castoreum, is set in clear water
in a narrow passageway frequented by the beaver, which is
caught at night.   The hunter, sleeping on the bank with the
draw string attached to his wrist, is awakened by the pull of the
struggling animal in the net.   To-day steel traps have taken the
place of all other devices, and water in which the castoreum has
stood is sprinkled about to attract the animal.

The land otter is not so abundant in the Tahltan country

Fig. 19.—Deadfall for marten.

as on the coast, and it is regarded with much superstition by
the people generally.   Its spirit is considered to be the property
of the shaman and in early days the animal was not molested;

but after the great demand for furs took possession of the whole country, this feeling was overcome. The otter is now shot, and also taken in deadfalls, but its flesh is never eaten.

The marten is very abundant throughout the lower woodland country and in the vicinity of water. It has always been esteemed for its rich, soft fur, which makes the most valuable blankets and robes, and is always marketable. It is taken in several varieties of deadfall baited with fish (Fig. 19). Its flesh is not eaten.

The mink and the weasel are trapped like the marten. More or less superstition attaches to both of these animals, and particularly to the latter, the skins of which are worn by the shaman in his incantations. The flesh of neither is considered edible.

In primitive days the marmot, next to the caribou, was possibly the most important animal found here, from an economic point of view. Its great abundance and the ease with which it was captured insured a supply of nutritious food for the winter. As soon as the salmon season was over, the people went to the mountains and hunted this animal until it hiber-

Fig. 20.—Deadfall for bear, fox, wolf, land otter, marmot, etc.

nated. It was taken with a snare set in front of its hole. The body was split and dried or smoked and packed away for the season of want. The skin was cleaned, dressed on the underside, and used for making blankets, robes, caps, and heavy winter shoes. The blankets were an important medium of trade with · the coast people.

Wolves are said to be more abundant to-day than in the past; they were formerly taken in deadfalls (Fig. 20) but now are little sought.

Foxes are the most valuable of the fur bearing animals of the country. The species that produces the black, silver, cross, and red, is very abundant, and the great value of the skins of the black and silver varieties makes their hunting very profitable. Foxes were formerly taken by the deadfall, but this device has been superseded by the steel trap.

The lynx is found wherever rabbits are plentiful, and has always been sought by the Tahltan. Its skin is very desirable for making winter robes, and its flesh is eaten. It is snared by means of the tossing pole set at the entrance of a corral of small sticks, at the lower end of which is placed a rabbit skin smeared with castoreum. Another form of snare is secured to a sapling trunk several feet long, with noose set in the rabbit trail, so that when the animal springs the snare the pole catches in the small wood, and in the struggle that ensues the animal is strangled. A peculiar tradition is current with all the interior people, and has even found its way to the island inhabitants of the coast, that in early days the lynx had relations with woman, consequently there are certain regulations regarding its treatment and the consumption of various parts of its body.

Rabbits are found everywhere, and can be had in winter and spring when other food supplies fail. They are still taken with the hide or sinew noose and the tossing pole, set in the runways as in the past. The flesh is eaten, and the skins are used for making shirts, robes, caps, and particularly for baby blankets.

The ground squirrel is snared and the skins made into blankets which are very light and durable. The flesh of the porcupine is highly esteemed; the animal can be had at any time, and is simply hunted with a dog and struck over the head with a stick.

Ptarmigan and grouse are snared, and are also shot with the blunt headed arrow.

As previously stated, before the introduction of firearms the capture of animals for food and clothing depended much more on trapping than on the efficiency of the arrow or the spear. The ingenuity of the Indian was taxed to the utmost to devise practical means to this end, inventing various forms of snares and traps. The former seem to have found more

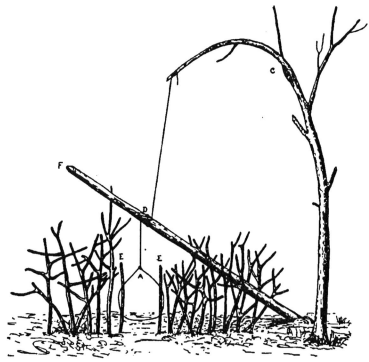

FIG. 21a.—Snare for rabbits.

favor, as might be expected in a land covered with snow during a large part of the year, and particularly when the fish and berry supplies were cut off and when the furs were in prime condition.

The snare for the larger animals consists of a rope of

twisted rawhide fitted with an eye at one or at each end, and secured at one end to a stake or a tree trunk, or to the tossing pole in the form of a stout tree trunk nicely balanced. The noose in the other end opens out over the trail, or an opening in the fence, and slipping over the animal's head, strangles it in its efforts to escape. For smaller animals the snare is of hide, or of twisted sinew or tree fiber, fitted with a wooden toggle about a third of its length from the noose end. The standing part is permanently secured to a sapling, bent over, or to a section of tree trunk balanced with the weight at the lower

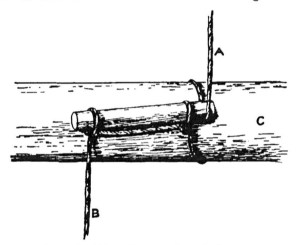

Fig. 21b.—Trigger for snare shown in figure 21a

end. By means of the toggle the strain of the sapling or tree-trunk is held until a slight disturbance of the noose releases the toggle when the sapling springs back into place or the trunk falls and the struggling animal is lifted and strangled (Fig. 21).

The second type of trap consists of a deadfall formed of a log or logs, weighted or not according to the size of the animal to be taken, and hung by means of a simple trigger held by a light rod which the animal springs by stepping upon or attempting to remove the bait rendered more attractive by smearing with castoreum.

SKIN-DRESSING

The tanning and dressing of hides and skins forms an industry in which the Tahltan women excel. It was their most important work in primitive times, for upon it the people depended for clothing, bags, babiche for snowshoes, nets, snares, rope, and cordage. The sale of tanned skins and babiche to the trading posts still constitutes a considerable item in the support of the household.

The hides of caribou, moose, mountain sheep, and mountain goat are tanned for clothing, while the skins of the smaller fur bearing animals, as the lynx, fox, marten, mink, marmot, squirrel, and rabbit, are dressed for blankets, robes, and head gear. Practically the same methods of treatment are employed to-day as in the past, and while an occasional iron tool may be found in use, implements of bone and stone, aboriginal in form and workmanship, are preferred.

The same methods are employed and the same tools are used in the treatment of caribou hide, moose hide, sheepskin, and goatskin; the latter two, however, are seldom tanned, but are superficially cleaned on the under side to serve for bedding and mats. Caribou and moose skins are utilized for clothing, the latter for the heaviest winter wear, for moccasins, and for the armored coat described on page 116.

The primitive skinning knife was of horn, or more often of a section of the rib or tibia of one of the larger animals sharpened at one end, and generally having a hole in the other end through which passed a string of hide for the purpose of sus-

Fig. 22.—Bone skining knife.

pending it around the neck or to hang it to the house post (Figs. 22, 23). It is one of the few Tahltan implements that generally show a rude attempt at ornamentation in etched lines and geometric figures, rarely in animal forms, brought out more distinctly by filling the incisions with red ochre.

The skin is first cleaned of all particles of adhering flesh by hanging it over an upright post standing about three feet out of the ground, and scraping it with a hand fleshing bone, the tibia of the caribou or of the moose, but better still of the grizzly bear (Fig. 24, A, B). The scraping edge at the end is generally serrated. The skin to be tanned, if green, is moistened and rolled up

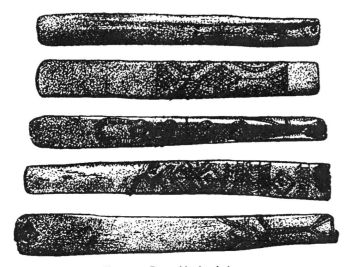

Fig. 23.—Bone skinning knives.

and allowed to remain for several days; or if an old skin it is moistened and rolled up, by which means the hair is loosened. It is then moistened again and placed over a section of sapling or half rounded tree trunk inclined at an angle of forty-five degrees and the hair removed with a bone shaving implement consisting of the tibia of the caribou, sharpened along the lower edge and used in both hands. This tool (Fig. 24, C, D) is practically a natural product, showing no attempt at workmanship beyond the cutting edge, but it serves its purpose perfectly, and is much more popular than the bent iron blade in single or double form sometimes seen.

The skin is next dried in the shade and then soaked in water with the brain of the animal for one night, when it is taken out and washed. This process is repeated several times. Slits are cut close to the edges, around the entire skin, through which passes the line that stretches it on the dressing frame.

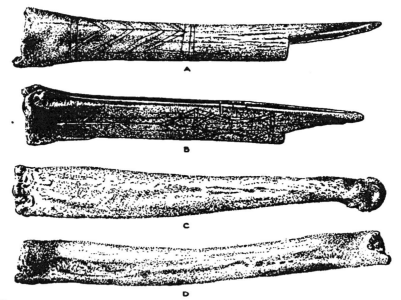

FIG. 24.—Bone fleshing and scraping implements used in dressing caribou and moose skins.

Before the introduction of iron these slits were made with sharp flakes of obsidian. The skin is now moistened, and, to soften it, rubbed with the brain or the liver boiled hard and reduced to meal. Sometimes a soft white clay procured in trade from Atlin is used in place of this preparation. The inner cuticle of the skin is now scraped off with the heavy chisel-like fleshing implement made from a leg bone of a bear, moose, or caribou, the blade of which is serrated to insure a better hold on the skin. This is the most laborious work, and the most necessary to insure the best results.

After drying, the skin is next treated with a stone dressing implement, and rubbed and softened first on the flesh side, then on the hair side. This rough stone consists of the split half of an oblong, flattened, small boulder or pebble of a character that can be picked up almost anywhere on the trail. The rounded working edge, if too sharp, is blunted to prevent it from cutting or tearing, for the use of this implement is simply for the purpose of softening the skin by rubbing and pressure. It may be necessary to chip the edges slightly to produce the desired shape, for in use it is inserted in the split end of a stick about four feet in length, and secured in place with a temporary hide lashing, as the handle is not carried from place to place although the stone blade is retained. Hand dressing stones, not hafted, used in the treatment of smaller skins, are of the same general character, but oval or circular in form because more convenient to grasp. Such implements are of very simple construction. A pebble of the desired size and shape being selected, it is placed on end and struck with a heavier pebble which causes it to split in halves along the natural line of cleavage of the broader faces, thus furnishing one or two suitable pieces that need only a few strokes of the chipping stone to bring them to shape. Of all implements these dressing stones are the most frequently met, as they are readily procured and are in constant use. Smaller ones are sometimes carried in small skin cases in the woman's workbag.

The skin is worked again and again, moistened alternately, rubbed with brain, and dried until it is as soft and pliable as a piece of cloth; then it is allowed to dry finally, after which it is removed from the stretching frame and folded.

If the skin is to be smoked, it is stitched together lengthwise, like a bag, and fitted over a light willow frame of saplings stuck in the ground around a circular depression, the tops being bent over and seized to one another. A fire kindled in the hollow beneath is later covered with decayed spruce and black pine cones that smoulder and produce a smudge, gradually changing the white skin to a rich brown.

Skins of the smaller fur bearing animals, which are used for making shirts, blankets, and robes, require little labor in dressing, if the animals are killed in season, and the skin is carefully removed; for except in the case of the marmot they are very thin, and need only to be cleaned, washed, and softened, with the least possible work. The process of scraping is performed with the flat bone skinning knife, which for this purpose is notched along the working edge, while the softening is done with the hand dressing stone already described.

At Tahltan and at the principal winter camps, permanent dressing frames for the treatment of moose and caribou skins are erected. They consist of two stout uprights, firmly planted in the ground (*AA*), each of which is supported by two braces (*BB*), and a horizontal bar that rests in the crotch of the braces against the upright (*C*), where all are secured together by a stout lashing. Near the ground another cross-bar (*D*) is lashed to the uprights. To accommodate the frame to a skin of any size a horizontal bar (*E*), suspended by two ropes from the upper bar, can be raised or lowered to any height. A perpendicular pole (*K*), adjustable laterally to any distance desired is lashed to the movable and the lower horizontal bars (See Fig. 2, p. 33).

Babiche, which serves for snowshoe netting, bags, beaver and fish nets, cordage, and thong, is made from caribou skin, dehaired, cleaned, and cut when wet in sizes according to its use. A strip is cut around the inner circumference of the skin in a continuous length, which is tied in a bundle and stored for use. At the present time a small straight-bladed steel knife is employed, but before the introduction of iron an obsidian chip or knife was used.

FISH AND FISHING

After the spring hunting the people return to the permanent villages, as the animals are with young and in poor condition, and their pelts valueless. Then follows a period of rest and relaxation after the long, severe winter season, when the temperature frequently registers −50° F.

In this inland country spring breaks while the coast, with its comparatively mild climate, is still enveloped in snow. This difference is most noticeable in coming from Wrangel by the Stikine as late as June. When the flats of the lower river valley are buried beneath two or more feet of snow and the chill of winter is in the air, the land beyond the cañon is taking on a shade of green, the air is soft and fragrant with the awakening of spring, which gets into the blood of the people and drives them out of their houses to the fishing grounds to await the coming of the salmon.

Five varieties of salmon come in from the sea and ascend the river to spawn during the summer. The first to appear, in June, is the king salmon, the largest and the most esteemed for cooking while fresh; and this is followed in succession by the small silver salmon, generally known as the sockeye; the humpback; the dog salmon, and the coho, besides several varieties of trout. Of these the sockeye is the main source of supply, from its greater abundance, and being a dry fish it cures readily. All varieties, however, are taken and eaten fresh, and greatly enjoyed after the winter diet of meat. In the days of primitive arms and appliances, when animals were more difficult to secure, the Tahltan were probably much more dependent on fish as a staple, as the supply never wholly failed, and fish were more easily captured than mammals. In the vicinity of old living and fishing places there may still be seen cache pits of considerable size where the catch was preserved for winter use. These caches were square pits of fair size, floored and lined with small saplings. After the fish were packed away, a covering of saplings and bark was laid over, on top of which were placed tree trunks, and all was concealed beneath an upper layer of earth and leaves, so that in event of a raid by hostile people and the destruction of the village, this source of supply would escape detection. The earth covering was also a protection against forest fires that have devastated this interior country from time to time. To-day the Tahltan eat fresh salmon throughout the summer season. They dry and smoke a certain amount, but the latter is traded and used as dog food rather than for their own consumption.

The Stikine river and its tributaries are swift streams, rushing through deep gorges with precipitous walls and offering few vantage grounds for fishing. When such occur, however, summer huts of sapling, roofed with bark and branches are built and these serve likewise for smokehouses. In streams of such swiftness as these, fences and traps are impossible, and in muddy water the spear is equally useless, therefore the gaff hook is to-day the main implement for fishing. This implement is similar to that used by the more southerly Tlingit, and consists of a pole armed with a sharp pointed detachable iron hook, which, by means of a couple of feet of hide line, is permanently attached to the fifteen foot shaft. When the fish is struck the hook detaches itself and remains attached to the pole only by the line. I believe that before the introduction of iron a similar hook was fashioned from caribou horn.

Formerly gill nets of twisted sinew and babiche were used for catching small fish in the lakes. Scoop nets of the same materials were used. The smaller streams were fenced for fishing, and long slit baskets with narrow conical mouths were placed at openings left for the purpose. The fish in their upward passage entered these baskets and were thus confined. At one point in the main river known as Ge-kah-ne-gah, where the water flows through a narrow and shallow passage, cylindrical rod baskets each with an inverted cone within the mouth were weighted down, and when filled were lifted and emptied. In the lakes several varieties of fish were taken, the most esteemed of which were whitefish and trout.

Spears of several varieties were formerly employed in fishing at different seasons. A salmon spear of primitive type was described to me by the Tahltan, but no example of it could be found. It consisted of a blade made of mountain goat horn, about three inches in length, pointed at both ends, and sharpened along one edge. A line of twisted sinew or hide passed through a hole about the center and was secured to a twelve-foot shaft near the head. One end of the toggle-like blade fitted in a socket in the end of the shaft, and in use, when the blade was driven into a fish, it was released from the end of the pole, and the strain on the line tended to turn the blade at an angle and prevent its withdrawal.

A type of spear for lake fishing through the ice is common to the entire country back of the coast range, and has been adopted by the Chilkat. It consists of a fifteen foot pole, to the end of which is lashed two short arms of tough wood or horn. At the end of each arm is a barb of horn, latterly of iron, lashed with sinew or hide, and a sharp pointed bone projects from the shaft-end, almost meeting the barb points. The fisher stands over a hole in the ice, through which a bait of salmon eggs has been lowered, and as the fish comes directly beneath, it is speared. These holes in the ice are made with a pointed section of caribou horn, one old specimen of which was fortunately found in an old fishing house on Tahltan river.

The salmon is split and cleaned, the head cut off, the back-bone removed, and the flesh scored and sundried for a day or two, and then hung on drying frames over a slow fire of willow or cottonwood in the curing houses. These frames are built in two or three tiers. The fresher fish are placed nearer the fire, and after a day or so they are placed on the tier next above until thoroughly cured, when they are tied up in bundles and stored in the caches or small storehouses for winter use.

Trout of several varieties, including the Dolly Varden,

cutthroat, rainbow, and lake trout, are taken with a gaff hook similar to the one for salmon described above but of smaller size. They are also caught in traps, baskets, and nets, and with a rude wooden hook barbed with wood, bone, or metal, baited with salmon eggs or meat.

Large fish, when caught, are killed with a small wooden club consisting merely of a section of sapling, free from any attempt at ornamentation.

GAMBLING

With that tendency toward adoption that characterized the Nahane, the Tahltan have sacrificed all their own games of chance in favor of modern cards. Gambling implements of the past were found among the rubbish of the cache houses, at the bottoms of old chests, and in the forgotten débris of the dwellings. More difficult still was it to obtain accurate particulars concerning the games themselves, for the men of the present generation in their desire to be considered as the white man disclaim any knowledge of the past, while the memory of the older people is not always dependable, although only the native games were known prior to the Cassiar gold excitement of 1874, which event strongly marks the past from the present.

Three different sets of implements were employed in gambling, all of which are common to the whole northwest coast, and two of them to an extended area of the interior, hence it is reasonably certain that none of them originated with the Tahltan.

The game of *tse-teh-lee* was played with a number of small, rounded, marked sticks, of the finer grained woods of the country, as maple, birch, ash, and sometimes spruce or willow, neatly fashioned to a definite size, smoothed with the native "sandpaper" of equisetum stalks, and painted in red and black encircling lines and bands of different widths variously placed. These markings determine the values and the names of the sticks. The value is fixed, and is represented by one character in each color on two sticks of a set, which are named *eh-kah*, "feet." These might be designated trumps as they are the winning sticks in the play. All the other marked sticks are termed *tchar*, "painted." In value they are equal to the plain ones, of which there are generally a few in each set. The painted lines and bands (Figs. 25–28), which in a number

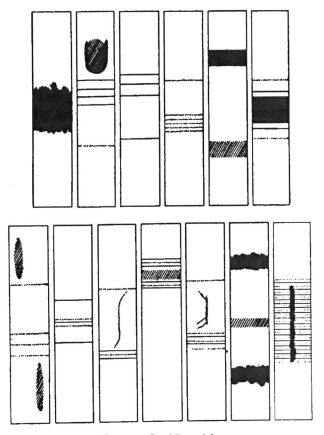

FIG. 25.—Gambling sticks.

of sets show only slight differences, give to each stick its name, but this does not affect its value in the play. These names are purely individual, given at the will of the owner, and are those of animals, parts of the body, and natural objects. While some marks are generally recognized by the same name, they follow no fixed rule, and this makes it impossible to identify them except through the one who has used them. In almost every set a few of the sticks are painted in picture designs, in red and black, entirely distinct from the encircling lines, which affect neither the value nor the name. These characters are entirely decorative and represent graphically or symbolically some animal form or natural object intimately associated with the life of the people (Pl. XIX). While these crude drawings sometimes rudely depict the object, generally they are in simple lines, sketchy and without apparent meaning; but to the older people they seem to convey distinct impressions, suggesting the existence of a system of picture writing in the past, which the Nahane are said to have practised. The sticks are slender, and the ends are squared or bluntly rounded. Those that have been used for a great length of time have received a fair polish, but all are well finished.

The gaming sticks are in double sets, each numbering from eighteen to more than thirty. Each set is carried in a cylindrical pocket in either end of a caribou skin band that serves as a carrying strap for the hand or to throw over the shoulder. The bags are generally trimmed with a strip of colored cloth and edged with beads, and in some instances are decorated with dentalium and tufts of yarn. The double set of gaming sticks and the peculiar carrying bag I have never met with elsewhere (Pl. XIII).

A necessary adjunct of the gambling sticks is a strip of hard tanned bear skin, about forty inches in length by ten inches in width, upon which the sticks were thrown in play. When not in use the skin is kept rolled around the shredded bark or hay in which the sticks are wrapped when in play, and is tied around one end with a hide string.

Before describing the manner in which the gaming sticks were used, it might be pertinent to compare them with those of the coast, in contradiction of the theory that they were borrowed from the people of the littoral, from whom the Tahltan have adopted so much.

In material each people used the finer woods of their own country, which, except for the maple and the spruce, are very

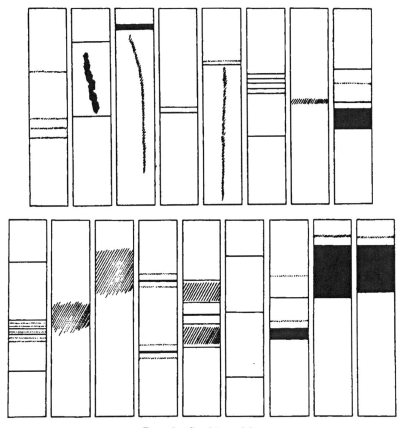

FIG. 26.—Gambling sticks.

different, and the maple is little found on the islands. The Tahltan gaming stick is uniformly slender and is squared or bluntly rounded at the end, while that used by the coast people is always thicker (sometimes two or more diameters larger), and the ends are often ornate, pointed, nipple-shaped, rounded, hollowed, and sometimes inlaid with shell. While the encircling lines bear a general resemblance, they are characteristic with each people, the arrangement being entirely different, and the rude pictography of the Tahltan sticks is archaic when compared with the artistic burnt and incised conventional designs of some of the coast sets, which also are often inlaid with shell and bone. The carrying bag of the Tahltan, as above noted, is unique both in its double arrangement and in its connecting strap, while the skin bag of the coast has but one pocket which is covered by a flap or wrapped around by the extension of the back of the bag that is carried to some length as a band. The number of sticks in the coast sets average many more than the number in the two sets of the Tahltan, reaching, in some instances, eighty or more. The strip of bear skin on which the sticks are thrown when played is replaced on the coast by a square or folded mat of heavy hide, cut or painted in totemic design. The Tahltan have no counterpart for the strip of caribou skin with the hair intact, and fringed and often painted along the sides, which the coast people roll around the paint sticks and the shredded cedar bark. So that it would seem that this game came to the Tahltan from some place other than the coast.

The game is played by two men seated opposite to each other. Each player is provided with his own paraphernalia, and carries several sets of sticks, which he uses as we do cards, throwing aside one set and taking up another for "better luck." The bear skins are stretched between the players. The sticks, in two bundles of plain and marked ones respectively, are placed within easy reach at the left, and a small bundle of shredded bark or fine hay is before each player. The dealer now takes one of the marked, or "trump," sticks, *eh-kah*, and three other sticks, wraps them in hay, and places them separately on the bear skin in front of him in four bundles. The opponent next points to one of them, indicating the bundle which he believes to contain the trump. The dealer then takes it up, and also a lot of ten or twelve of the other sticks, forces the former through the hay among these, and manipulates them with both hands, jostling them around; he then takes out one stick at a time, throws it down on the bear skin, and calls out the name if a marked stick, until he comes to the trump or has exhausted the bundle. If the trump is not shown, the opponent guesses again, and the process is repeated; and if the trump is not disclosed, he again guesses, and, if not successful, the dealer wins a half of the entire stake. The trump is now taken up by the dealer, and one other stick is taken from the pile to the left; each is wrapped in hay, and the two are placed separately in front of the dealer. The opponent now guesses which is the trump, and as before the concealed stick is forced into and manipulated with a bundle of other sticks and cast down on the bear skin, and if the trump does not appear, then the dealer wins half of the remaining stake, and the whole process, with the four sticks, is repeated, then with the two sticks. The dealer now sings, and if the trump is not guessed, the stake is won by the dealer; but if the opponent guesses the trump at any time, the deal passes to him, although the amount won by the dealer is retained.

Another and much more complicated game was played for the writer by one of the few older men who still remembered the play of the past.

The players seat themselves as before, with the implements similarly placed. The dealer takes one trump and one other stick which he first wraps in hay separately, then in one bundle together under the hay in front of him; he next jostles the bundle around in his hands until the opponent calls "*Ha!*" when he removes the outer wrapping and places the two wrapped sticks singly in front of him. Then the opponent waves his hand to right or left, indicating which bundle he wishes taken up. The dealer takes also a bundle of ten or twelve of the other sticks, and forces the wrapped stick out of the hay and among the other sticks, and jostles them about, and as he throws down each

stick on the bear skin in front of him he calls out its name, if
marked, until he produces the trump or exhausts the bundle.
If the trump is produced the dealer wins once, and the process is
repeated; should the dealer lose, the game is begun anew; but
if the dealer wins the second set, then he takes the trump and

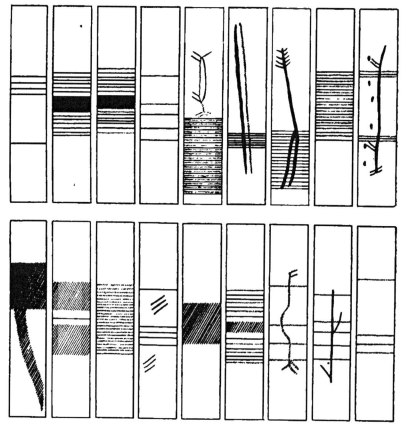

FIG. 27.—Gambling sticks.

three other sticks, wraps each one in hay, and places the four
bundles in front of him. The opponent points to one which is
taken up and manipulated with the bundle of sticks, as before
described, and if it is not the trump, then the opponent indicates

another one of the three bundles left, and if he fails the second
time to guess the trump, the two remaining bundles are taken up
and jostled in the hands, and when the opponent says "*Ha!*"
they are placed in the bundle of hay with the ends just protrud-

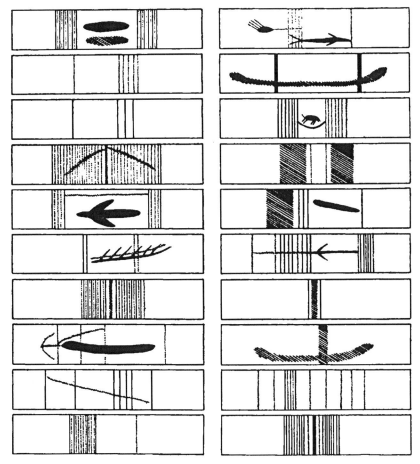

Fig. 28.—Gambling sticks.

ing, and by a wave of the hand to left or right he indicates which
one he wishes taken. As before, it is manipulated with a bundle
of sticks, and if the trump is not produced when the sticks are

thrown down, the dealer wins and takes half the stake, and commences again with two sticks as at first; the production of the trump winning for the dealer, and if he wins all four sets in succession he takes the remaining half of the stake. But should the opponent win twice when two sticks are used, and again when the four st cks are used, he takes the deal and the game begins. It will be seen that in this game the trump is both a losing and a winning stick, losing when guessed with two sticks, and winning when guessed with three or four.

Possibly there were other variations of this game, but to-day even the older people have little recollection of it, and there was great difficulty in finding two men who could interpret its intricacies. When playing, the dealer sings, as in all gambling games. The songs have little meaning, just a word or two long drawn out, and often in a foreign tongue.

The game of *nah-ar*, the guessing contest of odd or even, is played with bone toggles, averaging three inches in length, but sometimes smaller. They are generally rounded, and tapering from the middle to the ends, which are usually blunt or rounded; but sometimes they are flattened on two sides and of the same thickness throughout. No unvarying shape obtains, and they do not exhibit great care in the construction. They are in sets of two and four, in which half are plain and half are distinguished by a few turns of hide or wire around the middle. Undoubtedly this game has been borrowed from the coast, and the finer implements are clearly of coast manufacture, the Tahltan work being noticeably crude.

The game is played by two persons or by any number seated on the ground opposite each other in two lines. Each player bets with his opposite, and the two stakes are placed together between them. The play is conducted by one side at a time, each man of which has a marked and a plain toggle which he changes from hand to hand or manipulates behind his back or under the blanket that covers his knees. Sometimes instead of two toggles the players use but one, which is passed from hand to hand and serves the same purpose as the marked one. At a signal the hands of the players are produced and kept in motion in front of them while all join in an expressionless song consisting of a few long drawn out words in their own, or, very often, in the Nishka language. The leader of the opposing side with outstretched arm throws his hand to the right or left, at which signal all the players open the indicated hand in front of them, and according as the hands contain plain toggles (or if playing with a single toggle they display it), the guessing side wins that number, and loses from the plain toggles or empty hands. The difference in number between the two is indicated to the winning side by stick counters that are stuck up in the ground between the contesting parties. After every count the other side takes up the play, which continues until all the counters are accumulated by one or the other of the two sides, when the game is finished, and each man of the winning side takes the individual stake in front of him.

The counters, twenty or more in number according to agreement, may be small willow twigs a foot or so long, but the writer found a bundle of regularly cut stakes, pointed at each end, so that they could be stuck in the ground and the players could determine at any time how the game stood.

This game, with slight variation, is common to all the tribes of the northwest coast, and it probably came to the Tahltan from this source rather than from the interior. It is of later origin than the preceding game played with the small sticks, and is to-day well remembered by a majority of the people.

The only game of chance played by the women is known as *ketchee,* a Tlingit word referring to the hand and indicating the source of the game. It is played with a small die of wood or bone, and is a contest of dexterity rather than of guessing. The die is thrown in the air, and according to the way it falls it counts naught, one, or two. Small stick counters are used, and when one gains them all, the stake passes to her as the winner. Only a single specimen of die was found among all the

7

people. It is of wood, ornamentally carved in bird form, and most probably is of Tlingit manufacture.

Of children's games but little could be learned. In primitive days the Tahltan unquestionably had their time well employed in procuring the necessities of life, and the children from an early age had their share of labor to perform that occupied much of their time. Then their hunting, in small bands, and constant shifting of camp, all tended to retard the development of amusements. The girls had their dolls, which they have to-day. The boys played jump pole. They ran, they lifted weights, and they made bundles of the stems of fireweed or of brush which they placed in a thicket out of sight. This they tried to spear from a distance with sharpened sticks, the winner receiving a prize. In winter the same game was played, but the bundle of twigs was buried out of sight in the snow.

MARRIAGE

So far as the daughter is concerned, marriage is largely a matter of sale, for she belongs to the parents, more particularly in this case to the father, and is not consulted in the choice of a husband. Early marriage is the rule with both sexes, and this is generally consummated shortly after the girl is released from the confinement attending puberty, and the boy has attained maturity. Daughters are really more of an asset to the parents than sons, for besides the original price, or gift, if the wife proves satisfactory the husband honors the father-in-law with presents throughout life; and in the case of young couples, the husband more frequently comes to live with the wife's parents, thus adding materially to their support. In the case of sons, if they are not given to an uncle to rear, they live with and assist the father until marriage, when their connection with their parents practically ceases. Referring to the customs of the past, the proposal of marriage came from the man, who communicated his wishes to his mother, married sister, or aunt, who in turn went to the mother of the girl and asked her consent, at the same time intimating the number and value of presents to be made. This was discussed by her parents, and generally a demand for further gifts was made, and thus were the negotiations carried back and forth until an agreement was finally reached. The brothers or near totemic relations of the suitor then carr'ed the payment in skins or blankets to the father of the girl and placed them before him. If he was satisfied the time for the union was named. If it was the daughter of a chief, or of a man of standing, he held a feast, assisted by his family, and to this feast the family of the prospective bridegroom was invited. When all were assembled, the presents were brought forth and counted. The bride-elect was seated, with her back to the guests, in a corner of the house, near the entrance, and was completely covered with a blanket of caribou skin, and thus she remained throughout the feast. At its conclusion she was taken by her mother to the house of the groom, if he had one; if not then to the home of the man's parents, where they lived for a short time and then returned and lived with the parents of the bride. Etiquette required that the young husband hold no intercourse with the mother-in-law; when one came into the shelter, the other would often leave.

Although the girl is not permitted to choose her partner, marriage seems to be as productive of good results among the Tahltan as elsewhere. Although exacting under normal conditions of climate and country, the life of the woman is by no means one of oppression, and her position in the household is well assured.

Polygamy was both permitted and practised, but it was not the rule, and it has now practically disappeared. The old custom of requiring the nephew to marry the widow of his deceased uncle on attaining the succession was instituted that the old wife might continue to enjoy the benefits of a home and the support to which she had been accustomed, for she could inherit nothing from her husband's estate, owing to the social organization requiring her to be of the opposite totem. Such ill-assorted unions were generally responsible for the taking of another wife more congenial in point of years. Another reason for plural marriage was the privilege of hunting grounds and trade rights acquired with each wife. These advantages influenced intermarriage with the people of neighboring tribes, more particularly with the Taku and Kaska, whose language, customs, and pursuits were very similar, as well as with the Bear lake people, the Stikine Tlingit (with whom they constantly traded), and occasionally with the Nishka during periods of peace. On the death of the wife, should she have a marriageable sister the widower could have her at little or no extra cost. She would as a right come to him to supply the place of the dead in payment for the original cost. Divorce was not common. Indeed on the whole the domestic relations were and are as happy among them as elsewhere. Affection for their children is particularly noticeable, and this they richly deserve by reason of their unvarying obedience and helpfulness.

CHILDBIRTH

On reaching the period of confinement the woman seeks an outhouse of brush and bark that has been erected for her temporary seclusion, for both at this time and when isolated on reaching puberty she is considered unclean. In the retreat she is attended by one or more experienced older women. In delivery she assumes a squatting position directly over a shallow pit that has been lined and half filled with soft moss, and leans forward with her arms over a stout pole securely driven in the ground at an angle, which relieves the weight of the body and allows the muscles to relax. If labor is difficult, the midwife manipulates the abdomen and assists the delivery; and in extreme cases it is said that the shaman might be summoned. Should this be necessary he would come only to the shelter, holding concealed in his hand an object believed to possess medicine, or magic power, as a bit of fur, or a bird skin, and, reaching in, he might touch the patient's head with his hand, after which he would quickly disappear. This, as the informant expressed herself, "would scare child and make it come quick."

Upon delivery the child is slightly washed in warm water, but in the past it was wiped with a soft rabbit skin, then wrapped in a light fur blanket and placed in a bark cradle lined with soft-ground moss (*Hypnum capillifolium* Wornstorf) which had been carefully picked apart and dried, and the whole structure covered with tanned skin or fur. Regarding the form of the cradle, some of the older people claim that the primitive cradle was a hammock of skin with lines of babiche, a type that survives in the blanket of commerce and the rope line that may often be seen in Tahltan houses to-day. Neither of these forms is ever used more than once, and when it has served its purpose it is hidden away, as the connection between the life and the cradle can never be broken, although growing apart with age.

After delivery the mother rests for two or three days, and is given no solid food, only a tea of herbs, of dogberry root, or of the inner bark of the spruce, and later a soup made of salmon and dogberry root which is believed to increase the flow of milk. When she is able to take solid food a fish diet is preferred, grease and fats being avoided.

The placenta (*ethone ke-thla-ge*) is often retained for several days, no attempt is made to expel it, nature being allowed to take its course.

The umbilical cord (*ethone elboola*) is tied with sinew and then cut; before the introduction of iron this was done with a rude knife or splinter of obsidian. The life of the child is foretold by the length of the cord, which, after it comes off, is dried on a stick, wrapped with fine sinew thread, sewed in a tiny sack, and secured to the cradle or to the clothing. The mother carefully preserves the sack until the child reaches maturity, when she hides it away in a crevice in the rocks, in the nest of an eagle, or in a hollow tree.   Its relation to the life always exists, although after maturity it is less considered.   If it should be lost in childhood, a normal growth would not be attained.   If it were purposely destroyed, misfortune, or death would follow.   If it should fall into the hands of one evilly disposed, sickness could be produced that might result fatally; therefore, as my informant expressed herself, "that string is a child's life: that one thing they look out [for]."

The mother remains in the bark shelter during the two or three days following delivery, and then returns to the camp. She is still cared for until able to get up, and a wide abdominal band of skin is put on and worn until normal conditions are restored.

The child is given the breast as soon as the milk comes; but should there be any trouble, the infant is given to some other nursing mother in the camp.   The child continues to nurse as long as it can draw any sustenance from the breast, sometimes until it is two or three years of age, when it is running about and eating practically every variety of food.

The husband is excluded from the presence of the wife during confinement, but he may visit her immediately after delivery.   Before confinement, neither husband nor wife is permitted to eat the flesh of any young animal.

The Tahltan are a fairly prolific people.   Four or five children are of common occurrence, and two old women were pointed out who had borne nine and ten children respectively.   But their hard life, ignorance, and lack of sanitation have always been the means of retarding any material increase in numbers, the infant mortality being unduly great.   Children are not "taught" as we understand the process; they simply learn from intuition and observation.   In a working community every one finds employment.   The little girls help their mothers greatly in caring for the younger children, and at an early age the boys trap and hunt with their fathers, so that as they grow they learn unconsciously the duties and habits of life until they assume the full responsibilities that come with marriage and take their places in the family councils.

NAMING

Among those tribes of the northwest coast which acknowledge a legal succession in the mother's line and recognize an emblem of family that we commonly call a totem, the name is more than a personal attribute. It not only distinguishes the individual, but it identifies his clan or family, and tells of his social position and ancestry. So it will be seen that names are not given at will; they are inherited rights in the separate family divisions. Each has a meaning which more often refers to the emblem or to some incident in the life of the family, although from time to time individual happenings bring out new names.

A few days after birth the child is named after some maternal relation. This name is not of great importance, for while it makes clear the family connection, it serves only to distinguish the individual. A second name is given at any age from eight to fifteen years, and with people of the higher class this is done at the time of a feast, or memorial ceremony, given by the maternal uncle, who himself names the nephews while his sisters name the nieces, and these names are likewise of the mother's family. The baby name is now discarded, except possibly by the immediate family, and the new name is substituted as the more important. A third and more honorable name is taken by the individual himself on succeeding to the estate of a relative, when the memorial feast is held and property is distributed to those who assisted at the obsequies of the deceased whose name is now assumed. Another, the most honored of all names, may be taken later in life, that of some distinguished maternal ancestor or a great uncle or a great grandfather, but to do this it is necessary to give a feast and to present property to the opposite totemic families proportionate to the honor assumed. To this end the accumulations of a lifetime are sometimes distributed cheerfully, the giver accepting poverty for the remainder of his days   It can be seen how, during generations, names increase in importance, and each one endeavors to outdo the others in the distribution of property so that the old name may be still further honored in himself.

After the birth and the naming of a child the parents may become known as its father and mother. This custom is common among the Tlingit, and has probably been borrowed from the coast.

PUBERTY CUSTOMS

On the first appearance of catamenia the pubescent girl is separated from the family and is confined in a small brush or bark house in the rear of the dwelling. This seclusion covers a period of from six months to a year, and is more strictly observed with the daughter of a chief. Even to-day this custom is observed, but for a much shorter period, and a corner of the house may be partitioned off for the girl's seclusion to take the place of the out of doors structure formerly built. She is attended by her mother, aunt, sister or other female relation. The father is not permitted to see her for at least a month after the confinement and then but seldom. When taken out to walk at night she is completely enveloped in a caribou skin robe which covers the head and reaches to the ground. She wears around the neck a hollow tube, the tibia of the swan or a goose, through which she drinks. Were she to drink in the ordinary way it is believed that she would suffer from stomach trouble in old age. Attached to the tube by a hide string is a small pointed stick or bone with which to scratch the head, for during confinement the hair is not combed. Sometimes, the drinking tube is hung with beadwork which is purely ornamental (Pl. VIII, B, E). During this period of seclusion the girl's diet is generally restricted to dried fish and meat, although sometimes she is allowed fresh porcupine flesh and fresh berries. The uterus, the head, and generally the feet of animals the pubescent girl is prohibited from eating; if the head or brain is eaten, her child will suffer from an abscess in the ear. If the feet of the mountain goat are eaten the off-spring will be lazy and a poor traveler. Partaking of the beaver's feet will produce a stumbler, who can not run; and eating the fresh flesh of animals, besides being harmful to her, may bring bad luck to the hunter. During one of my visits to the Tahltan village in the fishing season, one family complained that they could not join their companions across the river, be-cause a daughter of the household was experiencing her monthly sickness, and her passage over the river at this period would drive the salmon from the sea.

On being released, the girl's skin robe is discarded, she is given the sweat bath and then dressed in new clothes, the hair is combed, and the horseshoe-like beaded ornament (*mossth*) is hung around her neck, if she is of high degree, and a feast is given in her honor to which the opposite totemic families are invited. The neck ring is very attractive. The frame is of bent wood in the shape of a horseshoe, with a lashing of hide in the rear. It is covered with tanned caribou skin or colored cloth ornamented with dentalium, beads, or pearl buttons, and is hung with shell beads and tufts of colored yarn (Pl. VIII, A, C, F, G).

This ring, which is the most highly prized of the ornaments of the woman, is worn as a sign of maturity after the period of confinement following puberty, for about a year, but never after marriage.

If at this time the wearer wishes to speak with her brother or with a male of her own phratry, she ties a bit of babiche or sinew to the mossth.

MORTUARY CUSTOMS

As the Tahltan live their lives in the enjoyment of the few pleasures that come to them, uncomplaining in hardship and adversity, so they accept the end with composure and resig-nation.

Death is announced immediately by one of the men of the family in a loud voice from without the doorway, when all assemble and strike the ground with sticks, chanting, "if the spirit does not hear, he will lose the trail." Then pointing the sticks to the sky, they sing, "you take this trail [upward]; do not lose the trail." The death song is never used or even repeated on any other occasion.

The family opposite that of the deceased, that is the family of the husband or the wife, as the case may be, performs all the mortuary services. The corpse is laid out, and the arms folded over the breast. It is then wrapped in a skin blanket, tied about the head, feet, and middle of the body, and placed opposite the doorway, which is the position of honor. The family ceremonial pieces and some personal property are placed about the dead by way of display. The corpse is kept in state a day or two, and in the case of a chief, four days.

During this period the family eats but once a day, but those of the opposite family who have charge of the funeral arrangements and are preparing the pyre are given food two or three times daily. If the deceased is a married man, the wife cuts her hair and blackens her face, and keeps the face blackened as a sign of mourning for one year. Each night while the corpse is lying in state the family assembles and sings four death and family songs.

On the death of a brother they sing: "he broke his own canoe, my poor brother!" The words are long drawn out and repeated, and during occasional intermissions in the singing, the covering is removed from the face of the dead. Other words were used in the place of "brother" and "canoe" when occasion demanded.

Etmetah, the oldest surviving shaman, sung his family song in a language of some other time or people—it was neither Tahltan nor Tlingit:—"outside [referring to the coast country] is good; go you there!"

The funeral pyre having been prepared and all made ready,

the members of the opposite family assigned to the task, carry the corpse by means of two long poles, one on each side, which pass through the three ropes tied around the body shrouded in the skin blanket. It is never taken through the doorway, else the spirit of death will return to the household, but through the side of the house, or lifted through the smoke hole or through the corner of the bark shelter or tent, and a dog is thrown out after the corpse to prevent the return of the death spirit, and also ashes are cast out. The members of the household, in their oldest clothes and with faces blackened with a preparation of charcoal, balsam, and tallow, follow the corpse, which is placed on the pyre and slowly cremated. During this process the women relatives cry, while the men of the clan sing the family songs, and the women of the clan, other than those of the immediate family, dance in their slow swaying motion from side to side. Among the Tahltan the body of a shaman is cremated the same as the others.

The charred bones are collected by one of the opposite family usually as soon as the fire has burned out, but sometimes not for several days, and are put in a box which is placed on top of a memorial column, on a crib of logs, or in a small box-like house situated on some prominent point on the outskirts of the village. That night the family of the deceased gives a smoking feast to the opposite family. Tobacco is thrown into the fire for the dead, and later a little food is given away to the guests. Generally about a year after death the family of the deceased honors the dead with a feast to the opposite family, when the guests in ceremonial dress sing and dance, first the women and afterward the men. Two years after the death a great feast is given, if the deceased were a person of standing, which lasts four days. The first day the guests dance and sing, first the women then the men. The second day the men of the family sing and the women dance, and a smoking feast is held, after which the guests dance and sing. On the third day the performance of the first day is repeated, and on the fourth day payment in property is made to those who took charge of and performed the funeral and cremation ceremonies, when all obligations on account of the dead are discharged.

The Tahltan believe in many spirits. Big Raven, "*Cheskea Cho,*" created the world, and when the people wanted game food they indicated their desire to this benefactor by burning eagle feathers and saying, "give me food."

Everyone possesses a spirit that is immortal. It is released at death and lives in an abode in the heart of the earth; but it is not confined to this place, as the spirits often return and inhabit the air around, and in most instances are born again in another of the same totemic family. In proof of this the writer was informed of a little boy who, in passing the grave house of an ancestor, turned to his father and said, pointing to it, "that is where I was once laid away." Another belief is indicated by the following narrative. A young girl just reaching maturity died. Her friend, about the same age, gave birth to a baby girl the following year, and in its coming the young mother recognized the return of the spirit of her dead companion. As the child grew she always preferred the parents of the dead to her own, and learned without teaching to call them mother and father, referring to her natural parents as uncle and aunt, while the younger sister of the deceased, although years older than herself, she always spoke of as her little sister.

These two incidents, insignificant in themselves perhaps, were given as evidence in support of their belief in reincarnation.

There is no recognized belief in future punishment, or in an abode of evil spirits. The only thing approaching this is when they speak of the spirit as "losing the trail," and it is for this reason that when a death occurs they beat the ground and sing to the spirit to "keep to the trail." As one informant expressed it, "the song is the same as a candle to light the trail." The concept of the lost spirit is very indefinite, it would simply wander aimlessly.

Generally the spirits of the dead are believed to be harmless, but there are maleficent witch spirits which live about the dead houses and are greatly feared. It is related that in early days four hunters were returning one night, and near the dead poles at the lava beds they heard voices, but could see no one. As they listened, they heard the words, "that [dead] house is filled and we can not go in." Then the voices sang.

"He's dead now,
He's dead no more.
We see him [and they heard the crying stick beating time].
Dead man you go;
This way is your trail!"

When the hunters reached the village they related what they had heard, and the following day they all died.

FEASTS, DANCES, AND OTHER CEREMONIES

The dances and feast ceremonies practiced by the Tahltan have been borrowed from the Tlingit. If they had any such ceremonies of their own, these have entirely disappeared and are forgotten by the living. Wherever the totemic system prevails, the death feast seems to occupy the first place, as it is designed to honor the departed and this is reflected on the whole family. The making of peace has always been regarded as an occasion to be celebrated with much formality.

The dances are given about midwinter, when the people have returned to the permanent village after the hunting season is over. The feasts occur at the close of summer, before the hunting season commences.

As mentioned in connection with the mortuary customs, the totemic family of the deceased entertains the opposite party which performs the obsequies and conducts the cremation, receiving food and tobacco. A year or two afterward they are again entertained and compensated for their services by the distribution of property, in return for which they dance. This final feast continues through four days, and at night a smoking feast is held. This ceremony is called *Ten-ar-lee* (dance), and is participated in by men, women, and children.

The ceremonial dress, except that part procured from the coast tribes, consisted formerly of skin clothing worked in porcupine quill and colored with red ochre; furs, bird skins and feathers; but this has all disappeared, and in its place beaded bags, belts, knife cases, and head pieces of colored cloth are used. The stuffed body of a wolf, the emblem of the family, I saw in a house at Tahltan. It was carried in the dance and placed in a conspicuous place. I also saw several Chilkat blankets, likewise chief's headdresses with the carved mask surmounted by sea lion whiskers and with the broad band of ermine skins depending behind, and carved wooden rattles of the Tsimshian type, all of which had been procured in trade from the coast; but nothing of any artistic value original with the people themselves was to be found. In the dances a whistle of bone is used by the master of ceremonies as a signal.

The Peace Dance, or *Kau-ah-kan*, a Tlingit word meaning "deer," by which term the hostages are known, is wholly of coast origin. After families or tribes have been in conflict and peace is restored, this performance is celebrated by an exchange of two or four hostages, who are treated with the greatest consideration. First one side dances with its prisoner or hostage before the other, and then the other side performs, during four days, each party performing one dance a day. A free translation of a song accompanying this dance is as follows.

My brother was killed fighting,
And when word came to me,
My heart was sad and I wanted to die.
But now I am Kan-ah-kan,
And I love peace,
And I do not want to kill
Now any more.
Now I do not bear hatred
Toward the one who killed my brother.

THE OTTER SPIRIT

The Tahltan have a strange belief in a spirit that they call *Kus-su-nar yar-za*, Young Otter. Almost every woman has one, two, or even three of these; the more one has the greater the dignity. If possessed of none, she commands little respect, therefore few if any women are willing to acknowledge this lack. The spirit generally acts for the good of the owner, but sometimes it may kill her. Living within her, just above the stomach, it makes itself known by a peculiar sound, and sometimes it rises to her lips, but is never seen, although some say that it has been seen when drawn out as a small black object. The possessor of a young otter spirit is always conscious of its existence. At death it escapes and seeks an abode in another human being. It is exceptional for a man to harbor this spirit, and it is not for his good. When he becomes possessed of it he seeks a woman doctor who can suck it from him through his lips, but only a woman having one already can remove it, and not all of these have the power. They do not like to speak of this to a stranger. It is not etiquette to refer to it, for it may offend the spirit and cause harm. Again it is said that only the shaman can treat this condition, and that once an otter not larger than one's hand was taken from a man. The ordinary treatment is believed to result in making the otter a good friend of the possessor. Dr. Ingles informed the writer that the manifestation of this strange belief is epilepsy.

The land otter has always been regarded with much superstitious awe and as sacred to the practice of shamanism. Before the advent of the Hudson's Bay Company it was never molested, and when the demand for its fur induced its capture, it was simply killed. The flesh was never eaten, the body never burned, nor the tongue cut, and it was never spoken of except with great respect.

SHAMANISM

Shamans among the Tahltan are born of ignorance and nurtured through superstition. They treat sickness not as of the flesh, but as due to the presence of an evil spirit within the body. Consequently they offer no material aid, but with the more powerful spirit that dominates them they exorcise the evil one that has entered the body of the patient.

Any one to whom the spirit comes in dreams may become a shaman. On receiving such a manifestation he goes out alone and lives in the woods for several months (some place the limit at four months), during which time he must exercise strict continence. He fasts during alternate periods of four days, drinking only a little water. During all this time he searches for a land otter, but if he can not find one he must be satisfied with a mink, a marten, a bush-tail rat, a frog, or some animal that is recognized as possessing a strong spirit (by reason of which such animals are not considered edible). When the animal is met with, it is killed and the tongue taken and concealed in a skin, fur, or feather bag, which constitutes his medicine, symbolic of his spirit power, hence he now controls the spirit of the animal which works his will. Having become possessed of a spirit, he returns to his people and announces his power. Cartoona, an old doctor, recounting the practice of early days, said that the novitiate during his period of fasting travelled the country over to find a pregnant moose, caribou, sheep, goat or porcupine, and then followed her to be present at the birth of the young, which he wiped with some twigs and then switched its legs to make it rise. He killed neither the mother nor the young, but in some unexplained manner he received magic power from his presence at the bringing forth of the young.

When one becomes ill some near relative visits the shaman and arranges with him to treat the patient, stating what quantity of skins or other property will be paid for his services. The shaman, accompanied by the men of his family, who carry his dress and implements, then go to the house of the sick. Seating himself by the patient, the shaman, without speaking, sometimes fills his pipe and smokes; then he commences to tremble, which indicates that his spirit is manifesting itself. He now takes off all of his clothing, puts on a waist cloth, lets down his hair and sprinkles it with swansdown, puts on his head the neck skin and head of a swan or a crown of grizzly bear claws, and around the neck, mink or ermine skins, swan or loon necks and heads, owls' claws, bird skins, a rope of cedar bark or small spirit chains, each sewed in a tiny skin case. When these things are employed water must not be drunk. Sometimes the shaman's wrists and arms to the elbow are painted with red ochre. He again seats himself by the side of the patient, and after again trembling for a while, commences to sing. Those who have accompanied him, and are seated at one side, take up the refrain, keeping time with the beating sticks and a small skin drum. While the shaman sings only a few words at a time, the others sing and drum continuously. Then he rises and dances around the patient, his eyes closed or partly closed. He may carry any part of an otter, mink, marten, ermine, loon, raven, or hawk skin in his hand, and he may put this on the patient or touch it to the part affected. He may put his hand on the sick person, or his own lips to those of the patient, in order to draw the evil spirit from him; or he may call the spirit with a bone whistle which he carries in his hand. The performance may take place at any time of the day or evening, and it lasts from half an hour to an hour. When he departs he may leave at the side of the patient anything that he has worn or carried, for the purpose of keeping evil spirits from him.

If after several visits from the shaman the patient does not improve, the shaman tells the family that a witch spirit possesses him, and that until it is liberated nothing can be accomplished; then after further payment he points out or reveals in song the person who has bewitched the patient. In thus indicating the witch, an enemy or an inoffensive person is usually made respon-

8

sible, and he is forthwith bound and placed in an outhouse without food. If the patient recovers, the accused person may be liberated, but if he dies, the one charged with the sorcery may be killed.

Should the patient recover and live for a year, the shaman retains the payment, but if he die within that period all of the property he has received in payment for his services is returned to the family.

Several of the old shamans still remain, but they have generally abandoned their practice, except in a mild form to treat some old unregenerate who still adheres to the customs of the past. An instance is recalled of an old chief, crippled with rheumatism, to whom the shaman had given small strips of the neck of the swan to bind around the arms above the elbows and the legs above the knees.

Regarding the witch spirit that causes sickness and death, the people know only what the shaman tells them for he alone can see this spirit, and if his power is the greater he can draw it from the patient.

MEDICAL PRACTICE

The physical treatment of disease or injuries is entirely distinct from the practice of the shaman. For many ailments the Tahltan gather herbs and root stocks which they prepare for both internal and external use. Knowledge of the preparation and application of these nostrums is possessed by all, but some of the older women are regarded as authorities. For inflammations of every description recourse is had to the lancet, which ordinarily is kept in the repair or workbag, and the puncture is dressed with bird's down. In the pure atmosphere wounds heal readily. When the disease is internal, and its cause not understood, it is attributed to the machinations of an evil spirit that has entered the body, when the services of the shaman are required.

For digestive troubles the stem of the soapberry bush

is boiled and given as a tea. For constipation bear grease is taken. For burns, spruce leaves are chewed and used as a poultice. For rheumatism, dog's hair is burned and the smoke inhaled under a blanket. Fractured limbs are set and bound in splints.

Of the many plants used for medicine, wild rhubarb root and the root and the stem of the devil's club are most freely used.

The old people say that when they lived in the open throughout the year, colds and the attending troubles were unknown.

Idiocy is believed to be produced in childhood or even later by the land otter eating food thrown away by the person afflicted or by his ridiculing an animal having a spirit, or by the killing of an animal having young, especially a bear or a mink and allowing the young to starve.

Idiocy at childbirth is attributed to a similar act on the part of the father at some previous time, consequently when an animal is encountered while carrying young it must be killed immediately, the front feet held tight in order that they may not move, and the throat cut quickly, otherwise the child of the hunter when born will develop convulsions. Deafness and dumbness are considered inherited from an ancestor owing to some neglect on his part in observing the laws governing killing the young of animals as above described.

WAR CUSTOMS

From the fragmentary stories of their fighting and wars it would appear that in early days the Tahltan were embroiled with their neighbors most of the time, and the names of a number of villages are remembered that were destroyed in these encounters. With the Nishka of upper Nass river they were constantly in conflict, and frequently so with the Taku over hunting rights; but with the Kaska, Bear lake people, and Stikine Tlingit their trade relations proved a bond of peace. Their last hostility was with the Nishka in 1862, since which period peace has prevailed, although they speak of occasional trouble with the latter people.

It is likely, however, that time has greatly exaggerated the importance of these conflicts, and while at times considerable parties may have taken the field, it seems probable that ambuscades, solitary killings, and the sacking of half deserted villages constituted the most serious results of their campaigns. While the Tahltan are fearless hunters, it is hardly probable that they were ever a fighting people except when forced to assume the defensive. They claim to have used in war a defensive dress of hard tanned moose or goat skin, beneath which was sometimes worn an armor of wooden rods bound together with a twining of twisted sinew and goat wool cord in alternate bands, and headpieces of wood. Spears, knives, bows and arrows, were their weapons. Of these accoutrements nothing remains except the war knives, and most of these, judging from the fine workmanship and the elaborately carved and ornamental heads, are of Tlingit manufacture (Pl. XII).

Before going on war parties the shaman might perform a ceremony, calling on his spirits to aid the people. To the leader and other members of the expedition he might give some medicine charms, as a piece of fur, the head of a water bird, the claw of an eagle or an owl, a piece of obsidian, or the like, to protect them against harm; but he fought just the same as the others.

For war the face was daubed with red ochre and black paint, and they say the scalp lock was tied up. The custom of scalping was practised, all the hair being taken, and these trophies were displayed only at family ceremonies. An old native informed me that in war the body of the dead enemy was sometimes roasted and the warriors cut a mouthful from it not as food but to fulfill an ancient custom, but this no one else confirmed. Prisoners taken in war were made slaves, but could be ransomed.

Before going to war they hardened their bodies by morning plunges in cold water, but this was also done at other times.

LEGENDS AND FOLKLORE

History and legends were generally known to all, but they were particularly in the keeping of individuals who taught them to the children at night about the fire. A few days after each lesson the children were all questioned and made to recite what they had been told, and the most apt pupils were given a thorough course of instruction. The writer's limited experience in this matter, however, led him to believe that the older women were generally the better informed in questions of history and legend, for in conversation with the men when relating old stories they would often appeal to the older women for aid.

In the legends of the Tahltan, the formation of the earth is not accounted for. In the beginning it was a chaotic mass of mountainous shore and ocean, without fresh water, and enveloped in semi-darkness. The elements, light, fire, and fresh water, existed in hiding and were zealously guarded by supernatural beings co-existent with nature, who resented the coming of man, and of whom little is known, for with the loss of their power·they disappeared.

The mediator and creator appeared and wrested from the mythical beings the elements, which were given to the earth to make it habitable. He then made man. He often assumed the form of Cheskea Cho—the Big Raven—as he was called. The principal folk tales of the Tahltan naturally relate to the acts and wanderings of the Raven, but they are so similar to those of the coast tribes, which have been told often, that they may be presented here merely in outline.

Light was hidden in three bundles, containing the sun, the moon, and the stars respectively, and carefully guarded by the master spirit who had a daughter approaching womanhood, whose every movement was watched. The Raven transformed himself into a tiny leaf and dropped into the spring from which the water she drank was dipped with a basket, and although the leaf was detected and thrown away several times, the young woman finally swallowed it. Thus was the Raven conceived and born again as her son. The grandfather became greatly attached to the child, and could refuse him nothing. He played with the bundles of light as a baby; but as he grew older these were withheld. When the boy became ill and cried incessantly for his old playthings they were given to him, when he released the light from the bundles and threw it into the air, to take its place in the firmament.

Fresh water was in the possession of another master, known as Kounugu, who slept throughout the day on top of the well that contained his treasure. The Raven came to him and asked for drink but was refused. Then he went away and catching a few drops of rain in his bill, hurried back to the water master and spat the water out before him, saying, "see, I too have fresh water!" After this he was allowed to remain working for Kounugu. Watching his chance when Kounugu slept, he rubbed dirt over him, and, waking him, told him to go out and wash. When the water master was about to wash his face Raven told him that he would do it for him and asked him to open his eyes. When he had done this Raven blinded him with urine, and quickly diving into the well, drank deeply of the water, but this so increased his size that he was caught in the smoke hole of the house in escaping.

Kounugu then built a fire of pitch kindlings, the smoke of which turned Raven black, for at first he was white. Escaping from the smoke hole, he flew over the earth, and where-ever he let fall a drop of water from his bill, a lake, a river or a creek was formed. Fire was likewise released from its keeper and stored in the trees and the rocks for the use of man.

Now the earth was made ready, and animal life already existed; but Raven, wandering far and wide, became lonely for human companionship. He came to Stikine river above the cañon, and as he sat on the bank he saw a salmon jump. He was very hungry, but he had neither spear nor hook to catch the fish, so he talked to it, saying, "come here and hit me right in the stomach." As he spoke the salmon jumped at him, striking him and knocking him over; and before he could recover himself the fish had wriggled back into the water. Then he thought to build himself a low stone wall at the water's edge (some say he dug a ditch), and standing within it he again spoke to the salmon; but when it again jumped at him it could not return to the water, and was caught. Raven then prepared and cooked the fish and invited all the smaller birds to a feast. When the salmon was cooked under the turned-up root of a tree, Raven took a piece of the flesh, and, talking to the root, offered it, saying, "*Nă Nᵃ*," "here take it," but quickly drew it back, deceiving the root, which dropped back, covering the salmon, and although all the birds dug in the ground, they could not find the fish. Then Raven told the little birds that he was going to make man, but they did not believe him, and as he asked each one, "have you young inside?" they all answered, "no." Then he turned to the rocks, and the trees, and asked them the same question, and they both answered affirmatively, whereupon he told them that the young first born would be man; and they each told him that at the break of day a child would be born. And so in the morning the tree first gave birth, and the offspring became man, therefore as the tree springs from the seed, lives, and dies, so human life is but for a season. Following the birth of the tree, the rock brought forth its offspring, which was of stone and which was rejected by Raven as having everlasting life.

Following the creation of man, when the world was still sparsely peopled, came a long period of rain that covered the surface of the earth and destroyed many. The few that were saved climbed to the top of the loftiest peaks, and after the subsidence of the water settled the earth.

These stories of the Raven, the creation, and the flood are common to all the tribes of the northwest coast from Puget Sound to the Arctic, and are localized at many points. Hence it is certain that the Tahltan borrowed them from others. Their great similarity to the stories of the Stikine Tlingit would seem to indicate that the Tahltan borrowed their myths from the same source as their social organization, their ceremonies, and so many of the customs that distinguish them from the more easterly and primitive Nahane.

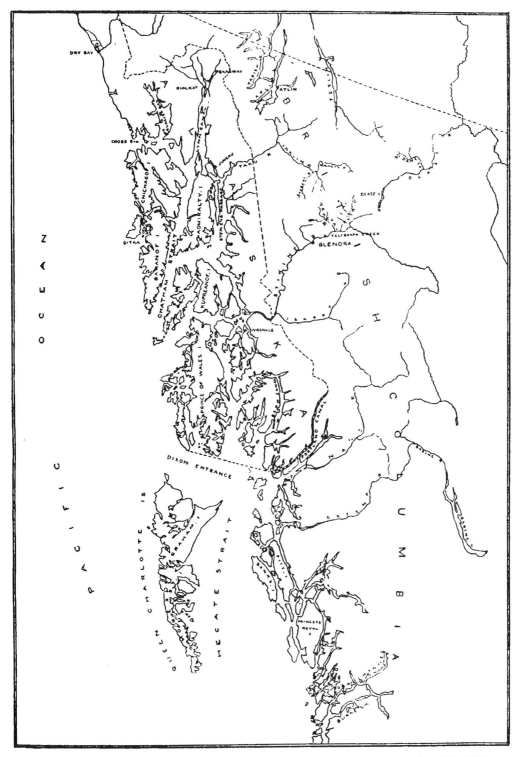

MAP SHOWING A PORTION OF THE NORTHWEST COAST OF AMERICA AND THE
COUNTRY INHABITED BY THE TAHLTAN.

PLATE I

Nan-nook head chief of the Tahltan.

PLATE I

ANTHR. PUB. UNIV. OF PA. MUSEUM VOL. IV

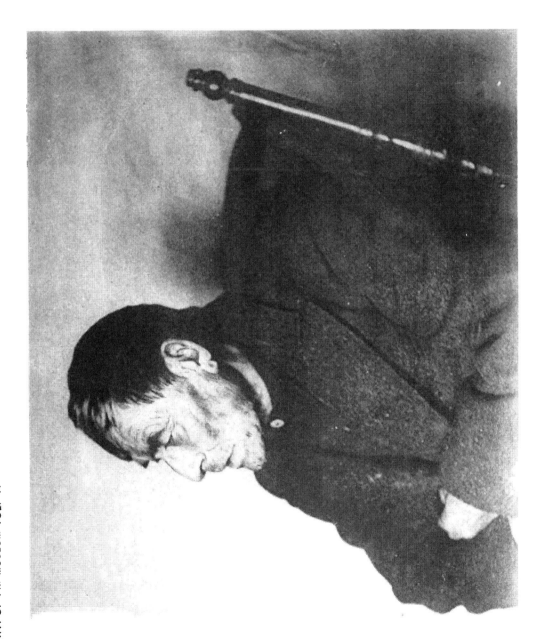

NAN NOOK. HEAD CHIEF OF THE TAHLTAN

PLATE II

KASKA JOHN AND HIS WIFE

PLATE III

Koshon (old wolf) and his wife Thlogosqin.

KOSHON AND HIS WIFE THLOGOSQIN

PLATE IV

THREE TAHLTAN SISTERS

PLATE V

An aged Tahltan woman.

AGED TAHLTAN WOMAN

PLATE VI

Tahltan camp showing structure of sweat bath in foreground.
Tahltan summer camp.
underground dog houses in a Tahltan village.
house of bark and brush.

PLATE VI

B

D

A

C

TYPES OF TAHLTAN HOUSES

PLATE VII

A: food cache with rude ladder made of a notched tree trunk.
B: Tahltan woman and her dogs with packs.

PLATE VII

A

TAHLTAN CACHE

B

TAHLTAN WOMAN AND HER DOGS

PLATE VIII

B and E: drinking tubes used by pubescent maidens.

A, C, F, G: collars worn by maidens after seclusion.

D: woman's ear ornament.

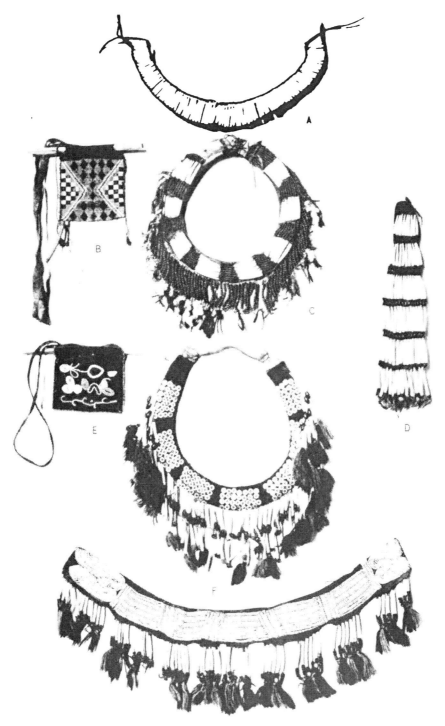

ARTICLES USED OR WORN BY WOMEN

PLATE IX

A and B: ornamental bags of caribou skin covered with colored cloth and beaded. This article represents an original firebag which has degenerated into an ornament.

C: packing bag of caribou skin with beadwork embroidery.

D: netted bag of babiche. This form of bag is carried by men to contain the provisions and necessaries for a day's travel. Also used as a game bag.

E: netted bag of cord made from the wool of the mountain goat. It is used for carrying fish.

B

A

D

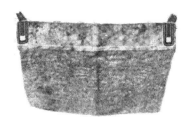

C

E

DIFFERENT FORMS OF BAGS

PLATE X

Man's workbag with outfit.

1: knife.   2: snowshoe chisel.   3: awl.   4: whetstone.   5: beaver teeth used as a knife sharpener.   6: caribou sinew for making cord.   7: lancet.   8: paint bag.   9: bone drinking tube.   10: bone gambling toggle.   11: bone skinning knife.   12: bone attachment for pack strap.   13: powder flask.   14: piece of punk.

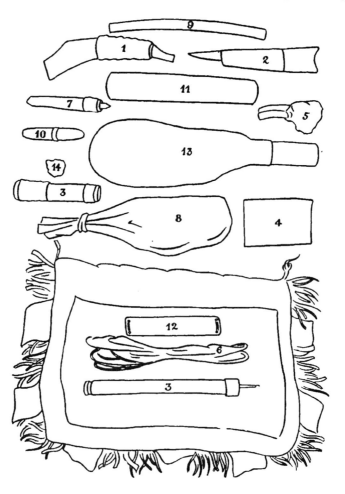

MAN'S WORKBAG AND CONTENTS

PLATE XI

Woman's workbags.

A, 1: knife. 2: awl. 3: sinew thread. 5: snowshoe netting needle. 6: stone implement for dressing skins. 7: bone attachment for pack strap.

B, 1: knife. 2: awl. 3: sinew thread. 5: snowshoe netting needle. 6: bone skinning knife and skin dresser. 7: bone drinking tube.

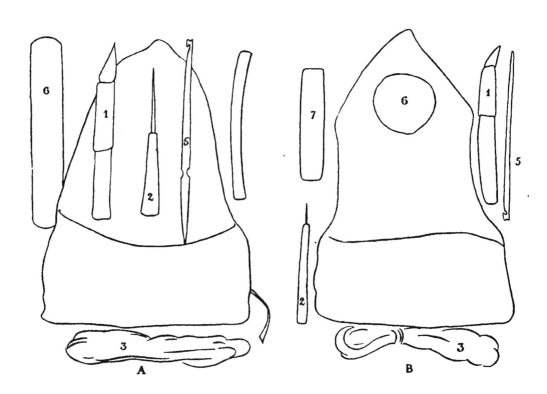

PLATE XI

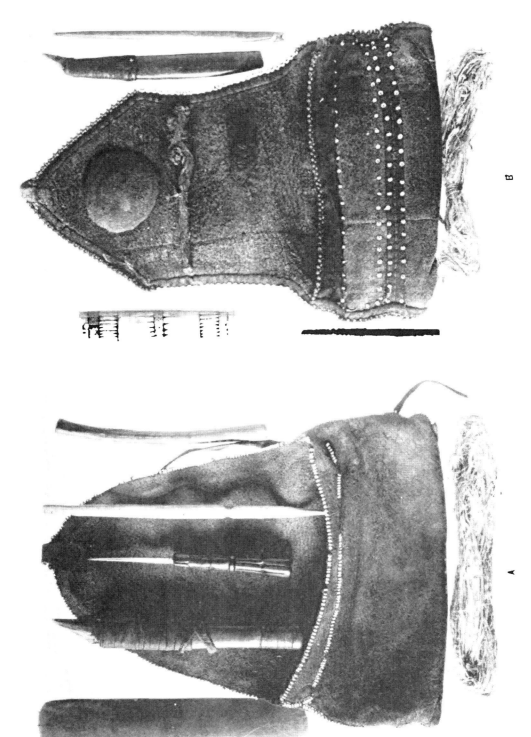

A

B

WOMAN'S WORKBAGS WITH CONTENTS

.

PLATE XII

War knives in sheaths of buckskin and cloth decorated with beadwork.

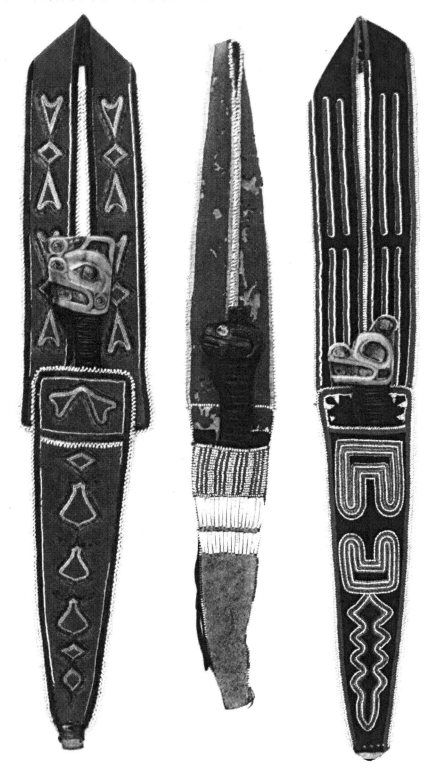

WAR KNIVES AND SHEATHS

PLATE XIII

Two double sets of gambling sticks in their carrying bags made of caribou skin ornamented with dentalium shells and colored beads.

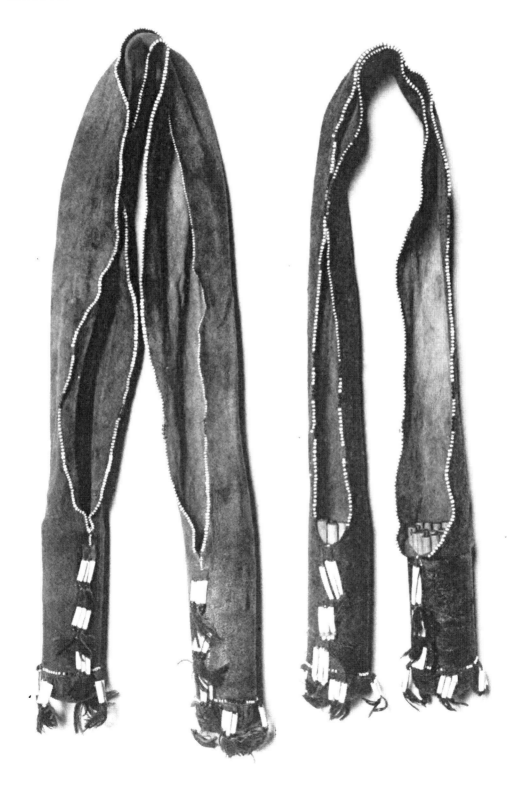

PLATE XIV

Three ceremonial bags of buckskin and cloth decorated with beadwork.

PLATE XIV

CEREMONIAL BAGS

PLATE XV

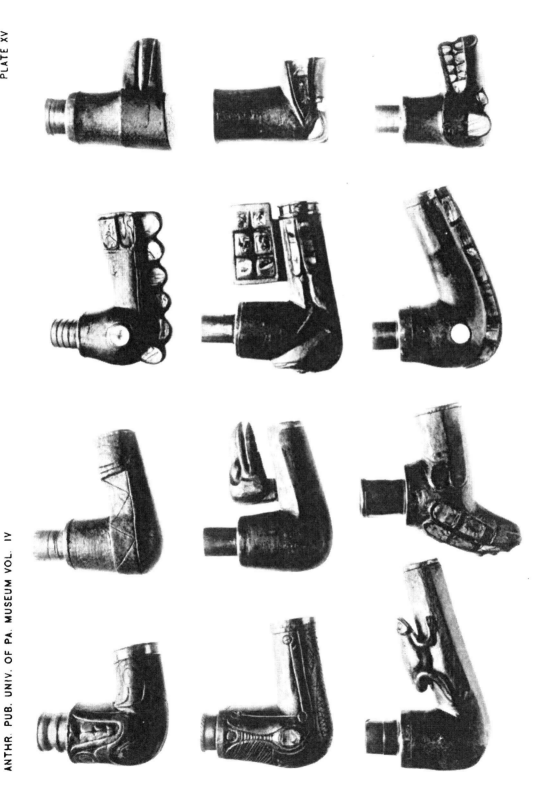

TAHLTAN PIPES

PLATE XVI

Ceremonial pipes used upon feast occasions. The ornamentation
in carving and inlaying generally represents the totemic emblem
of the family.

PLATE XVI

CEREMONIAL PIPES

PLATE XVII

Two ceremonial pipes. The upper one is made of walnut inlaid with haliotis shell and further decorated by carving. It was found in the possession of a very old shaman of the Tahltan in whose imagination it represents a beaver, the back bone being represented by the carving at the base which is inlaid with pieces of shell. The leaves and stems according to this interpretation represent the animal's food. This pipe like its companion is of Haida design and workmanship.

The lower pipe in the illustration is made of boxwood inlaid with white and black bone and further decorated by carving and painting. In shape it represents a canoe. At the fore end is an ivory figure which shows the bow man watching the water ahead. In the middle is a miniature house with windows and lattice. In the rear is an ornamental carving, flower-like in design. It was obtained from an old man at Tahltan who knew nothing of its history except that it had descended to him through five generations. It is unquestionably of Haida origin and is similar in design and workmanship to a number of pipes of both wood and slate in the U. S. National Museum gathered by the United States Exploring Expedition in 1841, in Oregon.

PLATE XVII

PIPES MADE BY THE HAIDA

PLATE XVIII

Fishing village at the mouth of the Tahltan river, near the site of the first known settlement of the Tahltan people. The houses are built of upright saplings stuck in the ground and bound together with rope of twisted bark and roofed with slabs of spruce bark.

MOUTH OF TAHLTAN RIVER WITH FISHING VILLAGE

PLATE XIX

Decorated gambling sticks.   The names given for the decorations are as follows.

Upper row: arrow, canoe in water, man, fresh water crab, fire, bear in water, dog, lakes, leg, musk rat.

Second row: fire, rock, man's eye, caribou horn, mouse, man's trail, man, osprey, ptarmigan arrow.

Third row: crab, porcupine hook, mink, ?, beaver, rope, ?, a stick across the trail, fish net, lynx.

Fourth row: fox, canoe, teeth, black bear, sheep, moose, arrow, belly, moose skin rope, ground hog.

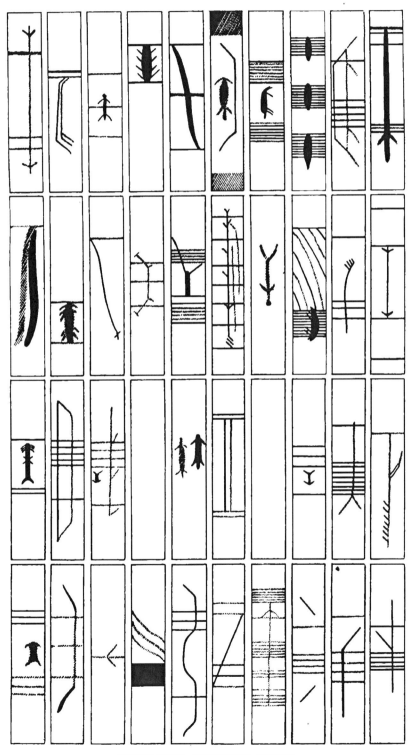

DECORATED GAMBLING STICKS.

ERRATA

Page 13, line 18, for "Giv-na-na," read Gu-na-na.

Plate VII, line 3, for "ear ornament," read hair ornament.

Key facing Plate XI, line 2, for "A," read B; line 5, for "B," read A.

Plate XIX, line 3, for "arrow," read caribou foot; line 4, for "bear in water," read beaver in water, and for "leg," read lake.

Line 6, insert comma after "ptarmigan."

UNIVERSITY OF PENNSYLVANIA

THE UNIVERSITY MUSEUM

ANTHROPOLOGICAL PUBLICATIONS

VOL. IV   No. 2

SACRED BUNDLES OF THE SAC AND FOX INDIANS

BY

M. R. HARRINGTON

ILLUSTRATED BY SPECIMENS IN THE
GEORGE G. HEYE COLLECTION

PHILADELPHIA

PUBLISHED BY THE UNIVERSITY MUSEUM

1914

CONTENTS

SACRED BUNDLES OF THE SAC AND FOX INDIANS.

INTRODUCTION.

The use of objects supposed to have mysterious power for magically influencing the affairs and conditions of life seems to have been almost universal among the native tribes of North America. Some groups, as might be expected, show a greater development along this line than others, while considerable variation in the character and use of the "powerful" objects is seen in the various types of culture.

Such facts of development and variation are well brought out in the collection secured by the expedition maintained by Mr. George G. Heye, among the various tribes now residing for the most part in Oklahoma—tribes representing a number of linguistic stocks and types of culture, and formerly widely distributed geographically, but now gathered within a comparatively limited area. During the progress of this work, which was under my immediate charge, we were fortunate enough to obtain a considerable number of these objects, including many of the sacred bundles which were objects of the highest veneration. In many cases the tribal religious observances had virtually centered about them.

To describe these objects, collected by the Expedition, and to set forth such information as could be obtained concerning

them, is the task I have before me.   A complete account,
however, is not possible, for not only is our series of "powerful" objects from any given tribe seldom even approximately
complete, but information was not always obtainable, even
concerning the specimens we were able to secure.   In many
cases the owners of the sacred bundles had died, and the
younger people inheriting them know little or nothing of their
history, use or ritual.   In other cases Indians would bring
themselves to the point of selling their bundles to get rid of
the responsibility of caring for them, but could not be induced
to give the information belonging to them, either through fear
of the supernatural, or fear of what their tribesmen might
say, or merely because they thought that we wanted to make
fun of their sacred beliefs.   For it must be remembered that
the traditions belonging to the bundles are as sacred to the
Indian as his Bible is to the orthodox Christian.

Among the tribes from which "powerful" objects were
obtained are the Sac and Fox, Pottawattomi, Kickapoo, Delaware and Shawnee, representing the Algonkian stock;   the
Osage, Kaw, Iowa, Otoe and Quapaw (all Siouan);   the Caddo
and Wichita (Caddoan);   the Comanche (Shoshonean);   the
Kiowa (Kiowan);   and the Chiricahua Apache (Athapaskan);
and the Seminole, Creek and Choctaw (Muskhogean).   Among
the last three, however, such objects are rarely seen.

The concepts underlying the beliefs and customs connected with these "powerful" objects, are usually quite obscure
and involved, but the basic idea is, apparently, that such
objects are endowed with a certain degree of supernatural
power, by which they can directly or indirectly influence the
phenomena of life, in the interest of their owner.   Classification
is rendered difficult by the vagueness of some of the concepts;

still a general classification is possible, and will be given here, with the definitions of the terms I shall use hereafter.

THE FETISH.

This is an object, natural or artificial, large or small, which is regarded as a living being, possessed of supernatural power, and as endowed with consciousness and volition, or is thought to be the dwelling or representation of such a being, and to possess its magical powers, wholly or in part. It is supposed to understand what is said to it, and to enjoy offerings.

THE AMULET.

An object, small, or at least readily portable, which is worn or carried by its owner, with the idea that it possesses the power of giving him good fortune, protecting him or imbuing him with powers or qualities not naturally his own; but without any definite idea that the object is alive or that it is the actual habitation of a spirit. The idea underlying this class is frequently that the amulet is a symbol or token of a supernatural being, who is pleased by seeing it worn and grants his protection and aid to the wearer. In other cases the idea is that of sympathetic magic, as when a portion of some animal's body is worn to endow the wearer with that animal's desirable qualities.

THE CHARM.

Like the amulets, the class of objects which for purposes of this paper we shall call charms are not generally regarded as living, supernatural beings, nor the abode of such, but are objects, substances or compounds of herbs (charm-medicines), which by their own inherent virtues or powers, can compel the supernatural beings or forces of nature to aid the manipulator of the charm, in some particular, invariable way, or can cause such abnormal results without the idea of the intervention of any spirit, but purely by properties inherent in the charm itself.   There is little if any difference in the mind of the Indian between the manner of action of the herbs that he compounds as a cathartic and the action of another compound that he makes to drive away witches.   The phenomena of chemical reaction to his mind would be comparable to the workings of a charm to produce rain or to give a rival hunter bad luck.   In this way the beliefs and practices connected with charms and charm-medicines merge into those accepted by modern medicine and chemistry.

The Sacred Bundle.

This is a bundle containing one or more charms, amulets or fetishes, often a collection, embracing objects of all these classes, together with paints, offerings and ceremonial paraphernalia. Many of these bundles, regarded with the greatest respect and even fear, are thought to have a consciousness of their own, to understand what is said to them, and to enjoy offerings.   In such cases, we have a collection of various kinds of "powerful" objects regarded, in its entirety, as a fetish.

This is almost invariably the case with the important bundles connected with the religious rites of the influential societies, the clans or the whole tribe; the war bundles and others of general public interest.   In a lesser degree, the same idea appears regarding some of the bundles of more or less personal use, such as those for hunting, love, friendship, healing the sick, preserving the health, athletic sports, gambling and witchcraft, and the general bundles, combining two or more of these functions. Bundles of this last group—those of personal rather than public appeal—are usually classed as "medicine" or "charm" bundles, as they usually contain many charms and charm-medicines, and but few fetishes or amulets. While frequently held by shamans, this was not the invariable rule, for a very large number of these bundles were in the hands of private individuals.

Most of the fetishes, amulets and charms collected, especially those from the central Algonkian tribes and those of Siouan language but similar culture, were not obtained separately, but as parts of bundles of one kind or another; but among some other tribes, such as the Comanche, Apache and Caddo, the few specimens of this kind that were found, had been kept and used separately and not enclosed with others in a bundle.

Inasmuch as the Heye Expedition has collected more "powerful" objects from the Sac and Fox tribe of the central Algonkian group than from any others, these have been selected as the subject of this paper.

SKETCH OF SAC AND FOX CULTURE.

Before taking up a detailed study of the Sac and Fox "powerful" objects it might be well to gain perspective by glancing for a moment at their life as a whole.

As might be inferred from their name, the Sac and Fox people were at one time two distinct but closely related tribes, who cast their lot together and thereby gained the compound name by which they are now known.   Later a split occurred which left one band, mainly Foxes, near Tama, Iowa; another in Kansas, and a third, mainly Sac (Sauk), near Shawnee, Oklahoma, far from their old haunts near Lake Michigan, where they were encountered by the whites at an early date.

Most of our "powerful" objects were secured from the Oklahoma contingent, but a few articles of this class were collected in Iowa.

Although they lived for the most part in the borderland between forest and prairie, the life and habits of this people were typically those of the woodland, with fairly permanent summer villages convenient, not only to good hunting grounds, but also to places where their great staple, corn (maize), and other vegetable foods, could be successfully raised.   Houses for summer use were rectangular structures of poles and bark, with gable roofs, sleeping platforms and adjacent arbors for shade; but in winter these were usually abandoned in favor of the warmer oval dome-shaped lodges covered with great mats (Pl. XXI, A) made of cat-tail flags.   These were portable, a decided advantage for the winter hunt.   Canoes were formerly in general use.

Their manufactures included baskets and many woven articles such as sacks and mats, some of them being excellent in workmanship and design, as well as the bowls, spoons and other articles of wood and the articles of buckskin, rawhide and the like, while their bead work shows a large proportion of curvilinear designs—a series of products typical of the central Algonkian peoples.

The tribes were divided into clans, most of which bore animal names and in which membership was inherited through the father. Among the Sac clans were: the Eagle, Thunder, Swan, Sturgeon, Bear-potato, Wolf, Elk and Bear.

Besides this, the tribes were divided into two parties, irrespective of clan or inheritance, the Ac kac'ᵃ and Kic'koᵃ, who played against each other in games, and were especially recognized in the ceremonies. As nearly as I can find out the first son of a couple belonged to the Ac kac'ᵃ party, the next to the Kic'koᵃ, the next Ac kac'ᵃ, and so on. It was said that an Ac kac'ᵃ must never change his mind nor give up what he has begun, and especially, must never retreat in war; but a Kic'koᵃ may do as he pleases. Black was the painting color of the Ac kac'ᵃ and white that of the Kic'koᵃ.[1]

The ceremonies connected with the sacred bundles of the different clans and the Me dä win or Medicine Society were their most important religious observances. At the present time Ge'tci Ma' ni to, the Great Spirit, is frequently mentioned in the traditions and in the ceremonies as chief of the Manitos; but whether this concept is of native or foreign origin I have no means of telling. There seems to be a tendency to assume a priori that because certain tribes of American Indians had no concept of a Supreme Being before the coming of the whites, or seem to have had none, no tribe had this concept; this, I think, is a mistake. To-day (1912) the Dream- or Drum-dance religion is in great vogue, and some of the people have taken up the Peyote Rite.

In disposition the Sac and Fox were proud and warlike and seem to have placed much importance on military achievement.

---

[1] "Besides the grouping into gentes the tribe was further divided into two great social groups or phratries: Kishkoᵃ and Oshkashᵃ. . . . A child entered the group at birth; sometimes the father, sometimes the mother, determining which group." Bureau of American Ethnology, Bulletin 30, Part 2, p. 478.

THE BUNDLES.

Hanging overhead from the smoke-stained rafter poles in the few remaining primitive lodges of bark or mats, may sometimes still be seen, the sacred bundles—mysterious oblong packages wrapped in blackened buckskin, stiff and crackled with age (Pl. XXV), from which often hang pendant clusters of gourd rattles, likewise black with age and smoke.

Well may the Indian view these bundles of mystery with reverence and respect, for within them still lingers the spirit of yesterday—memories of the days he loved—the days of the freedom of forests and prairies, of the glory of war, the excitement of the chase—the days when the Indian was a power in the land—the days now gone forever.   But the greatest basis of his regard for these relics of the past lies in his belief that the bundles were the direct gift of the Manitos, of the great powers that rule the world, to his people.   The glorious powerful Sun, the terrible Thunders, whose wings darken the sky, whose roar shakes the prairie, and whose dazzling fiery darts shatter the trees of the forest—all gave their power to mankind through the bundles.

The bold Eagle, the swift Hawk, the night-seeing Owl, the sturdy Buffalo, the tireless Wolf, the sly Weasel approaching his prey by stealth, the Snake slipping unseen through the grass—all gave their power; and the herbs that protect, that cure, that bewilder and bewitch—all contributed their potency. Moreover, the feasts, ceremonies and dances connected with the bundles formed a great part of the people's religious activities, and the consequent gatherings much of their opportunities for social intercourse.   It is not surprising then that the bundles were treasured, and that only of late years, when the old times are fading into the past, and the old beliefs are being rapidly forgotten by the rising generation, that the Indians have begun to let the bundles pass out of their hands.

The Sac and Fox visited by the Expedition denied that they had ever used shields such as were common among the plains tribes, asserting that the protective powers of the bundles were better than those of a shield. They affected to pity the tribes whose "medicine was so poor that they had to protect themselves with shields." Nevertheless, Catlin pictures the old Sac chief Keokuk carrying a shield, also the chief Pashepaho is similarly shown, and the use of shields is shown in his pictures of several Sac and Fox dances.[1]

[1] Catlin, Manners, Customs and Condition of the North American Indians, London 1841. Vol. II, Plates 280, 289.

HISTORICAL REFERENCES.

The earliest mention I have thus far encountered, regarding the sacred bundles of the Sac and Fox, is in Catlin,[1] where a short account is furnished, of the "Dance to the medicine of the Brave" as an explanation of the plate here reproduced (Pl. XXII).

"In the plate is reproduced," says Mr. Catlin, "a party of Sac warriors who have returned victorious from battle with the scalps they have taken from their enemies: but having lost one of their party, they appear and dance in front of his wigwam fifteen days in succession, about an hour every day, when the widow hangs his medicine bag on a green bush which she erects before her door, under which she sits and cries while the warriors brandish the scalps they have taken, and at the same time recount the deeds of bravery of their deceased comrade in arms, whilst they are throwing presents to the widow to heal her grief and afford her the means of a living." The picture shows a war bundle (Pl. XXV) with a gourd rattle (Pl. XXIX, D) attached, hanging in front of a mat lodge, while a company of shaven-headed warriors dance in a circle to the sound of two drums and a deer-hoof rattle. (See Pl. XXIX, A.) The three persons brandishing the scalps in the center of the circle have long hair and seem to be women.[2]

The next reference that I discovered, in point of time, is a quotation from the report of the Indian Agent at Tama City, Iowa, dated August 10, 1885.[3]   In speaking of the Sac and Fox religion he says: "Feasts are held before their crops are planted, and another series of prayers and thanksgivings

---

[1] *Ibid.*, Vol. II, p. 215.

[2] Another and much fuller account written about this time has been brought to my attention by Mr. Alanson Skinner, of the American Museum of Natural History, and is reproduced as an appendix to this paper.

[3] Smithsonian Report, 1885, p. 39.

after the crops are gathered. Blessings and invocations are said when a child is born. . . . Holy or consecrated tobacco is burned on certain occasions as incense, and they have something that profane eyes are never allowed to see, called 'Mesham,' corresponding to the Jewish Ark of the Covenant." This was, of course, a "mī camⁱ," or sacred bundle.

Incidental mention is made of the sacred bundles in Dr. William Jones' Fox Texts,[1] also under the head of Sauk in the Handbook of American Indians.[2]

---

[1] Publications of the American Ethnological Society, Vol. I, pp. 161, 165, 169.
[2] Bureau of American Ethnology, Bulletin 30, Part 2, p. 478.

MYTHS OF ORIGIN.

The origin of the different kinds of sacred bundles, in fact of many kinds of fetishes, amulets and charms, is generally traced, by tradition, to the custom of the youth's fast, widespread especially among the eastern and central tribes, in which the boy subjects himself to hunger and exposure in the hope that some supernatural being will appear to him and offer to be his guardian spirit and helper through life. At such a time, say the legends, the originator of the bundle, then a poor starving boy, was visited by the Manitos and told how to make the amulets and other things that would give him the power he craved. Such a bundle would then be handed down to the succeeding generations. Thus it happened that many a warrior used a bundle that was not the product of his own dream, but the vision of one of his ancestors. Bundles may be divided and made the basis of several new ones, and changes may be introduced in response to new revelations.

A tradition purporting to be the story of the origin of fasting for power, and of the first bundle ever made among the Sac and Fox, was obtained from Mecabékwa (Pl. XX, A), a man of Fox descent, living near Cushing, Oklahoma. This is given substantially as he related it, sentence by sentence, as translated by the expedition interpreter, Leo Walker. Mecabékwa's name means Big Back, but he goes by the name of U. S. Grant among the whites. The tradition runs as follows:

The man to whom the Great Manito first gave this bundle received the name of Pī toc kā h' (redoubled). The name he bore in childhood is not now remembered. He was poor and as he grew up he did not enjoy living, but was always dissatisfied, so at last he painted himself and made up his mind that he would go out and starve.

The morning he started he told his father and mother not to think about him any more, that he was going out to starve and did not care where death overtook him. As he left he sang:

1. Ä kwī nī gī a ni nī na (five times)
   - na
   - no
   - na
   - no

   (Since I was born)[1]
   Ä kwī nī ge',

   Nī kē kä nä mä kwī a'kī
   (I was known to the world)

2. Wī hī ni to no kwa nī
   (The way he will understand you)
   Wī hī ni to no kwa ně

   Wī hī ni to no kwa nī
   Wī hī ni to no kwa ně

   Wī hī ni to

   Hī na ka Ma ni to a
   (He above Spirit)
   Hī na ka Ma ni to a (four times more)

Ten days he was out, singing thus, then his relations began to think he was dead, and his father and mother began to fast. Tha ic' ki no was the old man's name. In his fast, some one called by name, saying, "Stop grieving, grieving will be changed to joyful feeling, I have heard it from above.

---

[1] The translations of these songs were furnished by the interpreter.

You will see your son. I have given your son something, you will like it. I am the one that owns the world, and I am the one that has helped him. I am the one who expected him to do as he has done. But fifteen days will pass before you see your son, as I want him to fast twenty-five days altogether. I have given him the power and strength and that is why he has not already starved to death. I have given your son the name Pī toc′ kä h‘ (redoubled), by which he shall be known to all people, spirits, monsters, animals, everything. You will see the things that I have given him, things that will make the people powerful." Two days before he came back the mother was also told to stop grieving. "Do not cry any more, as the day is coming when you will see him face to face. You will see what changes I have made in his body and features." At last they heard singing—their son's returning song:

> Ne pi a wē na (six times repeated)
> (I am coming to you)
>
> Ne pi a wi
>
> Yo ma nē ha‘ kī yē
> (With this world)
>
> Ne pi a wē na (six times repeated)
> (I am coming to you)

So when they heard him coming, they prepared the house for him, cleaned it, and fixed food for him. The Great Manito said to the old man, "Have water ready in a wooden spoon, and put dirt in the water, and stir it up. That is my power. Before you give him anything to eat, give this to your son." So he fixed it according to directions and when he was done he saw his son standing just before the door. Then the boy spoke: "My father, my mother, my brothers and sisters— I have come." Then the old man addressed him: "My son, we have cleaned and fixed a place where you will sit." "My

father," the boy replied, "you must hear me first."   So he
sang:

> Hä me no la pē to ma nä (eight times repeated)
> (My right of sitting [living])
>
> Yu ma nē ha' kī yä
> (In this world)
>
> Hä me no la pē to ma nä (eight times repeated)
> (My right of sitting)

When he had finished singing he took off a bundle that the
Great Manito had given him, and hung it up, although he did
not know what was in it; then he sat down.   The old man
then gave him the spoon containing muddy water, and he
drank.   When he had done this he felt good all over.   Then
they gave him food.   Some one spoke to him from above and
told him not to eat too much.   After he had eaten he sat still
and he and his father gazed at each other all day.   The father
thought, "The Great Manito has given my son something,"
and he thought of the bundle.   "He has been fasting many
days, and he must have been given something or has had
something made known to him."   His thoughts were understood by his son then.   "Yes, my father," he answered from
his heart, "the Great Manito has given me something, but
I want you to wait, as I am going out again."   He also told
the old man to save up deer hoofs for him, as he was going
to tie them on a stick and make a rattle (Pl. XXIX, A).   Next
morning he set off very early, unknown to his father.   When
he was a long ways from the camp he started to cry again,
and sang:

> Nī kē tē ma ke nī me ko to ka ⎫
> (I will receive sympathy)   ⎪
>   ⎬ repeat couplet three times
> Hī na ka Ma ni to wa nī na   ⎪
> (He above Spirit, me)   ⎭

While he was crying and singing, the Great Manito spoke to him and told him to stop crying. "I was the one that helped you before," he said. "You will see buffalo over there at the point of the draw, by the spring. Give them tobacco so you can get a tail and other parts from them." So he did this, and skinned off the tail of a buffalo so as to hurt it as little as possible (Pl. XXXIV, F, G, H); then he raised the tail and said, "I have done what you told me!" Then he cut a strip of skin from the buffalo's head (Pl. XXX, A), and, holding it up, repeated, "I have done what you told me!" Then the Great Manito told him to cut off some skin and hair from under the forelegs of the buffalo, first right and then left (Pl. XXXIV, A, D, E), and then a piece from its beard. Thereupon he raised everything up and exclaimed, "I have cut everything off the way you told me!" "Now you must go on," said the Great Manito. "As you cross the prairie down there you will see something standing. It is a raven; grab it by the neck and take it with you." He did this and went on his way, and finally found a camping place, and built a fire to warm himself, and spent the night there. Then came morning; he skinned the raven and dried the skin right there. Then he went his way. "You will come to a cut bank or bluff," said the Great Manito. The young man asked himself when he reached it, "Why did I come here?" "There," said the Manito, "pick up that red clay—it is paint!" Then he held it up to the Great Manito and exclaimed, "I have done what you said!" "Give me your right hand," he heard somebody say, so he held it up, and in it was placed a bluish soft stone or dirt. "What shall I do with this?" he asked. "Wait," was the answer; "you will know later." At this point he had been out eight days again, and now was told to go home and see his folks for a while. His father knew when he started home, that he was coming, so his bowl was already prepared for him when he arrived. When he came he hung his new things up by the bundle he had hanging there already, then sat down in his place. The women then gave him his wooden bowl and the spoon with the dirty water, which he drank before he started eating, as he had been instructed, but this time the Great Manito said, "Eat all you want." He stayed at home only two days, lying around. He could not talk to his father, or his father to him, because the old man felt sure the son was doing something great. The morning of the third day he started out again, first telling his father that he was going. Then he began to sing his first song and walk about the woods crying. Finally he asked the Great Manito what he wanted him to do about the bundle. "Well, I will tell you," was the answer. "Go to a certain plant, it is yellow, approaching it from the east; and go around it four times: then pull it up, root and all. Now go south until you come to a little hill of rock; when you get there I will tell you what to do." He did all this and stood waiting. "Another certain plant is growing there, it is red," he was told. "Go and do the same thing with that." Then he waited after he had made four rounds, and the Manito told him to pull this one up also. "Now go west. When you come to the creek, stop." When he arrived there he waited and was told to do the same to a certain black plant, pulling it up at the word. "Go straight north until you come to the head of a little branch (stream) on a hill." Here another black plant was secured in the same way; then he went back to his camping place and built his fire. Then and there he made up his mind that the Great Manito was really sympathizing with him and giving him power. While he was sitting there thinking, squatted wrapped up in his robe, he heard a rushing sound. Then something flew under his robe—it was a hawk. Then another bird came and lit on a tree near by. It was a prairie owl, the kind that lives in the prairie dog burrows. This owl spoke to the man, and asked him if he had seen the hawk he had been chasing. "Don't tell him," begged the hawk beneath his blanket. "Show me that hawk, my grandson!" the owl insisted, but the hawk pleaded, "Have pity on me, and I will do the same by you!" and the man remained silent. All night the owl sat watching, and all night the man sat hiding the hawk. Then he said to the owl, "I have not seen the hawk, but some one passed me last night." But the owl replied, "You have him under there. I know it, and if you will give him to me I will give you something in his place." But when day came the owl gave it up and flew away toward his home on the prairie. Then the hawk knew that he had gone, and showed himself at last. "Which way did he go?" he asked. The man pointed, and the hawk flew up and crosswise to try to get a glimpse of the owl, and finally set off as if he had sighted him and wished to overtake him. A little later he returned, bearing the owl's head. "I will help you this much for hiding me," he told the man, and gave the head to him. "In war time you will strike the first, and kill the first enemy." Then the Great Manito told the man to catch the hawk and take him along too. But when he caught the hawk, the bird died, so he left all the things he had secured hanging on a tree at his camping place, and started again on his wanderings. After traveling a while, he lay down to rest on a hill.

As he lay there he heard the Great Manito say, "I believe you are asleep," but he answered from his heart and said, "No!" "Look out, then, toward the west," said the Manito, "and you will see somebody coming toward you from that direction." He looked and saw a bird-hawk, the smallest kind, coming. "Take him and go," said the Manito. "Go on until you come to a prairie, where you will see a black wolf, which you must take with you back to your camp." When he saw the wolf the animal was apparently enraged, and rushing to attack him. "How can I kill a creature like that?" Pĭ toc kä h‘ said. "Grab him about the neck and carry him off," was the reply. "He does not amount to much." When he took hold, the wolf seemed very light, just like nothing; so he carried him back to his camp ground, and arriving here, he was told to skin the wolf and the other things that he had caught. This done, he started for home with all his things wrapped up in a bundle, and as he went along he sang his second returning song. When he arrived he found that his father had prepared the dirty water for him.

Again the young man stayed two days at home and on the morning of the third day told his father that he was going to start out once more into the wilderness. Four days again he fasted, and on the morning of the fifth, the Great Manito spoke to him saying, "I have now given you what will be the dependence and strength of you and your people. You will soon receive the last final medicine." When he went to his camp that night and lay down to rest, he began to wonder as to what all these things he had gathered might be, and what he was supposed to do with them. Next morning also he pondered on the things that had happened and on the articles he had in his possession. While he was thus thinking the Great Manito spoke: "Make your way northward until you come to a mountain; this you must climb, and wait upon its summit for further directions." He had reached this point and was lying waiting when once more the Manito spoke: "Two bands of Thunders will visit you when the sun stands overhead." At last they came amid rain and wind, the trees blowing down before them, and circling around alighted all around him, the black Thunders facing south, and the white ones north. After they had alighted the sky was perfectly clear. The black Thunders were Ac' kac ak, and the white ones Kic' ko uk. The black Thunders spoke first, and told him to cry no more; then the white ones told him not to grieve. The black ones then gave him a round object made of bone, which turns blue in the winter, and is said to represent the sky, and the white ones explained it to him, saying, "This is the strong power of all the Thunders. It was taken from the sky and is very powerful, and we have given it to you because the Great Manito told us to do so, and told us to help you. You, yourself, must keep and take care of this Kĭ cĕ kw' (sky) to be your guide and strength and help. In war you will use this, so the enemy cannot defeat you. Now we have finished the errand of the Great Manito. We want you to keep this gift and love it and open it in different seasons; it will change color according to the season. Now you must go home." So he started homeward.

As he walked along he began to think of his collection. "How shall I know what to do with these things?" he wondered. At once the Great Manito spoke to him: "I will now explain to you about these things, and you can finish the work I expect you to do. When you get home your father must get some young men to kill four dogs and cook them. When they start to boil the dogs you must spread the black wolf hide, and then arrange upon it the other things." When he reached home and had followed his instructions, he called to his father to come and sit beside him, and told him that he had been given these things because he had fasted so long. For the first time he unwrapped the first bag or bundle he had brought, and found inside a number of spotted fawn skins for wrappers to put on the various powerful objects he had obtained, together with two white deer skins. Then the Great Manito told him just what each article was intended for. "Take up that raven[1] first, and lay it upon the wolf hide; then split it and prepare it to use as a head band. Then the hawk skin—split that the same as the other (Pl. XXX, D), and the bird hawk as well; then place the raven to the right, and the other birds to the left, while the bone, gift of the thunders, goes on the right of the raven. The piece of hide from the head of the buffalo you must place to the right of this again, and the arm bands made of the skin of its forelegs to the right and left respectively of the piece from the head, and back of the headpiece, the tail. Then, still going to the right, the east medicine root must be laid down, then the south, the west and the north roots in order. Cut the white deer hide in four pieces for the medicine. Then cut a little off each of the roots, and upon these four piles scrape a little of the 'sky bone,' scraping it four times in all. Make these piles of medi-

---

[1] This may have been an ivory-bill or pileated woodpecker instead of a raven, due to error of interpretation.

cine into little bundles, and tie one of them on the raven head band, and two on the necklace, which must be made of the skin from the buffalo's head, one right, one left; then tie one on each arm band, and one on the buffalo tail, which is to be worn hanging down behind. Split the black wolf hide so that you can wear it with its head upon your breast and its rear parts and tail hanging down your back. Now spread everything out on the four fawn hides." What the Manito told him, that Pī toc kä h' did. Then he took up one fawn hide and put the head band in it, and the same way with everything else; thus the bundle was made.

All this time the four dogs had been cooking, so he sent the young men who were serving as helpers out to call the people to bring their wooden bowls and come to the feast. When they came and saw this stuff spread out, they were surprised, and wondered what it might be. Then the young man, sitting, spoke: "Now, my friends, what you see before me was given by the Great Manito. He told me to do this. When you have eaten the feast I shall start on the warpath." Then the people began to eat. Meanwhile he put on his robe and girded himself, thrusting extra moccasins under his belt as preparation for the journey, then he rolled up his bundle and tied it as may be seen to-day, then slinging it over his shoulder cried, "As many of you as wish to go with me, come on!" Now the Great Manito was advising him all this time.

So he started, and when night came, camped beside a creek. Here it was that many who wished to accompany him overtook him. "To-morrow at midday I will tell you where I want you to go," the Great Manito told him, so at midday he stopped, and was told, "On the third day you will see two mountains, between which there is a camp of A ca' hak' (Sioux), but stop on this side." So they traveled on. All this time he had eaten nothing.

At last the Great Manito told him, "To-morrow you will arrive, but do not make an attack until midday." So they camped when they came to the place, to wait for the time appointed, but the young man sent two spies, one Ac kac'ᵃ and one Kĭc'ko', to look around the mountains and see what was there. They saw the enemy, and returning, reported that by their appearance, they outnumbered the war party two to one. There were no guns at that time, but the weapons were nearly all of wood, clubs and bows and arrows, with some stone-headed hatchets and the like.

Then came the word from the Manito: "Now move up to the right distance!" When they came in view of the Sioux, it seemed as if they could see nothing else, there were so many. "Now we will make the attack, my people!" came the word. The Sioux knew by this time that they were coming. Pĭ toc kä h' put on the garments in his bundle—the head band, necklace and arm bands, for he was the only one that had them. "Do not be afraid," he told his comrades; "they are our protection." Then as they started in to fight he sang the attack song, keeping time with his deer hoof rattle, and dancing as he sang, repeating the songs over and over again as they fought, for he was their leader:

No ten wī ka o thä
(Wind blow, leg walk) (repeat five times)

Cī cī kwä wai ya ke
(Bull-snake hide)

Ne ta ma' ki sä hī
(Shoes I have)

No ten wī ka o thä
(Wind blow, leg walk) (repeat three times)

By this he meant, "I travel like the wind, or as a bull-snake slips through the grass." The fight was like running into a prairie fire, so he sang:

Sko tā wē ne na na thā ka
(Fire   I am going against) (repeat five times)

Ma ni to wī ne na na thā ka
(A Spirit I am going against)

Sko tā wē ne na na thā ka (repeat four times)
(Fire   I am going against)

Then referring to the black wolf's hide he wore which endowed him with the wolf's cunning, speed and endurance, and enabled him to travel at night like a wolf, he sang:

Ma w' ä wa[n] yo ha nē ya ha wē
(Wolf   my body is) (repeat five times)

Ma ni to wē ha nē nē ya ha wē
(A Spirit   my body is)

Ma w' ä wa[n] yo ha nē ya ha wē
(Wolf   my body is) (repeat four times)

Then came this song:

Ne na tä, ne na tä
(I am going after it, I am going after it) (repeat five times)

Hī nä ni wa ho tä hi
(Man's   heart)

Ne na tä ne na tä
(I am going after it, I am going after it) (repeat four times)

When the leader thought the fight had gone on long enough he stopped singing and his scouts, the Ac kac'[a] and Kic'ko[a], gave the yell for retreat, and then every one had to drop whatever he was doing and withdraw. If any one kept. on fighting after this, he was liable to lose his life. The leader had carried no weapon, not even a knife, for it was his place as leader to use the bundle only.

He then turned his black wolf hide around with its head to the rear, and as they started homeward he sang this song:

Yo wē nē ne wī ta
(Who will see me)
} (repeat couplet four times)
We pī ka pai nī nē
(Standing, me)

Yo wē nē

Yū mē no ta ha nī nī na
(In your village, I)

We pī ka pai nī nē
(Am standing, me)

Ne ke tī ma to nī na
(Treating them without pity, I)

We pī ka

Yo wē nē ne wī ta
(Who will see me)
} (repeat couplet)
We pī ka pai nī nē
(Standing, me)

He had turned the black wolf hide around, so that the enemy would see a wolf, not a man, and would think it was coming towards them. At last they arrived at their own village.

When his mother had given him food, he began to think again about what had passed. Then again the Great Manito spoke to him, and told him that hereafter he might eat and drink on the warpath, and gave him a song which he must always sing before drinking while on such an expedition:

> We mä no ya nī na
> (Now I will drink) (repeat four times)
>
> Ne pī nī na
> (Water, me)
>
> We mä no ya nī na
> (Now I will drink) (repeat four times)

Then he told Pī toc kä hʻ how to make the war whistle (Pl. XXIX, E, F, G) and how to blow it with medicine in it to weaken the power of the enemy. He also explained the bluish soft stone or dirt that had been given to the young man in his fast, saying, "This will be your medicine when somebody is wounded in the hollow part of his body. Fill a mussel shell with water, and scrape a little of the medicine into it, and let the wounded man drink it. It will make him throw out the blood, and will cure him." Then he instructed him as to what to do when he returned to his village after a war expedition. "If your father and mother have anything good to eat, let them ask the young men who help at such times to fix the meat and cook for a feast." This was done, and when they had put the meat in the pots, the young man, following the instructions of the Manito, took down the bundle and laid it upon the black wolf hide, and untied it, putting some Indian tobacco in it, which the Great Manito had given him for the purpose, with seed to plant to raise more. Then he sang:

> Hī na hī nī na
> (Now, myself)
>
> } (repeat couplet four times)
>
> Wī pa ka nī no nī na
> (Open me)

Wī pa ka nī

Ma ni to wa nī wa pa me kwa nī na
(Spirit will look at me)

Hī na hī nī na
(Now, myself)

⎫
⎪
⎬ (repeat couplet three times)
⎪
⎭

Wī pa ka nī no nī na
(Open me)

As he continued untying the bundle he suddenly saw beside him, a pile of sweet cedar (pa pa ka tā kwa) and the Great Manito told him to burn it and smoke the bundle, and to do this four times a year.   So he smoked the bundle, dipping it through the smoke four times to the eastward, and was then told that no one could destroy the power of a bundle thus smoked, and that even a woman in menstruation might approach it without injury (to the bundle) as it hangs to the rafters.   As a rule women are not allowed near when a bundle is open, especially when in their periodic condition.

Seeing what the young man had done, the other people took up the style and began to make and use these bundles, and to sacrifice to the Great Manito through them.   This was the beginning of fasting, and of Mī' cam an,[1] or Sacred Bundles.   From this first bundle all others are branches.

After I left the field, Mr. William Skye (Pl. XX, B), a member of the Peoria tribe, who had been my assistant during most of the Oklahoma work, tried to get further information about the bundles.   He met with considerable difficulty and opposition, as most of the Indians who knew these things thought it wrong to impart their knowledge to anyone who might write it down.

But he finally secured the following myth, another ver-

---

[1] Singular = mī'cam' or mī' ca m'.

sion apparently of the one just given, which is set forth here as nearly as possible as he wrote it (being merely rearranged) with the Indian words in his own spelling:

There were only five different bundles in the Sac tribe in early times, but after a while there were more bundles branched off from these, war bundles and namesake bundles. Pītoski (Pī toc kā h') was the name of the man who got the first bundle, after mourning (fasting) twelve days. It did not come through a dream in the night, but just as if someone was talking to him in the daytime.

This person (who spoke to him) told Pītoski to go and pick certain herbs, and that when he had his herbs gathered he would be told what to do. Then he was told: "Go over two mountains and you will see two buffaloes standing heads together; when you get there you must skin the tails from both the bull and the cow, and cut the long hair from the right foreleg of each—then you must take their heads, the skull of each one." These buffaloes talked to him, and one of them said, "I am giving you all my power: you must not be afraid of anyone hurting you, and you will not be harmed. You must put the buffalo bull's head on your head. And here is power I shall give you: you will be known when this is seen; one horn, on the right side shall be red, the one on the left, black." He was then told he must get a hawk, a small darting hawk, and after this was skinned he was told to get one more bird, the swallow. "Now," said the voice, "I will show you how to make your medicine." So he put all this together and made the bundle. The swallow was fixed to tie on the top of his head.

After the bundle was made, Pītoski's father came to him. "Father, I have had an awful experience from God," he said. "What can it be, son?" asked the father. "I want you to tell me." "I have made a bundle," was the reply. "He showed me how to make a bundle." "Well, my son, that is why I have asked you to mourn (fast); it is for yourself, for your own good."

"Now," Pĭtoski said, "I am going to quit mourning. Father, I am going home, and I am going to take my bundle with me to the place where we live." After he had brought the bundle to his place, he did not go away again for quite a while. (But) After a time, it seemed as if he had no more faith in his bundle. "Say, father," he said, "I have no more faith in this thing that I have made; it does not go as I was told." And so he started off again because he had no faith in his bundle.

He went to some wilderness and fasted four days. "Yes, this bundle is all right," someone told him. "You should have done as you were told." At this time, after he had been out four days, he was given paint, red and black. "Paint yourself in this way," he was told: "a zigzag line over the right eye, then a cross made of double lines on both arms, the left breast and the stomach, and a cross of single zigzag lines on the legs above the knees, and the calves of the legs the same; then a round spot on the forehead, on the palms of your hands, and on the inside of your feet just below the instep. Now you must also have a whistle to tie around your neck, and when you get the medicine and paint you must put (some of) it inside the whistle, and you must put this same medicine paint on your arrows and on your war club if you have one. Then if you ever (so much as) scratch an enemy with your arrow you will kill him."

Then the whole family and the tribe knew that he had been given a bundle, and the whole tribe went to mourning (fasting); some mourned four days and some eight days; then those that mourned found out that this man Pĭtoski had been given this bundle by the Spirit. Someone spoke to the mourners and told them, "I have given Pĭtoski this great power, he cannot deny it. That is the place to which you now must look. He has the bundle I have given him, you must go to this bundle and make known what you need."

(Later) Pĭtoski was told, "Now if you give a feast you must hunt deer or bear or turkey, but you must put dog meat first; dog is the head of all meats. Do as you are told and follow this.

"From this bundle you will find your names and clans; and hereafter, before your children are named they must fast for a certain number of days before they are entitled to names."

After this bundle was completed the people appointed four more men to mourn and find out the truth about the bundle, for there had not been anything given to them by the dream (vision). One stayed out four days, the rest eight days, but they could not find out anything, only about this same bundle. "You cannot get any more now. The bundle was given to Pītoski, and you should look to his bundle (to get yours). He has told you the truth."

(Something seems to have been omitted at this point, but it is evident that the men must have finally gone to "Pītoski" and received bundles from him.)

These first bundles that were given to the Sac Indians were called or named after each man who had received one: first the Pītoski bundle, then the Pī to kī mâ, Nī mâ ko mâ, Mâ cho kī mâ (Bad Chief), and Mâ shī wâ wīsquī.

"Now," they were told, "some of these men must not eat turkey at the feasts for their bundles, and you must be careful about the Bad Chief (Mâ cho kī mâ) bundle." This name means really not-powerful chief, he was just a common chief without special power of any kind. "You must be careful to sacrifice for his bundle a young buffalo calf. Just give him head or horn, that is just the same as if you were giving him medicine."

After Pītoski had given these medicines away, his father came. "Well, father," he said, "these spirits have given me truth. The men sent out to mourn have found it to be so."

"Well, son," was the answer, "that is why I have done as I have to you—so that you could find more power. I have abused you in your younger days so that you could get power to help yourself and the rest of us. I am glad you have found out that you have this power, and now have faith in your bundle. And this is why you should wear your whistle at your neck—so everyone may know you have had power given to you."

"Now, father," was the answer, "I am through. I will even quit fasting. After I had been out mourning the rest of the tribe found out that by mourning I was given power, so they began mourning too, so as to get power also."

"Feasts must be given for your bundles," said Pītoski to the four men. "First you must have fire and Indian tobacco; then you want dog first of all meats—dog will be chief leader of all meats in your feasts. Pītokīmâ and Mâchokīmâ do not eat turkey, and you must watch this. Pītokīmâ, you must get a pair of yearling buffalo horns and make a head band, and put these horns on it; and also get a young buffalo tail—this you shall wear in your feast dance. And Nīmâkomâ is another that must not eat any turkey. And when it is time to open a bundle and there are one or two or more of you there you must help one another, and put it back together after opening."

Now, as was said before, the names of their first owners were given to most of the bundles, Pītoski, Mâchokīmâ, Nīmâkomâ, and Pītokīmâ. But the Mâshīwâwīsquī was also (later) given to Pītokima, who gave it to Tekumse,[1] and gave him authority to keep it, and told him not to mourn any more, for he too had also been given power.

"This is what I want you to do—you must have your mind on your tribe and keep them together and not let anything happen to them. If any one of you gets hurt we have given you power to cure him, or cure them if any are sick. This is how you will be convinced that you have been given true power. If you are called upon to help you must always do so, even when people are hurt by accident in the tribe. In such cases you must doctor them and your power will help you just the same as if they had been wounded by the enemy.

---

[1] It seems hardly likely that the Shawnee chief Tecumseh is meant here. I think from what follows that Keokuk is meant.

If you are true to your bundles they will help you in your battles."

This Mâshīwâwīsquī bundle is a very powerful one, so powerful that no bundle in the other tribes could affect it, and the Sac[1] people became great in war with other tribes. All tribes fought with the Sacs and tried to wipe them out; but only one tribe, the Iowa, helped them. There were four cane whistles in that bundle that were worn by four men in battle. They had so much power that every time those whistles sounded it would make the enemy weak and the Sacs could kill them with clubs. (Here follows a digression concerning Keokuk's character and services, which will be omitted.)

Keokuk's bundle has never been taken care of as it should have been, since he died. We (the Sac tribe) are now suffering from the effects of this neglect.

---

[1] This would indicate that the bundle had been given to a Sac, and practically eliminates the Shawnee Tecumseh.

CLASSIFICATION AND USE OF BUNDLES.

The sacred bundles of the Sac and Fox can be roughly divided into three classes of differing functions, as follows:

1. Naming or Clan Bundles.—These are sacred bundles whose principal function seems to lie in the ceremonies for the naming of children. We were unable to obtain a specimen of this kind, not only because they were considered clan property and especially sacred, but because they are still in active use to-day.

2. War Bundles.—These are sacred bundles containing amulets, charms and other things thought to give magical protection and help in battle. Twenty-two examples were collected from the Sac and Fox, together with one small bundle which seems intermediate between this class and the following.

3. Medicine or Charm Bundles.—These people had many kinds of minor bundles, supposed to aid them in the various other affairs of life, such as hunting, love, gambling and even for injuring such of their own tribesmen as happened to offend the holders of the bundles devoted to witchcraft. All of these are classified as medicine or charm bundles, because of the large number of charm medicines and charms they contain, with few amulets and fetishes fewer still. Shapes and sizes are various. Most of these minor bundles serve several purposes, however, and may well be described as general bundles. Twelve were collected.

As we were unable to obtain naming bundles, and as they seem never to have functioned as "namesakes" except in the special naming rites of the clans, the meager information we have regarding their use will be taken up later under the head of "Ceremonies." A general account of the use of the war bundles, however, will not be out of place here.

The Expedition was very fortunate in obtaining war bundles, which, although held in great esteem by the Indians, are now, since war has become a thing of the past, of little use to them; on the contrary, merely a source of trouble and expense, for every bundle must have its feast and rites at stated times every year, the neglect of which is believed to cause some misfortune to the person responsible, the person who by inheritance or gift, happens to be its keeper.

Nevertheless it was very difficult to persuade the owners to give them up at first, but once they were satisfied that the bundles would not be ill treated, the task became a little easier.

The large number was due to two principal causes: the large number existing in the tribe, and the fact that the people had just arrived at that stage of civilization when they would dispose of them. In old times every warrior of any prominence had a bundle; thus it happened that with the thinning out of the tribe many families came to acquire several by inheritance. In such cases it was much easier to buy bundles that were superfluous than it would have been to obtain the only one in the possession of a family.

The typical method of using the war bundle may be set forth in brief as follows: When the war leader, after appropriate songs and ceremonies set forth with his followers, he bore upon his back the war bundle upon whose powers the success of the raid was supposed to depend. Every precaution was taken to care for the bundle, and every night it was hung on a tree or a lance thrust into the ground so that it might not touch the earth. But it was never opened until the enemy were actually sighted—but once they came in view, even if very close, the warriors, singing the song proper to the occasion, opened the bundle, stripped themselves and put on the "medicine" head bands, plumes, arm bands and other protective amulets it contained, painted themselves with its magic paint, and chewed and rubbed upon their bodies the herbs that would make them impervious to arrows or difficult to hit; then while the remains of the bundle were being wrapped up, and amid the shrilling of the war whistles and the sound of the rattles from the bundle, joined in a short dance. Then they were ready for the foe, who might have been firing on them in the mean time. After the encounter the amulets were returned to the bundle. If anyone had been wounded his injuries were treated with the herbs it contained.

Medicine or charm bundles are used in nearly as many ways as there are individual bundles, for which reason it will be better to leave the discussion of their use until the specimens themselves are described.

It was easier to obtain these minor bundles, except those connected with witchcraft or similar practices, where considerable difficulty was encountered. This was because few Indians wished to publicly admit that they had ever owned or used such things.

STORAGE.

In times of peace both war and naming bundles were kept hanging from the roof-poles of the lodge, and at stated times were taken down, opened and honored with feast and dance.

Many of them are kept to-day in special bark houses maintained by the men who act as priests, the important bundles of the clan being kept together in this way. These houses might really be called the ceremonial houses of the clans, for in them the clan feasts and dances take place (Pl. XXI, XXIV). Among the more primitive people, as at Tama, Iowa, the clan house is also the residence of the priest and his family; but among the more advanced, as in Oklahoma, the bark house stands beside the more comfortable frame dwelling of the priest. This is shown in Pl. XXIII, B. Some at least of the war bundles, and all of the minor varieties, are kept by their owners in their own homes, and not in the clan repository.

In these private homes, while the war bundles are of course hung up the medicine bundles are packed away in rawhide trunks, baskets and bags, along with other purely personal effects. The use of a clan repository is mentioned under the heading "Sauk" in the Handbook of American Indians.[1]

RULES.

There are certain rules connected with the handling of bundles, especially the war bundles, which must be obeyed. They must always be treated with respect, and never opened except for good cause, nor must they ever be allowed to touch the ground. One of the strictest rules provided that no woman should ever touch them or any part of them, or approach them when open; and no woman in her periodic condition approach them even when closed. Should this be allowed, it was believed that not only would the powers of the bundle be spoiled, but the woman would be likely to bleed to death. There are exceptions to this rule, however, certain bundles to which the taboo did not apply.

---

[1] Bureau of American Ethnology, Bulletin 30, Part 2, p. 478.

CEREMONIES.

Among these Indians the belief is prevalent that a child cannot receive a real and valid name except through the ceremonies connected with the naming bundle, usually that of its father's clan. To what extremes this idea may be carried out is seen in the case of a closely related tribe, the Kickapoo, whose children, born in Oklahoma, are frequently taken to Mexico to be named, for many if not all of the clan naming bundles are held by the bands of the tribe who have emigrated to Mexico in search of more primitive conditions, under which it is possible to continue their ancient manner of living.

Our only account of the Sac naming bundles, as recorded by Mr. Skye, is presented herewith:

"Now there are a number of clans in the Sac tribe: the Fish clans, Thunder clan, Fox, Bear, Wolf, Beaver, Eagle, Swan, Turkey, Turtle, Elk, Deer, Buffalo, Bear-potato, Sun or Daylight, Buzzard and Goose or Duck clans.[1] There are, however, only twelve namesake bundles, all taken from the first five.

"Children usually belong to the clan of the father, and so belong to a bundle of that clan, but sometimes, especially if children are sickly, they may be changed to or adopted by the clan of the mother, or possibly some other clan (with a

---

[1] Morgan's list (Ancient Society, p. 170) of the Sac and Fox clans is: Wolf, Bear, Deer, Elk, Hawk, Eagle, Fish, Buffalo, Thunder, Bone, Fox, Sea, Sturgeon, Big Tree; while the Handbook of American Indians gives for the Sauk division: the Trout, Bass, Sturgeon, Great Lynx or Fire Dragon, Sea, Fox, Wolf, Bear, Bear-potato, Elk, Swan, Grouse, Eagle and Thunder; and for the Fox: Bear, Fox, Wolf, Big Lynx, Elk, Buffalo, Swan, Pheasant, Eagle, Sea, Sturgeon, Bass, Thunder and Bear-potato. The only clans occurring on all four lists are: Fish clans (several kinds), Thunder, Fox, Wolf, Bear, Elk, Eagle; of these we may be reasonably sure for both the Sauk and the Fox; while the Bear-potato, Buffalo, Swan and Sea occurring on three lists, are probably correct. As for the rest a critical investigation is needed.

view to benefiting their health). This is the only way that a person can join a bundle. (This seems to be the case with war- as well as naming-bundles.)

"No one is allowed to marry into his own clan, for the people of each clan are related to one another, but must marry into a different clan. Now suppose a man belonging to the Bear clan marries a Bear woman, and a child is born to them. Such a child would not be recognized by the Sacs; they would not give him a name, for he is not entitled to one (according to their belief), nor can he belong to, or join a bundle.

"A child whose father belongs to the Buffalo clan, it is said, can, if his parents wish it, be adopted into any clan with a namesake bundle.

"When a child is four years old it is then entitled to a name; so the father goes to the head leader of a bundle, and says that he is going to name his child, that he wishes his child to belong to a certain bundle, and that he will give a feast. Any of the clans that keep, or belong to, a bundle, have the right to give names.

"The father then starts out early in the morning while breakfast is being prepared, to notify his hunters. He goes to each lodge and notifies the men he wants them to come and eat breakfast with him—eight men in all. They go at once and eat with him, and he tells them that he wants some meat for a feast. They go hunting and stay away four days, and bring back whatever they kill, such as deer, and leave it all with the father and his wife takes care of it. She can keep as much out as she needs for family use. The feast is held in four days, but in two days the people are notified to come and camp on the second day from that. In the meantime the father has selected the name, and has his attendants ('waiters') picked out, and is ready.

"Now they are all notified, and come and camp; and dogs are brought, and the other meat for the feast, and beans. Now they begin to kill the dogs and burn off the hair (Pl. XXIII, B) to prepare them for the feast, and four kettles are fixed for the cooking (Pl. XXIV). A set of firesticks is used to make the fire for singeing the dogs. One waiter takes the bow (of the fire drill) and holds the stick like an arrow, and pulls the string four times as if he was going to shoot; then they make the fire. When the dogs are cleaned nicely they are set to cook.

"When all this has been done, tobacco is put into a buckskin, as many pieces or pinches or handfuls as there are pieces of dog. Then they begin to sing, shaking their gourd rattles, while someone holds the bundle of tobacco out to the west, north, east and south.

"When the dogs are cooked and the rest of the meat is done, the kettles are taken up and hung on a tree or scaffold, then everything is ready for the feast. Then the invited people are divided up so that the Skushi can sit on the north and the Kishko on the south side; but all go in by the east door and walk around the fire four times before they are seated. Now there are an even number of wooden bowls brought in, the same in number as the pieces of dog meat, then they divide the dog and some of the other stuff cooked, putting the same number of pieces into each bowl.

"A man of the Thunder clan is next asked to take tobacco in his hand and hold it out to the west and whoop four times for rain. Then all whoop four times with their hands over their mouths—the war whoop—and after the fourth time they jump up, grab their bowls and eat up the food just as quickly as they can, each (side) trying to beat the other. After these specially invited people have finished eating, any one who wishes can share in what is left.

"Then they worship, each one for himself, and an old man is asked to pray for a blessing for all of them, and give thanks for plenty of meat, especially the dogs furnished by God to his people. Now he must also pray for the child's name, and for the one that gave him that name also.

"Now the Sun must know the child's name, so early in the morning they pray to the Sun, asking him to take care of the child until he turns gray. A man's life, they say, goes like the Sun. He rises and gets to a certain height, then begins to decline; so the man appointed tells the Sun they want this child to grow and live to old age, until, like the Sun, he finally goes down. 'Make this child live and believe as he has been taught,' the old man prays. 'He must believe in the Indian teachings. Let him then live until he is like someone with four legs'—meaning until he has to walk with two canes—'and his hair turns from gray to white.'

"This is prayed to the bundles too. When a man or a woman gets too old they keep quiet. They cannot go anywhere or do anything, so they depend altogether on the bundle they are keeping."

It would seem from the following item, also recorded by Mr. Skye, that the speakers, leaders and waiters chosen for a naming bundle ceremony must belong to other clans than that of the bundle.

"Now the name of Pītoski, to whom the first bundle was given, is from the Fox clan, so he (the keeper of the Pītoski or Fox bundle) chooses a chief of the Bear clan to help him arrange for feasts for his bundle—to talk over the way it ought to be done, and they get the nīmâwī okīmâ (Fish chief) to help them also. The Fox and Bear clans really came from the Fox tribe, originally, it is said. Then he selects from the Swan and Turkey clans the leaders in the feast; and two of the four waiters come from these and two from the Bald Eagle and Black Wolf clans. And, as was said before, the chief of the feast must be from the Bear clan. Now the Fish clan called 'Pa comwa' has for waiters men from Thunder, Eagle, Deer and Elk clans and the Bear clan takes from the Eagle, Rabbit and Bear-potato clans."

The following description of a war bundle ceremony was given by Mecabékwa, whose version of the myth relating the origin of the bundles has been related.

Certain persons are said to belong to one of these bundles, and these only have the right to get up a feast for it. When one of these wants to hold such a ceremony, he goes around and notifies his fellow members to gather at the place where the bundle is kept in four days. Then he appoints two men— the "waiters"—to go around and notify and invite the other people—anyone can come. When the time arrives, each member takes something to eat to the feast—turkey, pumpkin, anything he has handy—especially meat, like dog or venison. The ceremony begins before dawn, and all the morning, while the food is cooking, the songs go on, the singers being the people who belong to the bundle. In many cases there are dances to go with the songs (Pl. XXIV), and in these the public take part. About midday when the food is cooked one person is invited from the Ac kac'ᵃ division and one from the Kĭc ko⁺, and these compete with each other in eating the scalding food fresh from the kettles. In this contest a dog or a deer is divided in two equal parts, one for the Ac kac'ᵃ and one for the Kĭc'ko⁺, each of whom chooses an equal number of his own division to help him in the eating race.

This done, the leader of the bundle gives a pot of food to a certain one with a bundle of little sticks equal to the number of pieces of food in the pot. This person then goes out and gives the sticks around to anyone he wishes to eat with him, one stick to each person, and these join him in eating what is left of the food.

When everything has been eaten and there is silence in the lodge, a man known as a speaker, or preacher, stands up and relates the story of the origin of the bundle. When he has finished there is again silence for a while, then the leader of the bundle speaks: "Now, my friends, you have eaten the food that I have sacrificed to the Great Manito. Now you have the privilege of leaving us." To this the people respond, "Hao!" and get up and move about, even though they may stay longer.

The members of the bundle—the performers—all sit on the north side of the lodge (generally a rectangular bark house) (Pls. XXI, XXIV), while the invited ones sit opposite on the south side. When they start to go out the man furthest east on the south side gets down off the platform first, then walks westward, circling the fire, then eastward and out. Then the west one on the north platform circles the fire and goes out; then they all go. The ceremony is called Kī kă nu nī. It is sometimes preceded by a "medicine sweat" or steam bath for purification (Pl. XXIII, A).

As to the bundle, they dip it four times eastward through the smoke of burning cedar, when they first begin; then as they open it they sprinkle Indian tobacco in it, repeating a prayer. It lies open during the ceremony, in which condition it is smoked again, about the middle of the morning, by wafting the smoke over the outspread contents, sometimes with the aid of burning coals carried in an iron shovel. It is again smoked, about time for the feast, before being tied up again, and is once more passed through the smoke after it resumes its bundle form, four times to the eastward. Then they hang it back to the rafter poles overhead to await the next feast. Such feasts are held for some bundles four times a year.

One of the prayers used when sprinkling tobacco in the bundle was interpreted as follows:

Ne me co Pī toc' kă h' (Grandfather Pītoc'kăh'): "Do not think of me in the wrong way, but only in the right way. As the Great Manito has told you, that is how I want you to think of me. Think of my future life."

For most of the bundle ceremonies the water drum with curved drumstick (Pl. XXIX, B, C) is used to accompany the singing; the rattles, while sometimes made of deer hoofs in the old way (Pl. XXIX, A), are now usually of gourd (Pl. XXIX, D), which, the Sac and Fox say, is a comparative innovation. The screeching of the war whistles (Pl. XXIX, E, F, G) (frequently seen attached to the bundles) blown by the leading dancers is usually a feature of these ceremonies.

The opportunity was offered while the Expedition was working among the Fox Indians of Iowa to attend several such gatherings, or rather to look on, for outsiders were not .

permitted within the lodge where the ceremonies took place. One of these was a Wolf clan ceremony, in honor of a bundle whose principal "medicine" or patron was the wolf. In this case the musicians, who were profusely painted, sat on the south sleeping platform of the lodge, and here I was told the bundle lay open, although I could not see it from outside. The bark covered arbor adjoining the house on the east had been temporarily walled with such mats as are used to cover the winter lodges, and the end wall between house and arbor removed, throwing them together as one large room. In addition to the sound of the drum and rattles usually heard, a peculiar accompaniment to the singing was produced by rubbing a round stick of hard wood upon another long one, provided with a series of lateral notches (Pl. XXIX, H). The regular purring throb of several pairs of these sticks worked in unison produced an effect both unusual and agreeable. As the dancers passed the door outside which I was standing, circling contra-clockwise, it was noticed that the leaders were nearly naked and daubed profusely with paint, mostly white, while the rest of the dancers were fully attired in their best, both men and women. The leaders danced in imitation of the movements of the wolf, holding their hands drooping before their breasts as a dog holds its forepaws when standing upon its hind legs, and, as they stepped, constantly sounded the war whistles. This particular ceremony ended tragically, for the principal leader, an old man whose skilful dancing and effective use of paint had especially attracted my attention, dropped dead at the end of the first dance. A few days later I witnessed part of another bundle ceremony in which the dancers, in curved parallel rows facing the platform where the singers sat, danced without moving from their places.

WAR BUNDLES.

CONTENTS.—After tabulating the contents of the twenty-two Sac and Fox war bundles, it was seen that twenty of them contain parts of the buffalo; eighteen of them eagle feathers of one kind or another; twelve of them pieces of the downy skin of the young swan; seven, parts of the hawk (several species); six, parts of woodpeckers; four, parts of snakes; three, parts of weasels; and three, parts of small swallow-like birds. The animals represented in one or two bundles only were the wolf, bear, lynx, beaver, crow, wild duck and probably wild goose. In many cases the exact species is almost impossible to determine—in some cases quite impossible—owing to the alterations made by the Indians in preparing the skins and other parts for use as amulets, and to the ravages of time and insects.

Seventeen of the bundles contained war whistles made of cane, in one case as many as five in a single bundle; fourteen had fawn skin covers for the amulets; thirteen had packages of cedar leaves burned as incense; seven, Indian tobacco, and three, braids of sweet grass for the same purpose. Packages of magic herbs and roots were found in sixteen of the bundles, sometimes as many as twenty-three such packages in one; seven contained ground mixtures of herbs, and twelve, packages of magic war paint. Other articles occurred in lesser proportion.

The reasons given by different Indians to explain the presence of the more common kinds of animals and other things in the bundles agree to such an extent that it will be unnecessary to repeat them in enumerating the contents of each bundle, so they will be given here as general information; leaving for the descriptions of the separate bundles only such explanations as vary from the generally accepted ones, and explanations of unusual objects.

The popularity of the buffalo as a patron of war can be easily understood when we look at him from the Indian's standpoint. Unrivaled by any creature that roamed the prairies in strength, endurance and courage, this mighty warrior of nature, whose very appearance is enough to terrify, found his only dangerous foes in rivals among his own kind, and in man.

No wonder the budding warrior looked upon him with admiration, and craved a share of his awe-inspiring powers— his strength, endurance and bravery—in preference to all others. To this end the amulets were made from parts of the buffalo's body. A bit of the mane to tie on the warrior's scalp lock (Pl. XXXI), or a shaggy head band with the horns attached (Pl. XXX, A), arm bands (Pl. XXXIV, A, D, E) made of the skin of the forelegs, and a buffalo tail to hang from the belt behind (Pl. XXIV, F, G, H, I), all helped him to impersonate the mighty animal. The very fact that only two bundles out of the twenty-two were without some relic of this remarkable creature, would have told the story, even if several Indians had not explained the facts.

The warlike powers of the eagle are even better known, and to a lesser degree those of the hawk as well. Both are keen-sighted, quick and can take their victims by surprise. Both are notably successful raiders. And so, the Indian placed their feathers or skins in his war bundle, and wore them in battle, in the hope that he too would become imbued with eagle-like or hawk-like power—could surprise his foes just as if he had dropped out of the sky upon them, eagle fashion. Feathers dyed red symbolized blood and war.

Hawk and woodpecker skins were made into magic head bands by splitting the skins from shoulder to tail, strengthening the parts with buckskin or cloth, and arranging tie-strings so that the skin could be worn with the head of the bird projecting above the forehead of the warrior, the tail at the back of his head and the wings and feet at the sides (Pl. XXX).

Of course only the largest species of woodpeckers, the

pileated and ivory-bill, could be used for such a purpose. Woodpeckers are very skilful in finding their prey, even when well concealed—a quality which made their skins desirable as amulets, for either hunting or war, as by their aid the Indian believed he could locate his enemy or even a deer, just as the bird can locate the larvæ hidden away beneath the bark of a tree. Besides this, as one Indian put it, "The bird can peck a great hole in a tree in a short time; the warrior who wore the skin could do the same thing—it did not take him long to make a great hole in the enemy."

The downy skin of the young swan, seen in so many bundles, was not, so far as I could discover, supposed to impart any warlike powers to its wearer, but was merely worn on the scalp lock or elsewhere as a badge or sign to distinguish friends from foes, especially in the night (Pl. XXVI, B, H, Q).

As to snakes, the deadly power of the dreaded "rattler," which must have impressed every Indian, needs no explanation; while the little green snake was used on account of its ability to travel unseen and conceal itself readily and quickly.

The weasel has much the same qualities, and, in addition, quickness, cunning and the power of attacking and slaying creatures much larger than itself (Pl. XXVIII, A).

The small birds used, especially those of the swallow family, are very difficult to hit with an arrow or bullet, a power imparted to the warrior. Moreover, the person wearing such a bird skin properly prepared, would look small as the bird itself to the enemy, when they tried to shoot at him (Pl. XXVI, N). Such bird skins were sometimes attached to the mane or tail of the war pony to make it look small to the enemy and hard to hit (Pl. XXVI, P).

The tireless endurance of the wolf was much dwelt on by my informants as a desirable power for the warrior; the powers of the bear, lynx and mink can be inferred, although I have no direct information about them from the Sac and Fox tribe; but the properties of war amulets made from the

beaver, lizard, mallard duck and wild goose may only be sur-
mised, in the absence of any data.   They may merely represent
creatures appearing to the faster in his visions.

.Among the most powerful of the patrons of war, and yet
but scantily represented by amulets in this lot of war bundles,
are the Thunders, those awful supernatural beings, at the
same time bird-like and man-like, who wield the dreadful
lightning.   Their token is frequently the miniature war club
worn upon the scalp lock (Pl. XXVI, C), which symbolizes the
blows struck by the lightning, or balls of stone or other materials, of similar significance, both of which are supposed to
impart "Thunder-power" to the user.

All but five of the bundles contained war whistles made
of the bamboo-like cane found growing along streams in many
parts of the South, both east and west of the Mississippi.   In
earlier days, before the Sac and Fox left the north, they probably got their cane by exchange with other, more southern
tribes.   The whistles were blown in battle, after having been
treated with magic herbs, to weaken the power of the enemy
and bewilder his senses, and are also sounded in the dances
enacted at the war bundle feasts (Pl. XXIX, E, F, G).

The skins of little spotted fawns were usually employed
as covers for the different amulets in the bundles (Pl. XXXIII,
E), but in some cases buckskin was used instead.   Probably all
the bundles contained at one time, some form of incense, either
native tobacco, cedar leaves and twigs or sweet grass (Pl. XXVI,
R); but in some these have been used up and not replaced;
and all probably once contained packages of magic herbs and
paints, although these are now missing in some cases.

There was also a considerable number of tiny medicine packets usually from a quarter to half an inch in diameter,
tied fast to the different amulets;   these are enumerated
in the description of the individual bundles which follows.
They contain small portions of the roots, herbs and paints
supposed to have the power of magically turning aside bullets
and arrows, of "hypnotizing" the enemy and of curing the

wounded. Some of the roots are said to wake the magic power of the animal amulets and make them "alive," while one kind is carried to protect the warrior from possible boomerang effects of his own enchantments against others. Sometimes a number of these little packets were tied along a buckskin thong to form an amulet for the neck or arm.

When I asked for more definite information about the "hypnotic" effect of these magic herbs on the enemy, I was told that "The enemy seem to lose their minds. Sometimes they cannot see our warriors coming at all; again they may see us, but not in the place where we really are; sometimes they take us for a herd of buffalo or horses. One enemy said after the tribes had made friends again that he suddenly began to see different kinds of animals coming toward him in the air: he began to shoot at them and forgot all about the Sac and Fox warriors."

Some time in the future I hope to find a Sac and Fox Indian who will consent to open and explain each package of roots and herbs and give me the Indian names of each kind and a description of how they grow, so that I can have them identified; but so far I have not been able to accomplish much along this line.

DETAILED DESCRIPTION.

We had worked among the Sac and Fox for quite a long time before the slightest hope of obtaining a war bundle appeared. We had seen a number of them hanging in the bark lodges, but none of the owners would even consider selling. In fact, they refused with such indignation that we despaired of ever getting as much as one.

But at last a man was located who had too many bundles to care for, and finding them a burden, was willing to sell a few if he could be sure they would be well treated. This was Mecabe'kwa, known as U. S. Grant, the same whose version of the tradition accounting for the origin of war bundles has already been given. The first purchase consisted of two bundles, as follows:

BUNDLE 2/5317.

· Size closed, 18¾″ × 4½″. Buckskin cover badly broken and decayed; ties, braided blanket ravelings; calico sack of native tobacco attached to one of the ties; war whistle thrust beneath them.

Contents.—Headband made of the split skin of a female ivory-bill woodpecker (Pl. XXX, B). To each shoulder is fastened the red crest of a male, of the same species. At the throat are tied a bunch of buffalo hair and some deer hair dyed red, while here and there on the neck and wings are fastened nine little packets of medicine wrapped in buckskin. The strings for tying the amulet in place are of buckskin.

Amulet for attachment to the scalp lock, made of a piece of a buffalo tail, to the distal end of which are attached a piece of the downy skin of a young swan, some eagle down feathers dyed red, a little brass bell and four little buckskin packets of medicine.

Three buffalo tails; one in a fawn skin case painted red on the flesh side, but without attachments, and two with the proximal end bent forward upon itself to make a loop for the belt. One had a little packet of medicine, a hawk bill and a tuft of red cloth attached; the other, two medicine packets and a strip of faded yellow ribbon.

Neck amulet made of a strip of skin from a buffalo's neck, the hair now nearly gone.

Tuft of buffalo mane hair, perhaps part of a scalp lock amulet.

Two strips of downy young swan skin, one arranged as a scalp lock amulet with a bit of buffalo hair and a small white feather, the other plain. In length they measured respectively 8¾″ and 10″.

Fragments of fawn skin covers for amulets.

Black stone scraped and administered in water to wounded men as medicine.

· Four packages of magic roots and herbs.

One package of magic paint.

BUNDLE 2/5311.

Size closed, 20″ × 4½″. This is the second of the first two bundles bought from Mecabe′kwa, and seems to be one of the oldest in the collection. Buckskin cover nearly destroyed by age, ties of braided blanket ravelings and buckskin thongs. Gourd rattle (Pl. XXIX, D) attached to tie.

Contents.—An unusually interesting and very old necklace (Pl. XXXIII, B), consisting of a woven band about 30″ long and ¾″ wide, with a six-inch fringe at both ends. The material seems to be a sort of yarn of buffalo wool twisted fairly hard, the color, a deep reddish brown, apparently the result of age and dark red dye on fairly light colored wool. A zigzag line of large old white beads is woven in, down the center, and one side has an edging of similar beads. The band is folded longitudinally for the greater part of its length over a fringe of deer hair dyed red and yellow, and nine medicine packets are tied upon it at irregular intervals. Such an amulet is intended to give the wearer the powers of all the different herbs in the packets tied upon it.

A buffalo tail amulet for the belt, bent over to form a loop and bearing four little medicine packets and a bit of root knotted on a sinew string.

Amulet for the scalp lock made by tying together a bit of the downy skin of a young swan, a little buffalo hair, a braid of sweet grass for incense, a piece of red braid, and a small buckskin medicine packet.

Piece of colored braid with triangle designs, doubtful origin.

Remains of two fawn skin covers for amulets.

A little old metallic box, made by the whites, with a

Punchinello-like head painted upon the cover. As it was falling apart at the joints it had been wrapped in a strip of red cloth. It contained five packages of roots.

A package of magic red war paint.

A package of cedar leaves.

A skin package containing a piece of greenish stone imbedded in cedar leaves.

Three packages of roots.

A large cocoon, provided with a buckskin string for suspension.

Mecabe'kwa's remarks on these particular bundles may prove of interest here. "They are a little different now because some of the parts have been worn out, but once there were four of these bundles, all alike. On the warpath when the warriors get in front of the enemy they take off their clothes, open the bundles and put on the things inside, and open all the little sacks of medicine and take what they need to chew up and rub all over themselves, their horses and their ammunition. Then the bundle is closed and tied on the back of one of the warriors. This medicine prevents them from being hit, as the enemy are mesmerized[1] and cannot shoot straight. The warriors must not even turn toward the enemy until all is ready, but when all were done they whooped four times and turned on the enemy, who might have been shooting and coming all this time while they were fixing. The four songs were sung and a rattle shaken at this time While dressing they painted themselves, too, with red earth paint from the bundle, zigzag crossing lines on cheeks, arms and chest. A half-moon was painted on the forehead so that the enemy could not hit them, for they cannot hit the real moon in the sky, and they would have to hit the moon before they could hit the man."

At a later date another bundle was purchased from Mecabe'kwa, which, from its contents, appears to be the third

---

[1] The word used by Walker the interpreter.

of the four bundles that their late owner said were "once just alike." It is:

BUNDLE 2/6373.

Size closed, 20″ × 5¾″. Buckskin cover entirely fallen to pieces; a new one has been substituted.

Contents.—Head band made in the usual way from the split skin of a large hawk. About the neck, which was wrapped in faded ribbon, were hung three little brass bells. The hawk skin was protected by a fawn skin cover, the head of which contained a package of herbs.

Buffalo tail amulet bent over into a loop to slip upon the arm, or for attachment to the belt (Pl. XXXIV, C). Two buckskin thongs wrapped in porcupine quills dyed yellow and red were lashed in three places to the sides of the tail as ornaments. Below the third lashing each thong is split into two pieces, also wrapped in quills, and terminating in brass jinglers. To the right thong are tied six little medicine packets of buckskin. Three smaller thongs, wrapped in black, red and yellow quills hang from the back of the tail as a further decoration.

Another buffalo tail without medicine packets or quill work.

Scalp lock amulet consisting of part of a buffalo tail, a bit of swan's down, some eagle down feathers dyed red and a medicine packet.

Scalp lock amulet consisting of a bit of swan's down, some small feathers dyed red, part of the skin of a small bird, blue in color, and a fair sized medicine packet to which is attached a pendant eagle tail feather with strips of red cloth tied around its base.

Cane war whistle, with black ribbon to suspend from the neck.

Tail of a small bird.

Two deer hoofs, probably part of a rattle.

Two loose metal jinglers.

Birch bark package containing roots.

Buckskin package containing a bundle of roots and a paper package of roots and herbs.

Cloth bundle containing a buckskin packet of magic red paint (mixed with herbs) and the remains of a squirrel skin sack containing similar pigment of a slightly different shade.

Two globular objects, fibrous but fairly hard, possibly concretions from the digestive tract of some animal. Ball-like objects, whatever their origin, are usually symbols of the lightning when found in war bundles.

Three loose pieces of root.

Evidently belonging to the same class of bundles were three bought from Victor Neal, a Sac and Fox who unfortunately knew, or affected to know, very little about them. They were:

BUNDLE 2/8591.

Size closed, 20″ × 8″. Buckskin cover, stiffened and blackened by age and smoke. Three sets of ties, all buffalo hide, one set at each end and one in the middle. Beneath these are thrust four cane whistles. The outside appearance of this bundle is shown in Pl. XXV.

Contents.—Remains of five head bands made of the skins of hawks of at least two species. Only one was near being perfect. This was $16\frac{3}{4}$″ in length from beak to tail-tip and split and lined in the usual way (Pl. XXX, D), the tail being left attached to the right half of the skin. Tying strings of both buckskin and cloth were provided. Down, dyed red, protruded from the nostrils, while about the neck was a collar of red and black yarn into which were woven four rows of beads. On a separate buckskin string encircling the neck in front of the collar, were seven little medicine packets. The next head band in point of preservation was made of the skin of a larger hawk, 20″ long, about the neck of which was a red ribbon with two medicine packets, and seven medicine packets on a buckskin string. The next had seven such packets and three little bundles of roots without covering, attached to a woven yarn and bead band about the neck. This head band was in very bad order, but the remaining two were worse, mere fragments without points of interest.

Arm band decorated with porcupine quills (Pl. XXXII, B). This is the best thing of the kind I have ever seen. The band part, measuring $9\frac{3}{4}'' \times 2\frac{1}{4}''$, is made of buckskin, with thongs at the corners for tying the ends together about the arm. On the outside this is covered with porcupine quill decoration, the quills being wrapped around fourteen flat thongs of skin, attached, parallel and adjacent to one another, to the buckskin band. The ground color is yellow, the field bordered on all four sides with a narrow thong wrapped in red quills. The design consists of five brown bird-like figures in a row, a narrow brown line forming a rectangle about them. At one end of the band is a tab of netted quill work, two yellow truncated triangles on a red ground, with a buckskin fringe wrapped in quills; while at the other end, is a flat, quilled streamer 20″ long terminating in the tassel of a buffalo tail, the proximal end wrapped in swan's down; a few strips of faded red ribbon and an eagle feather. The streamer is composed of eleven strands or thongs of buckskin, the two outer ones wrapped in strips of bird quill dyed dark brown, green and red; the inner nine wrapped in porcupine quills dyed green, red and yellow, the colors so arranged as to form, when the strands lie flat and side by side, three human figures in red on a yellow ground, each with a green stripe down the center of the body. The quilled strands were formerly fastened together so as to lie flat, once at 6″ and again 5″ further down, but have now worked loose. From the point where the streamer joins the band, hang several very slender quilled thongs, provided with copper jinglers. Similar jinglers had once been attached to the side strands of the streamer at intervals of about an inch, but many of these are now missing. Where the streamer joins the band were also four little packets of magic medicines and paint, also a buckskin string to which are tied two sets of bits of root without covering, two in each set, and knots from which four other similar sets have fallen. At the point where the eagle feather is attached are two packets. The whole amulet seems to be a development from the simple buffalo tail bent over to form a loop. While often worn on the belt, these amulets could be used as arm bands by simply passing the hand through the loop. An intermediate form may be seen in the quilled buffalo tail already described as part of the contents of bundle 2/6373 (Pl. XXXIV, C), which was used as an arm band, and a further development in the specimen in bundle 2/8739 (Pl. XXXIV, B). The complexity of the amulet was not in form only, but in its powers also, for it was not only supposed to confer upon its wearer, the power of the buffalo and all the powers of the little packets of herbs and paints, but the eagle feather invoked the warlike abilities of that powerful bird; and the five bird-like figures on the band, the awesome might of the Thunder Beings, which they were supposed to represent.

A simple buffalo tail amulet, folded over in the usual way for attachment to the belt, bearing the remains of some red ribbon, two medicine packets, two pairs of little roots and one single root, all tied to a buckskin string (Pl. XXXIV, H).

Two other tails, nearly worn out, bore one medicine packet each (Pl. XXXIV, G); one tail, four strips of red cloth; and three tails, nothing. Two of these last had lost nearly all their hair.

Two arm bands, made of the skin of the buffalo's forelegs. One of these embodies a lock from the mane but nothing else (Pl. XXXIV, A); the other eight medicine packets and two little packages of exposed rootlets in addition, knotted on a buckskin string (Pl. XXXIV, D).

Three amulets for the scalp lock. The most complex was made on a strip of red cloth $5\frac{1}{2}'' \times 1\frac{3}{4}''$, rounded at the anterior end and provided with a border of ribbon work (appliqué) in blue and yellow with a bead edging (Pl. XXXI, D). To the upper surface was fastened the terminal tuft of a buffalo tail, some eagle down feathers, part white, part dyed red, a medicine packet, four bits of root tied with a buckskin thong and a few strands of faded ribbon. On the lower side, attached to the thong intended for fastening the amulet to the wearer's hair, was the remains of a tassel composed of a few down feathers and a tuft of buffalo hair bound together with ribbon and a buckskin thong which shows traces of having been wrapped with quills and still bears a medicine packet and a little brass bell. The second amulet was merely a bunch of buffalo hair to which was tied some reddened down feathers and faded yellow ribbons (Pl. XXXI, C); while the third was a piece of buffalo tail bound fast to a strip of downy young swan's skin $12\frac{1}{4}''$ long.

A buffalo horn, with the edges more or less rounded served, it is said, for a cup in which medicine was administered (Pl. XXXVI, B).

A cane war whistle.

A fine curved drumstick, $13''$ long, painted red (Pl. XXIX, C).

A coil of braided fibre rope or sennit about $12'$ long, both ends divided into four braided ornamental strands $8''$ long, said to be for binding captives (Pl. XXXVI, D).

Two deer skin covers, one for the quilled arm band, one for the best head band.

Buckskin thong bearing seven medicine packets, probably once part of a hawk skin head band.

Similar but smaller thong with six packets.

Two buckskin thongs, each with two bits of root knotted in.

Cloth package of cedar leaves.

Twenty-two packages of roots and herbs, one of them also containing:

One package of green paint.

Two packages of ground herb mixture.

One empty buckskin package.

Two tiny rolls of paper containing roots fastened together with sinew.

Eleven loose pieces of root.

Another somewhat similar bundle from the same man, Victor Neal, was:

BUNDLE 2/6376.

Size closed, 18″ × 6″. Buckskin cover, new, the original having fallen to pieces. Three buckskin ties, the end ones connected by a carrying cord braided from native fibre. Beneath the ties was thrust a war whistle.

Contents.—Two head bands, made in the usual way of the skins of large hawks, both in poor condition. The best preserved skin as it lies measures 26″ from the tip of the beak to the end of the tail. About the neck is a piece of red cloth 3½″ wide, bound with a cord made of hair, and a buckskin string to which seven little bags of medicine are attached, besides two bits of root on a separate string, two more tied together and a red down feather. Each wing is decorated with a slender, tapering flat stick, wrapped in colored porcupine quills, lashed fast to it with sinew. These are about 9″ long, and each has a tuft of hair, dyed red, fastened to base and tip. The skin is lined with bluish cloth.

The second head band is similar with the exception that there is a faded yellow ribbon on the neck of the hawk, that there are eight buckskin packets, one paper packet and one exposed bit of root on the neck thong, and that one of the wing ornaments is missing. This amulet is in very poor condition.

A tail and portions of the two wings of a similar hawk are also in the bundle.

Amulet for the scalp lock, made of a hawk wing to which has been fastened an eagle tail feather, a piece of red cotton cloth, and a bunch of red woolen cloth ravelings, together with a thong for attaching the amulet to the hair.

Three tail feathers, apparently those of a very large hawk.

Two buffalo tail amulets. One of these had apparently seen much use. About 4″ of the proximal end has been bent over and fastened with a buckskin string in the usual way to form a loop for the belt; while three little packets of roots, the remains of a red down feather and a looped piece of sinew, which had once held a number of little bits of root, were fastened to the tail at different points. There was no belt loop on the second tail, but a medicine package, wrapped in cloth was tied to the proximal end in such a way as to form a toggle which could be slipped under the belt.

An arm band made from the skin of a buffalo foreleg, provided with buckskin tie strings.

Amulet for the scalp lock, consisting of a long soft brown lock of buffalo hair, a bunch of darker buffalo hair, a piece of a young swan's downy skin, 7″ long, two eagle wing feathers, loosely attached, a bunch of eagle down feathers dyed red, a packet of medicine, a piece of sinew with five bits of root knotted in and a thong of buckskin with two, all tied together and provided with buckskin thongs to tie the amulet to the hair. The whole combination measured about 13″ in length (Pl. XXXI, B).

Another amulet for the scalp lock, comprising a bunch of buffalo hair, a number of eagle down feathers dyed red, some of them 9″ long, and two medicine packets, beside the tying thong.

An amulet of buckskin, called for convenience a "war apron," resembling a short apron in appearance (Pl. XXXV, A), but not in use, being worn in back instead of in front. In its present state, doubtless somewhat shrunken, it is approximately 15″ from side to side, and 14″ from top to bottom. The edge at the top is folded over to form a flap $2\frac{1}{4}$″ wide, which is decorated with crude ribbon appliqué in red and blue, and which is protracted at both sides to form a belt. From the center of this flap hangs a battered eagle feather, to the proximal end of which is tied a little packet of medicine and a green ribbon. A little below the flap, and not far from the edge on both sides is a seven-pointed star or sun figure, in ribbon appliqué, the left one red, the right blue. The lower edge of the amulet has two deep indentations, forming three points, which are fringed and decorated with copper jinglers. No one could enlighten me as to the special powers of this amulet, but judging from the patterns it may have been credited with sun or star power in addition to that derived from the eagle feather and medicine packet.

War whistle of cane, with dark longitudinal stripes (Pl. XXIX, E).

Calico package of eagle down.

Double cloth package, with eight packages of herbs and roots.

Part of fawn skin amulet cover.

A few loose bits of root, and loose jinglers from the apron.

Victor Neal sold us also two small bundles, which he said were "branches" of the bundle just described, No. 2/6376. Their contents seem to bear this out. They are kept tied together with a twisted rope of yarn and a buckskin thong. They are:

BUNDLES 2/6377, A AND B.

Bundle A.—Size closed, $15\frac{3}{4}'' \times 3\frac{1}{4}''$. Buckskin cover much blackened by smoke; ties, buffalo hide, buckskin and cloth strips.

Contents.—Two buffalo tail amulets, one looped over for the belt, the other with a buckskin thong at the proximal end for the same purpose.

Arm band made of skin of buffalo foreleg.

Amulet for the scalp lock made of a strip of the young swan's downy skin, a few eagle down feathers dyed red, and three packets of medicine.

Amulet similar to the last except for the addition of some undyed eagle down feathers.

Loose strip of downy swan skin.

Loose red down feather.

Remains of a fawn skin amulet case.

Bundle B.—Size closed, 17½″ × 3¾″. Buckskin cover much blackened by smoke; ties, twisted rope of buckskin, rope of green and red yarn, buckskin thong.

Contents.—Two buffalo tail amulets, one with a roll of buckskin at the end of a string as a toggle to slip under the belt, the other with a simple buckskin thong for a tie.

Part of an arm band made from the skin of a buffalo foreleg.

Amulet for the scalp lock consisting of a piece of the downy skin of a young swan, some small eagle feathers dyed red, and three packets of medicine.

Three loose eagle down feathers dyed red.

Remains of two fawn skin covers.

Of the same general sort as the preceding, including the two original Mecabe′kwa bundles, are three from Albert Moore, a Sac and Fox. As in one of the original two, however, the woodpecker takes the place of the hawk. They are:

Bundle 2/8772.

Size closed, 22″ × 6½″. Outside cover of coarse cotton cloth, much smoke-stained, then the remains of a very old buckskin cover, then a newer one with a cane war whistle tied upon it.

Contents.—Buffalo tail amulet, looped for attachment to the belt, bears fifteen medicine packets.

Two similar looped buffalo tails with only one packet apiece.

Four looped buffalo tails without packets.

Cane war whistle with thong for suspension, medicine packet, eagle down feathers dyed red and bits of gold braid attached.

Bag of coarse cotton fabric, empty. Probably once contained cedar leaves or tobacco.

Package containing herb mixture.

Package containing herb seeds.

Package containing magic red paint.

Small buckskin bundle containing:

Two head bands made of split woodpecker skins, one, the best preserved, of the ivory-bill woodpecker. This had six medicine packets attached.

Amulet for the scalp lock consisting of a buffalo tail to which are attached two medicine packets, part of a snake rattle and a few eagle down feathers dyed red.

Two empty packages, one of cloth, one buckskin.

Package of cedar twigs and leaves.

Package small seeds.

Calico package containing three buckskin packets, one of magic red paint, one of fine roots and one of the same small seeds noticed elsewhere in the bundle.

Whistle reed of cedar.

BUNDLE 2/8739.

Size closed, 18″ × 5″. Cover of buckskin, nearly fallen to pieces. This bundle had not been opened for a long time and the contents were badly damaged in consequence.

Contents.—Head band made of the skin of a pileated woodpecker, split in the usual way, and bearing nineteen medicine packets.

Buffalo tail arm band (Pl. XXXIV, B), decorated with porcupine quills, square blocks of brown on a field of white. The quills are wrapped around narrow strips of birch bark, fastened side by side upon the skin forming the band. Such a use of birch bark is rarely seen, strips of buckskin or rawhide being generally used for this purpose. Seventeen medicine packets and a bit of otter fur were attached to the band, while two more strips of the same fur, loose in the bundle, may once have served the same purpose. This amulet can be taken to illustrate an intermediate stage of development between a simpler form of buffalo tail arm band as in bundle No. 2/6373 and the more complex, in bundle No. 2/8591.

Buffalo tail, probably intended for a belt amulet, but apparently little if ever used.

Amulet for scalp lock consisting of a bunch of buffalo hair, some eagle down feathers dyed red, and a bit of rattle-snake skin with rattle attached.

Four pieces of fawn skin covers for amulets.

Three jinglers, two of brass, one of copper.

BUNDLE 2/8561.

Size closed, 16″ × 4¾″. Cover, buckskin; ties, fibre rope and cloth strips.

Contents.—Head band made of the split skin of a pileated woodpecker (Pl. XXX, C), bearing two medicine packets.

Buffalo tail amulet, large, the proximal end bent over into a loop and fastened for attachment to the belt; has eleven packets of medicine (Pl. XXXIV, F).

Buffalo tail amulet, small, thong for attachment.

Amulet for scalp lock consisting of a buffalo tail, to which has been tied a few eagle down feathers dyed red and two medicine packets.

Strip of basswood bark, coiled.

Cedar leaves and the terminal button of a snake rattle, wrapped together in a piece of calico.

Cane war whistle, four bits of root tied just above the air-hole, with thong for suspension from the neck (Pl. XXIX, F).

All the buffalo amulets in this bundle were notably well preserved.

Resembling the preceding, except that buffalo amulets are absent, is the following bundle, obtained also from Albert Moore, who said it was the same kind as 2/5317, one of the two original Mecabe'kwa bundles:

BUNDLE 2/6508.

Size closed, 12¼″ × 4″. Cover, buckskin; ties, buckskin, to which is attached the handle of an old gourd rattle.

Contents.—Head band made of the split skin of an ivory-bill woodpecker, with a band of white beads and red yarn about the neck, a faded green ribbon on the head, and three medicine packets attached.

Cane war whistle with ribbon for suspension.

Two packages of white mineral substance used as paint.

Two small packages magic red paint mixed with herbs, etc.

Two packages of herbs.

This was the smallest war bundle found by the Expedition among the Sac and Fox.

Two small bundles were obtained from Aveline Givens, a Sac and Fox, that bear a strong resemblance to the preceding series of bundles, except the last specimen described. They are:

BUNDLE 2/8448.

Size closed, 16″ × 4″. Cover of buckskin, blackened and crackled by age and smoke; ties of buffalo hide, buckskin and cloth, beneath which a war whistle is thrust.

Contents.—Four buffalo tail amulets, three of them bent to form loops for the belt, one with a thong for attachment.

An unusually long strip of young swan's down (22″), to one end of which was lashed a bunch of buffalo hair, a few eagle down feathers dyed red and two packets of medicine, the whole forming an amulet for the scalp lock which could, however, be worn around the neck if desired.

Two smaller amulets for the scalp lock, each composed of a bunch of buffalo hair, a few eagle down feathers dyed red and a packet of roots.

Woven necklace of blanket ravelings, in yellow and blue, edged with white beads. It bore seven packets of herbs and paints, three packets of roots and two exposed bits of root.

A cover of fawn skin, into which all the amulets had been packed.

BUNDLE 2/8534.

Size closed, 15½″ × 5″. Cover of buckskin, badly decayed; ties of buckskin, war whistle.

Contents.—Buffalo tail amulet for the belt, provided with two medicine packets.

Buffalo tail amulet, for either belt or scalp lock, to which were tied three medicine packets, one of them double, and a bit of root without covering.

Amulet for the scalp lock, composed of a small buffalo tail, a strip of young swan's down, and some eagle down feathers dyed red.

Woven necklace made of red and yellow ravelings, with white beads woven in. It bore eight packets of various magic medicines and two that were clearly roots, one of them without covering; and was enclosed in a fawn skin.

Part of what seems to have been a white buffalo or steer's tail, now a sort of sickly yellow—the only unusual thing in the bundle. At the proximal end was fastened a buckskin thong connecting with a wooden toggle intended to slip under the belt and keep the amulet in place (Pl. XXXIV, I).

Two fine bundles were bought from Co'kwīwa (Pl. XX, C, D) Smooth-surface, a member of the Bear-potato clan of the Sac and Fox, who is known to the whites as Sam Houston. While apparently very similar to many of the bundles already described, they are, he says, to be placed in quite a different class, the Mä me skwa pa yē no hun, or Bloody Thighs, so called because the usual taboo against menstruating women does not apply to them.

Co'kwīwa's remarks on these bundles should prove of interest here. "These bundles," he said, "were given by the Great Manito in a dream, but I do not know the dream well enough to tell it. Black Dog is said to be the owner of the original bundle taken from the first dream, and all the others are branches of his. The Bear-potato clan, Mu' ko ⌐

pe ni, owned these bundles from the first. But they can sometimes, if everybody is willing, be given to a man belonging
to some other clan. They are war bundles, and very different
from the 'namesake' bundles belonging to the different clans.
But they are not like most war bundles because a woman,
even in her monthly sickness, can come near them and touch
them without hurting her or weakening the bundle. That
is why they are called Bloody Thigh.

"Every warrior had a bundle—it was his shield, it protected him in battle.

"These bundles must be kept dry. Meetings or feasts
were held for them in the spring; this was the regular meeting.
Other meetings could be held whenever the owners wished.

"Both these bundles are the same medicine, but the contents are not quite the same. One belonged to my father and
one to my uncle. There is a medicine necklace in each one
which was worn in battle. The little packages of medicine
gave the warrior all the powers of all the roots and herbs
in them. What was left of the bundle after all the things
had been put on, was wrapped up in the cover and carried
along. They painted themselves in different ways, each man
in his own style. Blue paint means winter; green is spring;
light green, summer; and red, fall.

"The words of the songs sung while they were opening
the bundle and putting on the things went something like this:

"Wa bī ne thwa kä cī wa neth'
(White buffalo under the earth)

"Mä ka tä mo thä mo' kī ya n[i]!
(Black buffalo   I am coming out!)

"There should be seven kinds of herbs in each bundle,
all called thä ko wä' thon[i]. The leading kind is mä ka tä -
tca bi ku puk[i], or 'black root'—a black, round kind. When

it is chewed and rubbed over the body it makes all the animals in the bundle come to life, and hypnotizes the enemy.

"Mä' no wä^{hi}, or Angelica root, is another powerful one. It holds them spellbound. This is chewed and rubbed on the body the same way.

"Me ci ne' bī tho n^i, or calamus, is good for stopping blood; this is chewed too.

"Wa bec ki a gī me teg^{wi}, or 'white wood,' is used to harden one's self so as to be strong as a tree.

"Cī ka' wī, or 'widow medicine.' Round, hard, looks like 'black root,' only a little larger. Eaten to protect the warrior against his companion's medicine. It must be taken if mä' no wä^{hi} is used.

"Pă kī wuk^i, a round rough root, used to cure wounded men, by chewing up and blowing the resulting pulp on the wound.

"Mī thuk i puk^w, long thin black roots. A plaster is made of these roots and put on the wound."

The first of these bundles was:

BUNDLE 2/6371.

Size closed, 19″ × 7½″. Double cover of buckskin, two buckskin ties, beneath them a cane war whistle.

Contents.—Fawn skin cover, containing:

Two buffalo tail amulets looped for attachment to the belt.

Three arm bands made of the hide and hair of a buffalo's forelegs (Pl. XXXIV, E).

Amulet for the scalp lock composed of a piece of buffalo mane, with skin still attached, to which are fastened eagle down feathers dyed red, a packet of medicine and a wrapping strip of red cloth.

Another scalp lock amulet, comprising a long lock of buffalo hair, a fine piece of downy young swan's skin about 14″ long, a black-tipped eagle feather, some eagle down feathers dyed red, a strip of red ribbon and two packets of medicine.

A splinter of wood wrapped in colored porcupine quills and tipped with tufts of hair dyed red is said to have been once attached to the eagle feather as an ornament (Pl. XXXI, E).

The remains of a hawk skin with two similar quilled strips of wood tied to the wings. This amulet, it is said, was slung from the neck and not worn on the head.

In another fawn skin, the head of which was filled with down dyed red, was a woven necklace of native manufacture (Pl. XXXIII, D), a band nearly $1\frac{1}{2}''$ wide and about 27″ long, which seems to be woven wholly, or at least mainly, of buffalo wool yarn. The color is deep red with occasional rather irregular spots of yellow, evidently dyed after the fabric had been woven. This is frequently seen in the old buffalo wool fabrics. Apparently, the finished fabric was either first dyed yellow or left its natural yellowish color, then certain areas were covered with some substance, perhaps of a waxy or gummy nature, that was proof against the dye, then the whole object was immersed in the red dye. After dyeing, the waxy material could be removed, leaving certain spots untouched by the color. Or it may be possible, that the fabric was first dyed red all over, and then some bleaching material applied to certain spots. Or the color may have been daubed on where wanted and allowed to soak through. Additional decoration was supplied in this specimen by large white beads, interwoven in double rows running diagonally across the band, each pair about $\frac{3}{4}''$ from the next. At irregular intervals are tied seven little packets of medicine, one of magic paint and seven little bundles of exposed roots. These little packets and bundles are supposed to contain all the different kinds of herbs, roots and the like used in the war bundle.

The articles loose in the bundle were:

Deer hoof rattle, apparently very old, 16″ long (Pl. XXIX, A). The handle is a slender stick, the lower four inches of which are bare. The remainder is covered with buckskin to which the deer hoof-sheaths are attached, each on a separate string.

Near the tip, claws of some kind, possibly those of a badger, take the place of the hoof-sheaths. This rattle was used to keep time to the songs of the bundle ceremonies at home, and on the warpath, while the warriors were putting on their amulets before attacking the enemy.

Buffalo tail. This apparently has never been used as an amulet, but was saved as material.

Amulet for the scalp lock made of the tail of a buffalo calf with a packet of medicine attached.

Head and part of the neck of a young aquatic bird, probably a species of wild goose, formerly part of a scalp lock amulet.

Piece of the downy skin of a young swan.

Part of a network sash, apparently made of yellow buffalo wool yarn, afterward dyed deep red. The edges are beaded. Lying naturally, the sash was about 5″ wide, and the meshes each $2\frac{3}{4}$″ long and 1″ wide.

Lump of black earthy material, a″ki, used as paint. It symbolized the earth and, with a similar but finer material which was sometimes taken internally, was supposed to keep the warrior from "losing his foothold on the earth."

Part of a scalp—a trophy.

Four down feathers of the eagle, dyed red.

Buffalo bladder case containing two packages of roots, one of herb mixture.

Package containing native tobacco.

Package of down dyed red, supposed to have a protective effect when rubbed on the body.

Two packages of black earth paint, explained above.

Package containing an herb mixture imbedded in red down.

Two little packages tied together, one containing a mixture of roots, the other an incense made of cedar leaves and sweet grass.

One braid and one bundle of sweet grass, used as incense for smoking the bundle and its contents.

Twenty packages of roots and herbs.

Nine loose bits of root.

Part of a spotted fawn skin amulet case, head stuffed with down.

The following bundle, the second from Co'kwīwa, is probably the best, taken as a whole, secured from the Sac and Fox tribe, and is especially notable for the number and variety of the articles contained and their excellent state of preservation. The entire contents, excepting some of the medicine packages, are shown in Pl. XXVI.

BUNDLE 2/6372.

Size closed, 18″ × 8″. Cover, buckskin; ties, buffalo hide and buckskin, two near the ends, one in the middle, cane war whistle thrust beneath.

Contents (Pl. XXVI).—Wolf tail (A), worn as an amulet tied to the scalp lock or at the back of the belt, like the buffalo tails.

Arm band made of the downy skin of the young swan (B). From one end hangs an eagle feather.

Miniature wooden war-club (C) of the so-called "gunstock" type, worn on the head in obedience to a vision. Such objects usually symbolize the striking power of lightning, and are supposed to convey that power to their owner, but Co'-kwīwa did not explain this.

Part of a network sash (D), of brownish yellow buffalo wool yarn. Each mesh, hanging naturally, is about $1\frac{1}{4}″$ wide and 4″ long, the sash being four meshes wide. Only about 13″ of the length, exclusive of the remnants of a fringe, are left. Large white beads are strung along the sides.

Arm amulet (E), made from a piece of a red woven sash, of buffalo wool yarn, $2\frac{1}{2}″$ wide and $9\frac{3}{4}″$ long, besides a fringe at one end of $4\frac{1}{2}″$. The fabric has been folded lengthwise, and five packets of medicine, two packets of magic red paint, and one bit of root have been fastened to it at irregular intervals, together with buckskin strings to tie about the arm.

Another magic arm band (F), made of half a woven sash of buffalo wool yarn, 2¼″ wide and 14¼″ long, with an additional fringe of 10″. The buffalo wool is dyed red, the weave diagonal. A double zigzag row of large old white beads runs down the middle, strung on vegetable fibre. Eight packets of medicine and two fair-sized pieces of root fastened together have been tied upon it, also one very small packet of roots far down on the fringe. Tie strings of buckskin were provided.

Magic woven arm band (G), the fabric apparently expressly constructed for such use. It is rather irregular in width, but averages about 1½″, while the length, without fringes is 8½″, with fringes 15½″. A triple zigzag line of large old white beads runs down the middle of the band. Halfway between the ends is an area of dark yellow running entirely across the belt on both sides; the rest was red, a peculiar deep, rich tint. Both fringes began red, then came a yellow stripe across all the strands 1¼″ wide, then red again. It is clear from the fact that the separate strands of yarn are different colors in different parts of their length, that the dyeing has been done in some very different way than the method practiced to-day. The question has already been discussed (p. 190).

Another arm amulet (H) made from a short piece of a similar woven buffalo wool band, in red and yellow, pieced out with a downy piece of young swan's skin, 8¾″ long. Nine medicine packets and six bits of root were tied to the woven part, also two buckskin fastening strings.

Three arm bands (I, J, K) made from the skin of the buffalo's foreleg, one with three medicine packets.

Buffalo tail amulet (L), looped over for attachment to the belt and bearing a medicine packet and two little bunches of roots.

Rope (M), a square sennit of vegetable fibre, probably inner elm bark, 14′ 7″ long and about ¼″ in diameter. About

6″ of the extreme ends are wrapped in porcupine quills dyed red, yellow, green and black, and terminate in a bunch of copper and brass jinglers with red deer-hair tassels. Halfway between the extremities 18″ of the rope is wrapped in the colored quills. The whole affair was doubled several times and used as a sash. Ostensibly a rope for tying captives, it seems to have served more as an amulet to magically aid in the taking of captives and horses than for any practical purpose.

Amulet for the scalp lock (N) composed of a long piece of the downy skin of some young aquatic bird (not a swan), the tuft of a buffalo tail, the skin of a small swallow-like bird, a tuft of eagle down dyed red, a faded piece of red ribbon and one medicine packet.

Amulet for the scalp lock (Q) consisting of a strip, 19″ long, of the downy skin of a young swan, with a buckskin string at one end for attachment.

Amulet for the scalp lock (O) consisting of a tuft of buffalo hair, three eagle down feathers dyed red, two hawk feathers, the head and part of the skin of a little green snake and two medicine packets.

Amulet made of a sparrow-hawk skin (P), the nostrils stuffed with eagle down dyed red. About the neck is the remains of a red buffalo wool woven band with large white beads, two bits of root tied together and two medicine packets. Attached to the feet are three medicine packets and five little bunches of root tied on with sinew, and two long buckskin strings served for attachment. The amulet looks as if it had been slung about the neck or tied to the scalp lock, but Co'-kwīwa says it was most used to tie to the war pony's tail, "to make him look small as a sparrow-hawk to the enemy."

Five spotted fawn skins, covers for the amulets.

Eleven braids of sweet grass (R), used as incense.

Woven sack $3\frac{7}{8}″ \times 2\frac{3}{4}″$ (S), made apparently of ravelings from blankets or other fabrics, containing three little packets of herb mixture tied together; one separate similar packet, a small package containing a little greenish powder wrapped in paper; a piece of lava (U), some loose bits of root, and a buckskin package containing a mixture of down dyed red, cedar leaves, Indian tobacco and perhaps some other herbs. All the objects in this bag were packed in a mixture of white down and down dyed red, producing a very pretty effect.

Woven sack (T), 3″ × 4″, to all appearances made largely of buffalo wool yarn in black, red, yellow and green. It contains six small medicine packets tied on a buckskin string and a bit of root tied with a shred of sinew.

Two packages cedar twigs.

Nineteen packages herbs and roots.

Eight packages herb mixture.

Two loose pieces green soft stone, also two cloth packages of similar stones showing traces of scraping. The greenish powder in the first woven sack is evidently made from this stone, which seems to be a sort of indurated clay, stained green, perhaps, with copper salts.

Fifty-one loose roots representing at least seven species of plants.

Notched deer hoof.

The coverings of the packages of roots, herbs and the like were of buckskin, fawn skin, bladder, cloth, birch bark and paper (V, W, X). Paper has largely taken the place of birch bark since the tribe moved south of the birch tree's habitat.

A third bundle was bought from Co'kwīwa some time after the first two were purchased. The greater part of it is quite modern. It is:

BUNDLE 2/6511.

Size closed, 15″ × 5″. Cover, coarse cotton sheeting; ties, red trade cloth, buckskin and red cord, beneath which was a cane war whistle.

Contents.—When the outside cover was removed, two packages were disclosed. One of old red calico tied with strips of otter skin, enclosed a head band of buffalo hide, with the long hair well preserved.

The second package is wrapped in cotton sheeting. It contains:

Mink skin, flesh side painted yellow.

Package of magic paint mixed with herbs, to which is attached a string of large glass beads, terminating in a thimble, from which hangs an eagle down feather and some shreds of red and blue ribbon.

Small brass bell.

Miniature belt of black imitation wampum and green glass beads, trimmed with green and purple ribbon.

Square of purple cotton cloth containing two cloth packets of medicine, some bits of root, a small soft black stone, a piece of fungus tinder and a small chert arrowhead.

Package of fine ground herb mixture.

Package of small seeds.

Package of Indian tobacco.

Package of cedar leaves.

From Mecabe'kwa, the same man who sold us the first three buffalo-hawk and buffalo-woodpecker bundles, was obtained a bundle of quite different character; a bundle in which the weasel takes a prominent place. The contents is shown complete in Pl. XXVIII.

BUNDLE 2/6375.

Size closed, 14″ × 6½″. Covers, two, of buckskin, in fair preservation. Ties, on inner cover, two, both of braided buffalo hair; on outer cover, three, one a braided fibre rope, one a yarn rope and one a buckskin thong with package of native tobacco attached.

Contents (Pl. XXVIII).—Woven sack (F), 9½″ × 5½″, apparently made in part if not entirely of dyed buffalo wool yarn, and provided with a buckskin carrying thong. It contained:

White weasel skin amulet (A), worn on the neck. The skin is folded transversely and held fast in that position by a woven band a little over $\frac{1}{2}''$ wide, which is apparently made of buffalo wool yarn in black and yellow, with two parallel rows of large white beads. About the neck were hung a buckskin packet of magic red paint, another of herbs and a few bits of root tied together. The nose, mouth and throat of the skin were painted red; the top of the head, green. The band for suspending the amulet from the neck, $\frac{5}{8}''$ wide, seems to be made of buffalo wool yarn dyed in sections, dark red alternating with natural brownish yellow. A larger packet of magic red paint mixed with herbs is tied to this band, also a very small fragment of a root, tied on with sinew.

A piece of beaver (?) skin with fur (B).

A piece of dried meat(?) (C).

Package of cedar leaves (E).

Part of a bladder or pericardium (buffalo?) (D).

Remains of a paper package of cedar leaves (E).

Three packages, each containing herbs and cedar leaves mixed (E).

Similar package containing a piece of root and cedar leaves (E).

Loose in the bundle were:

Small buffalo tail (G), the proximal end bent over to form a loop for the belt. The terminal tuft has been broken off, but fastened on again with a buckskin string.

Squirrel skin package (H) of magic red paint, tied with a woven band dyed red and yellow in alternate sections. The band is $1\frac{1}{8}''$ wide.

Two calico bags of cedar leaves (I, J).

A very unusual bundle was bought from Albert Moore, who said it had been the property of the late Bena'nakw', also a Sac and Fox. It is illustrated complete in Pl. XXVII.

BUNDLE 2/8737.

Size closed, 18" × 5½". Cover, of buckskin; ties, two, of buckskin and buffalo hide, beneath which, besides the usual cane whistle, was a flat case about 14" × 4", made by folding lengthwise a rectangular piece of thick buffalo hide. Within this was another case of somewhat smaller size, this time made of a folded piece of birch bark (A), the whole enclosing an eagle feather, decorated with a slender strip of wood wrapped in colored porcupine quills and further ornamented with tufts of hair and down dyed red. The proximal end of the feather is provided with a buckskin string, by which it could be attached to the hair.

Contents (Pl. XXVII).—Inside the bundle proper, within a special buckskin sheath, was one of the most remarkable objects found in any of the bundles thus far examined, a belt of buffalo hide (B) completely covered on one side with bird quill decoration, the other side bearing more simple work in bird quill and buffalo wool yarn, the whole being 1¾" wide and 29½" long. Most of the quills are dyed red or black, but some are left their natural white, giving three colors in all. They are laid side by side transversely of the belt, and are held in place by six parallel lines of sinew sewing which run through corresponding longitudinal slits in the material. Beginning at the left we have three black stripes and three white stripes, each three quills wide; then a section of red reaching nearly to the middle, in the center of which is a black block, outlined in white, enclosing a white cross with a smaller black block in its center. Another similar cross balances this in the middle of the right side, while the middle of the belt itself is occupied by twenty-one stripes, most of them only two quills wide, eleven white, seven black and three red. At the right end are three white, two red and one black stripes. On the back, we have alternating blocks of yellow and black buffalo wool yarn, with bird quills appearing in some places. Tie straps of buckskin and buffalo hide are provided. From the middle of the belt, hangs the skin, minus the head, of what seems to be a crow, to the neck of which are attached two bunches of eagle down feathers dyed red, some slender thongs of buckskin wrapped in red and yellow quills and terminating in brass jinglers, a hawk feather dyed red and three little bunches of root tied on with sinew. To the belt itself is fastened a brass sleigh bell. One wing and the tail of the bird are decorated with wooden strips so wrapped in porcupine quills as to produce a pattern in black and white, and terminating in tufts of colored hair.

Buffalo tail amulet (C), the proximal end bent over to form a loop for the belt, bearing three medicine packets, two bits of root and a brass hawk bell. The flesh side of the tail skin is painted red. The most unusual thing is a tiny white weasel skin, wrapped in a piece of bladder with only the nose protruding at one end and the hind feet and tail at the other, and held fast to the amulet by a woven bead strap $\frac{3}{8}''$ in width on yellow and red yarn, possibly buffalo wool. The beads are very small.

Brown weasel skin (D), probably used as an amulet.

Polished slender stick, $7\frac{1}{4}''$ long (E).

Bag of cedar leaves (F).

Piece fungus (G).

Braid of sweet grass (H).

Five packages roots, the wrappings being cloth, birch bark and parts of pages from some Indian primer (I, J, K, L, M).

Another bundle from Albert Moore was once, he said, the property of the late Benan'akw, as was the last one described. This specimen Moore characterized as "Wi tce ka no bi kwe[1] ni ma gun," for which I did not get a satisfactory interpretation. He also remarked that it was a "leading" bundle, but professed ignorance as to any details. It is:

---

[1] This word may refer to the mythic horned serpents.

BUNDLE 2/8738.

Size closed, 18¾″ × 6½″. Covers, two, of buckskin, the outer one in fair condition, the inner in fragments. Ties, three, of leather and buckskin. To this last is fastened the shell of a gourd rattle and a bag of Indian tobacco. Beneath the ties is a cane war whistle.

Contents.—Some of the objects are so badly injured by insects and other destructive agencies that they can hardly be identified.

Remains of a hawk skin, split for a head band, now stripped nearly bare of feathers by insects. Two medicine packets were tied to the neck, where may also be seen a tangled mass of the large white beads, strung on fibre, such as were sold to the Indians in the early days of the frontier by "pony traders" who carried their stock on horse- or mule-back. The beads probably once formed part of a woven band now destroyed.

Weasel skin, now bare of fur, folded and attached head down, to a woven necklace of red yarn, into which were woven some of the same large white beads. At the back of the weasel's neck, just behind the ears, were tied two medicine packets. Three bunches of dark feathers, each on a separate buckskin string, were also tied to the necklace; and bits of root were attached at intervals of about ¾″ with sinew, a feature not seen in the other bundles.

Weasel skin, loose.

Another woven necklace, similar to the first, except that there is no weasel, the black feathers are larger and many of the bits of root have fallen off and been lost.

A third woven necklace (Pl. XXXIII, A), apparently of buffalo wool yarn in brown and black, with interwoven white beads. In this case there was but one bunch of feathers, short ones, and many of them brown instead of black; there was no weasel, but there were four medicine packets (besides the roots) instead of two. The sinew wrapping on some of the roots has been replaced with coarse cotton thread.

Small roach head dress (Pl. XXXI, A), the hair dyed red and black, to the front of which is attached part of the scalp of the pileated woodpecker.

Eagle feather, loosely hung in a bone tube, probably used with the preceding. An ivory-bill woodpecker's scalp was attached to the tube.

Scalp lock amulet, consisting of four black feathers (origin unknown), an eagle wing feather, a bit of the downy skin of a young swan and a medicine packet.

Single eagle feather, bearing medicine packet, probably a scalp lock amulet.

Parts of three quilled sticks used as ornaments for feathers, probably once used on the hawk skin head band or the eagle feathers.

Tuft of buffalo hair, the only relic of the buffalo in the bundle.

Pair of woven bead garters (Pl. XXXVI, C), the most archaic I have seen. The beads are the large white and blue variety, brought by the early "pony traders," woven on a native yarn, probably buffalo wool. The more perfect of the garters measures 11" long by $2\frac{1}{8}$" wide, but how much longer the yarn may have extended would be hard to tell, as it is badly broken and frayed. It seems, however, to have been woven on for about an inch beyond the bead work at both ends, beyond which it evidently hung loose as a kind of fringe, like the woven bead garters made by different tribes to-day. The design consists of three hour-glass shaped figures, outlined with a double row of white beads on a blue ground and connected by two rows of white beads with a blue row between running down the center of each garter.

Steel lance head (Pl. XXXVI, F) $11\frac{3}{4}$" long and nearly 2" wide at the base.

Two fawn skin covers for the amulets.

Package of vermillion done up in a page of the *Congressional Globe*, dated December 6, 1836.

Package of cedar leaves.

Metal salt shaker containing a small stone.
Piece of dried flesh.
Fifteen packages of roots.
Three loose pieces of root.

Another of the late Benan'akw's bundles, bought from Albert Moore, is said to belong to the "Bloody Thigh" class like those purchased from Co'kwīwa, so called because they are exempted from the taboo forbidding a menstruating woman to touch or even approach a sacred bundle. The contents, however, are different. It is:

BUNDLE 2/8593.

Size closed, $20\frac{1}{2}''\times7\frac{1}{2}''$. Outer cover of buckskin, fairly well preserved; inner cover a native rush mat, $32''\times20''$. The use of mats as bundle covers is rare among the Sac and Fox, although common enough among the Iowa and other tribes. Ties of buffalo hide and rope of coarse fibre, apparently native. Three war whistles were thrust beneath these ties, and to the central tie was attached a bag of Indian tobacco.

Contents.—Buckskin war apron (Pl. XXXV, B), measuring $20''$ from side to side, and $9''$ from top to bottom. It is doubtless somewhat shrunken. At each end the lower edge is protracted into a triangular point about $3''$ long, at whose apex is attached a bunch of hawk feathers and a deer hair tassel dyed red. The whole lower edge is sparsely fringed, each strand wrapped in red and yellow quills and terminating in a metal jingler, as a rule, of copper. The upper edge is hemmed and terminates at each end in a buckskin string for encircling the waist. At each end also hang two $10''$ strands of buckskin wrapped in porcupine quills dyed red and yellow, and terminating in a jingler of brass or copper with a red deer hair tassel. A similar pair of quilled strands hangs from the middle of the upper edge, making six in all. One side of the apron is badly stained, apparently with blood.

Head band made from a split hawk skin. The beak and front part of the head are missing, but the remainder, to the tip of the tail, measures 20½″ in length. One of the eyes, a brass-headed tack, still remains in place. About the neck is a woven band of buffalo wool yarn dyed yellow and red. The amulet was protected by a fawn skin case.

Fur head band, apparently beaver or otter (Pl. XXXII, A), long enough to encircle the head and hang down behind nearly 3′. The skin is folded in such a way as to make a band about an inch wide, with fur on both sides. There may be medicine packets within, but none are apparent from outside. Near the front of the portion encircling the head are two large tufts of long eagle down feathers dyed red, one tuft on each side, slanting backward, and just back of these again, two long eagle tail feathers, also slanting backward, ornamented with quilled wooden strips in red and yellow and tufts of down feathers and horsehair, both dyed red. A single eagle feather, hangs pendent from the trailer about 4″ below the head band.

Hand-made steel knife, 11″ long.

Cane war whistle, 16¾″ long, with part of a woven band of buffalo wool yarn knotted about it just above the reed (Pl. XXIX, G). This is 1⅝″ wide and about 22″ long, not counting some 7″ of fringe at one end. The weave is diagonal, like most of the yarn sashes woven by these Indians to-day, and the pattern consists of a series of pairs of chevrons side by side in a kind of greenish blue on a background of brownish yellow. There has been a white bead edging on both sides of the band, some of which has partially disappeared, and beads strung on the outermost strands of the fringe.

Large piece of bladder-like material.

Long sack, empty, of similar stuff.

Package of cedar leaves.

Package of white down.

Package containing six pieces partially indurated clay, almost white, packed well in white down. They seem to have been scraped for medicine.

Two packages of white earth paint.

Bladder package containing a few herbs.

Woven sack of buffalo tail hair (much coarser than the wool), 14″ × 8¾″. This is in very good condition and contains a number of objects:

Carved hardwood stick, 9″ long, representing a deer's foot and lower leg (Pl. XXXVI, A).

Skin of a mallard duck's neck containing a package of herb mixture.

Skin of a mallard duck's head and part of neck.

Long shell bead, broken.

Disk of wood ¼″ thick and 1″ in diameter, grooved around periphery, probably for use as a toggle.

Six pieces greenish stone.

Buckskin roll containing strip of fibrous inner bark from some shrub or tree.

Small buckskin roll, containing a sprouted seed, dried.

Large roll made from a complete spotted fawn skin, enclosing a few pieces of cloth and some bits of fungus tinder or punk for lighting fires.

Another bundle, bought from Albert Moore, is said to be a "Night War Bundle" because the ceremonies connected with it took place only at night. It is:

BUNDLE 2/6506.

Size closed, 22″ × 7″. Cover, of buckskin, in bad shape from age, smoke and exposure; ties, two, of buckskin.

Contents.—Thong or strip of buffalo hide, ⅜″ wide and 13′ 8″ long, terminating in a broader piece of the hide cut in the form of a lance head (Pl. XXXVI, E), 9¾″ long and at the base 3½″ wide, which had been painted longitudinally half black and half red. A loose piece about 4″ in length had evidently been broken from the opposite end of the thong. Several conflicting accounts were given by as many Indians as to its use, but the most intrinsically probable is, that the thong was placed in the bundle for binding captives, not so much for actual use, perhaps, as for a charm to insure by magic the capture of numerous prisoners and horses. This is particularly plausible in view of the similar use of thongs and ropes in other bundles. Another story related that the thong had been tied on the head as an amulet, which seems improbable in view of its weight; while still another stated that it had been used for carrying home the wounded.

Skin of a small bird, apparently a species of swallow, the plumage of the back being a metallic blue. This was swathed in faded yellow ribbon and provided with a buckskin thong (Pl. XXXIII, C), by which it could be suspended from the woven neck band wrapped around, but not attached to the bird skin. This band, apparently of buffalo wool yarn, was 14″ long, exclusive of fringe, and ½″ wide, and was decorated with two rows of old large white trade beads running down the middle, with similar beads on the fringe, and forming an edging on one side. Between the fringe and the bead work at both ends was a short bare strip, where it was seen that the band had been striped, half red and half yellow.

Another woven band 3′ 1″ long and 1¼″ wide, in brown, yellow and red, resembles native work to a certain extent, but the character of the weave causes me to class it as doubtful. It serves as a belt for a buffalo tail amulet, now nearly bare of hair, once worn hanging at the back. The tail was provided with a little buckskin medicine packet and a medicine package covered with bladder, flat, and measuring 3½″ × 1¼″ tied to the proximal end.

Two other buffalo tail amulets, with nine medicine packets apiece, and five more, two of them entirely bare of hair, with no packets at all.

Cane war whistle.

Wampum bead.

Two bits of greenish stone.

Package containing three bits of similar stone.

Two pieces of cane used as material for whistle reeds.

Brass jingler.

Section of buckskin thong wrapped in porcupine quills.

Piece dry buffalo meat, hide still attached.

Package cedar leaves.

Package yellowish scales.

Package roots.

Five eagle down feathers dyed red.

Empty cloth package.

Pieces of fawn skin amulet covers.

Aveline Givens, the Sac and Fox Indian from whom the following large and complex bundle was purchased, claimed that it was of Kickapoo origin;[1] but the evidence connecting it with the Kickapoo is not satisfactory or conclusive to my mind. I have presented it here as the final war bundle in our Sac and Fox series. It will be seen, however, that it differs considerably from the average Sac and Fox war bundle. It is:

BUNDLE 2/8452.

Size closed, about 21″ × 8″. Cover, of buckskin, so badly rotted that the bundle had to be wrapped in coarse sheeting. Ties, of buckskin and buffalo hide, beneath which were two unusually long cane war whistles (21½″).

Contents.—Buffalo hide head band with horns attached (Pl. XXX, A)—a fine one and the only amulet of consequence in the bundle. The hide has been taken from the animal's head (the matted wool is still fairly well preserved) and has been folded lengthwise in such a way that there is wool both inside and outside, and the band is about 2″ wide. The horn on the wearer's left has been smeared with red paint, the other remaining black. At the top of the band in front, loosely attached are three eagle feathers, the middle one dyed red

---

[1] I heard later that the bundle is really of Sac and Fox origin.

and decorated with a slender stick wrapped in colored porcupine quills and tipped with deer hair dyed red; back of these are eagle down feathers dyed red, and on each side a black ostrich plume, of course obtained from the whites. No medicine packets were seen; but of course there may be some folded away within the head band.

Dew-claw of a buffalo, notched on the edges and provided with a perforation through which runs a fibre string. This may have been an amulet or part of a hoof rattle.

Two pieces of buffalo skin from which the hair is now missing, possibly once parts of amulets for the scalp lock.

Bunch of felted buffalo wool.

Crude, much worn, bent drumstick of wood (Pl. XXIX, B).

Trade knife stamped "W. Dunn" on the blade.

Nine bits of cane, material for whistle reeds, in various stages of manufacture.

Claw of lynx.

Two bits of soft greenish stone.

Bag made of the entire skin of a bear cub, only about 20″ long, apparently for native tobacco. The opening was just below the throat, its edges bound with bird quills dyed yellow and dark red. A fawn skin cover, now much dilapidated, had been provided for this object.

Cloth bag, about 7″ x 5″, packed full of soft white down. It had been covered with buckskin, then a layer of bladder, and then another layer of buckskin; but only parts of these outer coverings remain.

Two smaller sacks of white down, to one of which is tied a buckskin packet of the same.

Small round box of wood, obtained from the whites, containing herb mixture.

Metal snuff-box, containing the following buckskin packages: One with piece of obsidian, packed in red down; one of roots and red down; one of herb mixture, ground; one of ground herbs and loose fur (otter?); one of mica. All these packages as they lay in the box were imbedded in down dyed red.

Piece of an old painted buckskin garment, containing roots. This was first thought to be the sleeve of a shirt, but more careful inspection seems to show that it is part of a fringed legging. The painting consists of red horizontal stripes about $\frac{3}{4}''$ apart, encircling the leg. Between the upper stripes are black parallel lines, the alternate ones terminating in arrowheads pointing inward.

Empty buckskin pouch of unusual interest (Pl. XXXVI, G), the main part of which measures $2\frac{3}{4}'' \times 3''$. To the bottom is attached an ornament of porcupine quill work in the rare netted technique, $2\frac{1}{4}'' \times 3\frac{1}{8}''$, in red, black and yellow; the design consisting of three black rectangles, with yellow centers, horizontal on a red ground. About the mouth of the pouch are four triangular points of skin, $3''$ long, and two on each side. These are fringed and the fringes wrapped in quills. In considering these quilled objects, one must remember that such work has not been done among the Sac and Fox for many years, and home-made quilled articles are now never seen in common use, although modern Cheyenne quill work is occasionally observed.

Another unusual buckskin pouch (Pl. XXXVI, H) measured $6\frac{1}{2}'' \times 4\frac{1}{2}''$. This also had four triangular points, two on each side of the mouth, each $4''$ long and decorated with a short quill-wrapped fringe, the quills dyed yellow. At their apices were three metal jinglers with tassels of deer hair dyed yellow, attached to the fringe, at these points wrapped in red and yellow quills instead of the plain yellow. At each end of the pouch hung four slender strands of buckskin, wrapped with alternate red and yellow quills, $4''$ long; and between the points on both sides were two similar strands. All the strands had once been provided with metal jinglers and yellow tassels. The pouch contains a buckskin package enclosing a piece of fossil bone (Pl. XXXVI, I) packed in red down, two bits of gypsum crystals, three packages of herb mixture and a small cloth sack, empty.

Woven sack, largely of buffalo wool yarn, $7\frac{3}{8}'' \times 5\frac{1}{4}''$, in two colors, brownish yellow and black. It contained, imbedded in down dyed red, the following: Four buckskin packets, tied side by side, containing herb mixture; another package with a piece of fossil bone wrapped in red yarn and showing many traces of scraping for use as medicine, the powder being taken internally; a bit of birch bark folded about some roots; part of the scaly skin of a lizard(?) packed in red down and wrapped in cloth; two packages of roots and the remains of two bladder packages containing herb mixture.

Another woven sack, $5\frac{1}{4}'' \times 5\frac{3}{4}''$, is apparently made partly of buffalo wool yarn, and partly ravelings from fabrics introduced by the whites. It enclosed a package containing two pieces of large fossil bone, piece of fossil bone or tooth wrapped in red down and a bit of bladder, package of gypsum crystals, and package of roots.

Two packages, one containing four pieces of a large fossil leg bone, the other part of a joint of a similar bone, both packed in red down.

Package cedar twigs.

Package magic red paint, mixed with herbs.

Bunch of leaves resembling "bear grass," tied with a woven band, probably not of Indian origin.

Ten packages roots and herbs.

One package herb mixture.

Twenty-three loose bits of root; at least eight species.

Two empty packages.

A FOX "WAR MEDICINE."

Somewhat resembling the war bundles in use, but decidedly not in the same class in point of sacredness or importance, is the small bundle bought from Joe Tessen, a Fox, belonging to the Tama band in Iowa, who claimed that it was a "war medicine." Further than that he could give no information. I am not entirely satisfied that the specimen was really intended for war, but I will describe it here, nevertheless, for what it is worth.

BUNDLE 2/7975.

The outer cover is merely a piece of figured calico.

Contents.—Leather bag containing, at bottom, a few pieces of herbs, then an empty buckskin package from which they had probably escaped; a rabbit's foot with a string to tie on the scalp lock. This is usually an amulet for swift running, and does not seem very appropriate for a war medicine, as the rabbit always runs *away* from his enemy.

Buckskin package, containing slender black roots.

Small medicine pouch of woven bead work, empty.

Piece of braided rope or sennit of native fibre, 6' 4" long, doubled and made into a loop. Such things are often seen in war bundles.

Small braid of sweet grass.

Piece of reddish indurated clay.

Woven sack of yarn, $3\frac{3}{8}" \times 2\frac{5}{8}"$, in red, yellowish white, black, yellow and purple, bearing on one side the white figure of a deer on a black ground; on the other a black figure of a man on a white ground. It contained two balls of stone, about 1" in diameter, one natural, the other perhaps partly artificially shaped; one disk of stone, natural, about $\frac{7}{8}"$ in diameter; one disk of bone about the same size, but slightly oval; one iron ring $1\frac{3}{8}"$ in outside diameter; ring of lead $\frac{7}{8}"$ in diameter; three packages herb mixture and one package native tobacco.

A strip of calico 9" long and 3" wide at one end, tapering to $1\frac{1}{2}"$ at the other, to which were sewed, all on one side, four pockets of the same material, the whole rolled up and tied with a strip of rag. The pockets contained: One package Indian tobacco, one package roots, five packages herb mixture, one of which, of buckskin, looked as if it had been carried a long time on the person.

MEDICINE BUNDLES.

Contents.—No attempt was made to tabulate the contents of the medicine or charm bundles, because there was too little resemblance between them; but the fact was noted that out of thirteen bundles, all contained charm medicines; eight, magic paint; five, "high-toned medicine" (to be explained later); four, amulets; and four, fetishes.

General Medicine Bundles.

Bundle 2/5327.

From Mecabe′kwa, also known as U. S. Grant (Pl. XX, A), who sold us the first war bundles, we were able to secure a small bundle for general purposes. This the owner called "Mĭ ca′ dus kwe," or "high-toned medicine," although the "good-will producing" compound generally known by that name forms only part of the contents of the bundle, which also contains medicines for war, gambling and hunting. Mecabé′kwa furnished the following information concerning the bundle.

The account is especially complete, thanks to Mecabé′kwa, who wanted every detail recorded. It seems a pity that there were not more like him among his people.

This bundle started from a dream or vision a long time ago. A man had painted himself black with charcoal and had fasted as much as ten days when Ge″ tcī Ma′ ni to spoke to him, and told him to get some hawk feathers. Next day he looked for a hawk and found one sitting low. Then he spoke to it and offered it Indian tobacco, telling it that the great Manito had directed him to get feathers. So the hawk let him go up to it and pull one feather from each wing—then it flew away.   Then he fasted again and was told to get down feathers from under an eagle's tail.   Next day he saw an eagle sitting on a log, gave him tobacco, and told him what the great Manito had said; whereupon the eagle let him take some feathers—then flew away.   Similarly, other things were also found for the bundle.   When the man went to war he wore the feathers tied on his scalp lock, the hawk feathers and one bunch of down feathers hanging down, the other two bunches of down feathers sticking out crosswise, and these protected him by their power, so that no one could hit him from behind.   At such times he used to put red paint on his face from the bundle, four spots on each cheek.

Another time when he was fasting, he had a little house or shelter built of long grass into which a small weasel made its way one day.   "Do not hit it!" said the Manito.   "Tie it up in a rag."   The man did as directed, but when he had finished fasting and looked in the rag the weasel was dead, so he skinned it and made a little medicine bag at the direction of the Manito, and this he wore when he went to war, hung about his neck.   The weasel runs close to the ground, or under it; he is hard to see and harder still to hit.   So the man was, when he rode to war with the little weasel hanging from its cord about his neck.   The Sioux could not see him— they could only hear his war whoop.   That is how the bundle started.   Later nine similar bundles or "branches" were made.

The snake rattle in the bundle was once larger, but has been broken off in the course of years.   It was tied on the feathers worn in the owner's hair in battle.   Some rattlesnake spoke to him in his fast, and offered to help him, and gave him his tail.   Often you cannot see the snake as it lies or moves through the grass.   That is how the snake helped him —you could not see the man either.

Some of the songs said by Mĕcabĕ′kwa to belong to the bundle, in its warlike aspect, were given as follows:

Kē cī no ko thī a ne
(I will resemble) (six times)

Kīc eth wa ä pī ä tcī ke tcidj
(The sun   coming up)

Kī na ha na ba mik'
(I will look like to them)

Kě cī no ko thī a ne
(I will resemble) (five times)

The above was sung, they say, on leaving camp to go on the warpath. As they traveled along the following was sung by the leader of the party who carried the bundle, the first form being for day use, the second for night. This is the first form:

Ni kē wī ka wē ha ne ne wa^n
(I am leading them   men) (four times)

Ne ko tī kī cē kw' ne ne wa^n
(One   day   men) (four times)

Ni kē wī ka wē ha ne ne wa^n
(I am leading them   men) (four times)

The second form differs from the first merely in the substitution of the syllables "ne ko tī te bä kwä" (one night) in place of "ne ko tī kī cē kw'" (one day). Before making an attack the warrior always danced after putting on the amulets from the bundle. The words given for this dance song are as follows:

Ne ne wē hē ma' yo ma' yo hē tē ta wē
(Men let us make each other mourn) (four times)

Ne ne wē yo ho ho ya^n!
(Men   yo ho ho ya^n!)

The following was sung as the warriors journeyed homeward, in which the singer is supposed to voice the sentiments of the weasel carried by the leader:

Ha ya ci ta pu' kwe pi an 'ē ye nī we
(Against the wall of the mat house
   sitting in the same place)

                             (repeat couplet four times)

'E ye nī we pia nī ne ne nī we
(Same place coming back men)

Not alone in war was the bundle useful, but in love also; in fact, the "good-will" medicine Mī ca' dus kwe, here used as a love charm, has given its name to the whole bundle in which it was included.

To attract a woman it was only necessary to put a little of the green paint on one's cheeks and chew the medicine that is in the little iron box in the bundle and rub it on the arms and chest, also on one of the eagle down feathers, which should be then fastened in the hair.   Thus equipped a man can attract the woman of his choice.

Mecabe'kwa tells that one time he tried to speak to a woman, but she hit him and made his mouth bleed.   Angered by such treatment Mecabe'kwa vowed to "get even;" so when he had the opportunity he put on the paint and feather from the bundle.   That night she came to his house crying, and told him that she loved him, and even proposed that she lie with him, although his wife was there and she knew it. After a while Mecabe'kwa saddled a horse and took her to her home.   On arriving at her place he told her, "Go inside and fix a bed for us while I tie my horse."   As soon as she had entered the house he rode away home.   But she came back later and bothered him for a long time.   The following song is used after painting with the green paint:

Ha na mo na ke te cī
(Paint   you name me)

Ha na mo na ke te cī he
(Paint   you name me)

⎫
⎬ (repeat couplet)
⎭

Ha yo wa hē na
(meaningless)

Ha na mo na ke ne' the kwa
(Paint   kill [bewitch] her)

Ha na mo na ke te cī
(Paint you name me)

Ha na mo na ke te cī he
(Paint you name me)

Ha yo wa he he na
(meaningless)

Also the following, which refers to the use of the feather as a charm:

Ni ki tī mī ko na
(My   eagle feather)

Hä yo na na
(Using it on you)

⎫
⎬ (repeat couplet four times)
⎭

Kī na he ti mo thä
(You my old lady)

Ni ki tī mī ko na
(My eagle feather)

Hä yo na na
(Using it on you)

⎫
⎬ (repeat couplet four times)
⎭

A song somewhat similar to the above was used also by a war leader wearing the feather.

If a woman uses this medicine she must be of decent life and good habits. If the husband of such a woman, a good man, leaves her for some reason unknown to her she is supposed to send for him four times, and then if he does not come back to her she may use this bundle. When she applies for it the owner says to her, "Daughter (or sister), do not cry. I have this bundle by which I can get him back for you. to live with you until old age and death. Only I must ask you not to scold him in any way if it can be helped." The woman must then fast two days, after which she takes the bundle east of the house, beyond earshot, and there she paints her cheeks and begins to cry. The man might be close or he might be far away, but he is bound to come to her while she is weeping. Four days she stays there, and even when the man comes she pays no attention to him until the time is up, even though he tries to stop her crying, builds fires for her and does everything he can. In this way he begins to take care of her. "Stop crying, sister," he says. "I will take care of you until death."

The song sung by the woman while crying runs as follows:

> Nă to nă w'a kă
> (I think I will look for him) (four times)

> Hai yo w'a!
> (Alas!)

> Hī ne ne nī wa ta
> (That man)

> Nă to nă w'a kă
> (I think I will look for him) (four times)

> Hai yo w'a!
> (Alas!)

The Sac and Fox still maintain the practice, well known to their ancestors, of separating into families or small parties for the hunt, at certain times, usually in the fall. Each family or party wanders off alone, sometimes not to return for months to the regular settlements of their tribe. Should it happen that the hunters of such a party find themselves unable to kill any game, day after day, they begin to suspect that some witch is spoiling their luck, and proceed to make use of a medicine in this bundle to counteract the spell. Dipping the bundle four times through the smoke of burning cedar toward the east at sunrise, they opened the bundle and removing certain herbs, macerated them by chewing, and rubbed them upon their bodies, also placing a little of the mixture in their hunting pouches. Each hunter then took a little stick which he dipped in the green paint and applied four times to his cheeks, making two little green spots on each side. As he applied the first spot he might say, "I will even kill the most difficult animal, the white raccoon;" then as he touched the other cheek, "the red raccoon." Or it might be that he would say, "the white deer" and "the red deer." This done, the hunter would start eastward to look for game. If there were as many as four hunters in the party, one would go in each of the four directions. It was thought that one of the rare animals mentioned would surely be killed that day. If a deer of any kind or similar animal was killed its head was laid to the east as soon as possible, or in the case of animals like the raccoon, the carcass was hung up with face toward the east. When the deer had been skinned, they cut out and left behind the head, neck and breast, just as they lay, while the blood was thrown to the four directions. This not only "spoils the witch medicine" that has been acting against the party, but also causes animals wounded thereafter to bleed freely, facilitating tracking. In the meantime the women back at the hunting camp had thrown away the old fire and built a new one with flint and steel, and fixed a place to hang the meat. When it is brought in they cut off all the lower part of the legs, and tying them together hung them up, being very careful not to break any bones or let the dogs get hold of them, or they would have the same bad luck again.   Under no circumstances was a menstruating woman allowed to touch any of this meat, for this would spoil the whole spell against the witch.   The best parts were then cooked for a feast, and some pieces laid on the fire for the dead, including the founder of the bundle the benefits of which they were enjoying, to show their gratitude.   The bundle is opened while the feast is in progress and a little grease placed on the teeth of the weasel, which thus eats with them.   Other unlucky hunters could join the gathering at this time and receive the benefit of the ceremonies.   The witch knew every time they were using the bundle against him, and would try four times to counteract the spell, but never could approach the camp in the absence of the hunters, for when they started they would always tell the weasel in the bundle to keep guard and not let the witch come near.   It is said that if a witch tries to do anything four times and fails, he is likely to die, for his power is broken.   It was not given to him by the Great Manito.   The two hunting songs given herewith are said to belong to this bundle, and to be used with it when functioning as a hunting medicine:

Ne wa kwä w'ï ne wa kwä
(We will see, then we will see)

A tha pa na wa pa thi to
(Raccoon   white)

W 'ï ne wa kwä
(Then we will see)

Ne wa kwä
(We will see)

The second was described as a deer song:

Pīä tce wī ne ka pa wa
(Toward me horns protruding)

Wī na ma nä ne nī wa
(This   man [buck])

Yo ta tua kī wa nī
(In   the   draw [hollow])

Wī na ma nä ne nī wa
(This   man [buck])

A song of this sort was sung when starting out on the hunt.

In addition to the uses already mentioned, the contents of the bundle, or rather a portion of them, were used in gambling. One little package of herb mixture was employed in foot races when valuable bets were at stake, such as fine horses and blankets. In such a case the runner would chew the herbs and rub them on his feet and on the little down feather worn in his hair, in the hopes that this would help him to win. In horse racing they would tie one of the eagle down feathers in the horse's tail, and a little red yarn in the mane, after which a medicine usually kept in the weasel skin in the bundle was chewed to a pulp and placed in the horse's mouth and nostrils, and rubbed on his head, back and legs, and on his hoofs. This was thought not only to give the horse the weasel's power of running swiftly, but to keep rivals off the trail. Other horses, catching the scent of the charmed horse's tracks, would bolt the course and buck off their riders. A feather song similar to the one used in courting was used when preparing a horse for the race, or for that matter when preparing for any sort of gambling. At the end of a race another compound would be given to the horse which would bring him back to his normal condition.

Similarly, whenever any of the medicines were used by a man or woman, the "curing medicine" found in the bundle was taken to counteract the bad effects on the user, effects which, it was thought, might mean sickness or insanity. A sweat bath and a swim were often taken as additional purification.

When not in use the bundle is kept wrapped in half a yard of calico, and laid on the sleeping platform up against the wall of the bark house. It is not hung up, because they say that the weasel within the wrappings might not like it.

Every spring and fall the bundle was opened and the weasel "fed" by rubbing a little grease from a fat duck, turkey or other wild fowl on its teeth and upon its nose. Whenever the bundle was to be opened it was smoked at dawn, over burning branches of what seems to be a species of cedar, dipping four times to the eastward. This cedar is called Pa pu ka de kw'.

The cover of the bundle is a bandana handkerchief, the calico mentioned above having been wrapped outside of this.

Contents (shown in Pl. XXXVII): Weasel skin (C), a large brown one, but so folded as to be only 9″ long, and held in that position by ties of buckskin and brown ribbon. A carrying cord of braided red yarn by which to suspend the amulet from the wearer's neck is fastened to the middle of the skin, while the head is ingeniously arranged to make a rattling sound when shaken. At the throat is a tiny buckskin packet smeared with green paint, and the same color is seen on the flesh side of the skin wherever exposed. A packet of magic red paint is tied to the carrying cord, also a little packet of roots.

Amulet for the scalp lock (E) consisting of eagle down feathers, hawk feathers, red yarn and one medicine packet.

Amulet for the scalp lock (D) comprising two bunches of eagle down feathers, some dyed red, some discolored white ribbon and a medicine packet. Both feather amulets had buckskin strings for attachment.

Metal snuff-box (F) containing slender black roots wrapped in pink cotton cloth.

The snake rattle mentioned by Mecabe'kwa, may be inside the weasel skin, or, like some of the herbs, may have been lost.

Another general bundle of different character was obtained from Jim Mamesa, a Fox belonging to the Tama band in Iowa. It is as follows:

BUNDLE 2/8598.

The cover is an unusually handsome and perfect woven sack, 15″ × 9⅜″, largely of native materials, such as Indian hemp and buffalo wool yarn. The design on one side represents eight long-tailed monsters or "dream panthers"; on each end, 4½ human figures. The remainder of the specimen was covered with geometric designs, especially fine in form and color.

Contents.—(A) Three packages containing love medicine. One of these, a cloth package, has a mixture of three varieties: Wi ko bī jä bi kī, or "sweet root;" A pe nyī gec kīk, or "Indian potato;" and Te pī kis ka kīk, a weed that grows beside the lakes. The lover puts a little of this mixture into his mouth when he sees the girl he wishes to attract, and takes pains to go around behind her and approach her on the right side. In a red calico package is a piece of blue cloth, in one end of which is tied a sort of powder, Nä thä tcī gun, used internally to remove from one's self the evil effects of the other medicines. In the other end is a bundle of herb mixture, containing sumach top, We cī hon, painted on the cheeks while courting. The third love medicine is contained in a piece of blue calico, and consists of a lot of scale-like seeds, Mī ca dji a gwi, in which are mixed a few round seeds, I kwä mi nī wä. It is supposed to have the power of attracting women when smoked.

Then there is a gambling medicine, three little packages done up in a piece of gay calico. One, of paper, contains a mixture of two herbs, Cī ka wī and Mic kwa na kī, chewed while gambling, and the cards and money rubbed with the spittle. Another package, in a plaid rag, contains the same mixture ground finer; while the third, in a black calico rag, contains a fine ground herb, Bec ki buk, used as a "curing medicine" to counteract the evil effects of the magic.

There are several medicines against witches in this bundle, one of which is a small red calico packet containing the powdered medicine, Be kī kī ak, a little of which is chewed every night to keep away "night travelers" or witches. Another protective medicine is a dark calico package of berry-like seeds, name not given, which look like fire to the witches when they come around at night, and frighten them away. A necklace of horsehair, braided into the form of a square sennit and decorated with strips of otter fur bore a cloth packet containing a wampum bead and two red "mescal" beans, Mes kwī na da wī nōn, and a buckskin packet, containing another similar bean, the whole forming a protective amulet against witches. Similarly a bead necklace in the bundle was considered a good amulet for this purpose. It also bore some otter fur; and all the owner had to do when he suspected some one of trying to bewitch him was to burn a little of the fur. It was worn with this strip of fur at the back, under the coat or shirt. A little red packet held a few calamus roots, Mi ci ne bi son, which were chewed and rubbed all over the person to make a scent which will "mesmerize" (the interpreter's word) the "night travelers." The person using this medicine can call a witch any number of "hard names" and the sorcerer will not become angry or wish to retaliate. The charm is improved if the contents of a little skin packet wrapped in a piece of red fabric—said to be pounded Măn wă hi (angelica root) is chewed and rubbed on with the calamus. It will be remembered that both these last two herbs were mentioned by Co'kwiwa in explaining his war bundles (p. 189). Angelica root, he said, would "hold the enemy spellbound" if chewed and rubbed on the person of the warrior. But to calamus, although used the same way, he only ascribed the property of stopping bleeding. Differences in recording the names of these herbs may lie for dialectic reasons in the names themselves (Co'kwiwa being a Sac and the former owner of the present bundle a Fox) or it may lie in my imperfect hearing of the same words spoken by two different persons. There is a larger black cloth package of calamus in the bundle.

Three small packages of "curing medicine," powdered vegetable mixtures in which Bec ki buk (a prairie plant with a thimble-shaped head) and sassafras bark, Thā kī jä bi kī, figure, were found in the bundle. These are used to counteract the bad effect of using other magic medicines.

The last outfit in the bundle, a red leather bag, contains medicine for foot racing. It consists of the tail of a newborn colt to tie on the hair for power and endurance in running, two rabbits' feet to tie on the necklace for speed, a pawpaw seed to hold in the mouth, and two cylindrical magic stones, one of them artificially shaped, to hold in the hands while running.

BUNDLE 2/7812.

A third general "medicine bundle" was bought from the Sac and Fox woman known as Laura Carter, which consists of two distinct parts, each of which might be almost called a bundle in itself, their only relation to each other being that they were kept in the same cover, a woven sack $8'' \times 11\frac{1}{2}''$, made of ravelings of woolen fabrics in soft colors and artistic geometrical patterns.

(A) The first part is called No cä wus kw', and is supposed to facilitate delivery in childbirth. It contains a piece of fossil tooth, apparently that of a mastodon, five pieces of fossil bone, a fresh-water mussel shell, a little wooden paddle and a common store-bought file. These things had been wrapped in three pieces of cotton cloth, the inner one purple, the next red and the outside a square piece of blue with a lining of figured red calico and hemmed edges.

According to Mrs. Carter the medicine originated with her grandfather's grandmother, "Me cā no kw'," one of the greatest "dreamers" known to the tribe, who was a noted lodge woman of the Me dä, her name being still heard in some of the songs of that order, and whose fame as a doctor has lived to this day. It is said that one time she fasted ten days, during which time this medicine and other medicines and powers were revealed to her. In her vision she was taken to the abode of the Great Spirit (Ge' tcī Ma' ni to wī ga' nik), where the Manito Under Water Animals are said to have appeared to her and to have given her this medicine, with which she was able to establish a record of one hundred cures. At the same time she received a white weasel skin which she afterwards used as a "medicine bag" in the rites of the Me dä' win. The medicine has descended directly from this old lady to Laura Carter, but inspection makes it evident that certain parts have been renewed.

The use of the medicine was given as follows: If a woman has a hard time in giving birth to a child, and wishes to try this medicine, she sends tobacco to the woman having the bundle in charge, with a present, such as ponies or goods of some kind. Then, if the practitioner wishes to take the case, she accepts the tobacco and throws it into some running stream, praying to the Manito Under Water Animals, and begging them to help the suffering woman. In order to get water for the doctoring, she then dips the shell into the same stream, dipping with the current, which is supposed to make the discharges run freely from the patient.

Taking the shell to the patient's home, she empties the water from it until it does not come above a natural mark in the shell, then sets it down with point to the east. With the file each of the fossil bones is scratched a few times, beginning with the small black one which is considered the best, and a little pile made of the resulting dust. Using the tip of the small paddle, which thus serves as a measure, a little of the dust is placed gently on the surface of the water at the east end of the shell, then south, then west, then north, after which, beginning at the east, they stir it four times around clockwise. If the dust sinks they believe the patient cannot live, but if it scatters out over the surface of the water she will recover. Then the patient drinks the preparation. If the dust has sunk, it is given to her but once, for it will do her no good, but if it floats, it is given to her four times, about half an hour or an hour apart. If this brings no result after the fourth time the following song is sung:

> Ne the wi nī ne pī ä to ī ne nī we
> (Curing medicine I bring to you, man)
>
> Ī nī wī tca me ko cī no wī no
> (Now you can come out)

And the following, but slightly different:

> Ne the wī nī ne pī ä to i kwä w'
> (Curing medicine I bring to you, woman)
>
> Ī nī wi tca me ko cī no wī no
> (Now you can come out)

They use both verses, addressing the child first as a man and then as a woman, because they have no way of telling whether a man child or a woman child will appear. When not in use the medicine was simply put away with other medicines, perhaps in a raw hide trunk. The mastodon's tooth is called "ma ni to wī pīts," or mysterious being's tooth, and the bone, similarly "ma ni to ha ka nun," or mysterious being's bones. The shell is "ä'thi," the little paddle, "pu" kī tha hī - gun," and the file, "ka' wī poi."

(B) The second part is contained in a pouch of red trade-cloth, $4\frac{1}{2}'' \times 5\frac{1}{4}''$, provided with a flap and decorated with crude ribbon appliqué in dark blue, pale blue and yellow. It may at one time have been slung on a strap or ribbon. The little bundle is known as Ci că wus kw', and is used to bring success to the hunter. The dried head of an ivory-bill wood-pecker within is supposed to give the man the woodpecker's power of seeking out and capturing his concealed prey, no matter how well hidden. The bird can by his own efforts cut a hole in the tree where the raccoon is hiding, and the hunter may share this power also. There is also tied on the head a little bag of paint supposed to have magical properties, with which the hunter bedecks himself, and a buckskin pack-age, inside, of herbs and tobacco, burned on the coals as a kind of incense. The woodpecker head is called mă mä wu', the paint, wă ci hon', and the package, no' thi gun[i].

The following account of its use was given by Mrs. Carter.

The hunter who wishes to use this medicine must purify himself by taking a sweat-bath every day for four days; then the next morning he goes out to some spot not frequented by women and builds a new fire, upon which he throws some of the compound of tobacco and herbs, fumigating his body, hunting pouch, blankets, bullets, everything he is to use, in the resulting smoke. Then he lays tobacco on the wood-pecker's head and asks or prays that he may kill a spike buck or a yearling doe, which are said to be the hardest to find and kill. If I understood correctly, each man who is to hunt does all these things, and then the leader, if there is a party, ties the woodpecker head to his scalp lock. They go the first day to their hunting ground and make camp, then at dawn the next day they sally forth, the leader, wearing the wood-pecker, to the east, the others different directions. One of them will kill the spike buck or young doe. because they asked for it. Whoever accomplishes the feat cuts the head off and throws it to the east, then skins and cuts up the carcass, leaving a strip of hide and hair on the breast. When this is cut loose and pulled back the blood inside is thrown to the four directions, in this order: E., S., W., N., after which the breast is given to the owner of the medicine to make a feast. After this everything becomes easy for the hunters. The breast, "o ka' kai ya," is fat and good. When it is cooked with fat from the rump, for the feast, it is considered very fine. A piece of this is always burned as an offering to the "medicine." Should the yearling doe be killed on the spring hunt, the milk-bag, or udder, is made into soup, but great care must be taken that no dogs eat any of this until four days have elasped. No one is allowed to waste the venison or make fun of the deer at any time. Mrs. Carter said she had forgotten the songs used with this medicine, although she had often heard them.

FETISH BUNDLES.

Resembling the general bundles in that they may serve for several purposes, yet forming a distinct class by themselves, are those containing little human figures (of wood as a rule) usually accompanied by various packets of herbs, and passing under the general name of Mi thi' ni ni (rigid-man). Somewhat similar images are found among the Pottawattomi, Delaware and the Iroquois tribes to my certain knowledge, and perhaps among many others.

It will be seen on reading the following pages that these little "rigid men" fill very well the definition of "fetish" as given in the first part of this paper.

BUNDLE 2/6507.

The best example secured was a bundle, the entire contents of which are shown in Pl. XXXVIII, containing a very old image of this class, which was bought, after much trouble, from the same Laura Carter who sold us the general bundle just described. The "rigid man" (A) measured $10\frac{1}{8}''$ in height, and was made of some hard wood resembling maple. The head is a separate piece, and is furnished with a pivot which works loosely in a socket in the upper part of the trunk, giving the head a more or less lifelike motion when the image is picked up. On the back of the head is carved a roach or crest, painted red and provided with a hole for the reception of a feather, now missing. The hair about the roach, supposed to be short, was represented by burning the wood until black. The eyes are long oval black glass beads. Each ear is pierced twice, once through the lobe and again near the top. From the upper perforations hang a pair of trade earrings of metal, from the lower hole in one ear three wampum beads and a smaller trade earring on a thread, but these are missing from the other ear. The image wears a fringed shirt and leggings of buckskin with moccasins of the same, while the breech cloth is of coarse cotton print. The legs are solid wood, and immovable, but the arms are merely the shirt sleeves, stuffed, the lower ends cut in the form of hands.

The image was kept wrapped in two pieces of figured calico, tied with strips of rag, together with the following objects, mostly magic medicines, which are lettered for identification on the photograph.

Contents (Pl. XXXVIII).—Pouch of red trade cloth (N) $3\frac{1}{2}''$ square, ornamented with a few rude patterns in black stitching. It contained a buckskin package (B) enclosing a powder made of red paint and magic herbs ground fine called Mī ca' dus kwe ("high-toned medicine"), a very popular mixture. This medicine obtains for the user the good opinion of others and helps her to get what she wants. If a woman wants a husband, all she has to do is to say to the fetish, as she sprinkles tobacco upon it, "I want to meet so-and-so," naming the man she has in mind, and then to paint a little of the medicine on her cheeks. Then her wish will come true.

Another use for "Mī ca' dus kwe" is in the "pony smoke" when the tribes visit each other and make presents of ponies. When the Sac and Fox visited another tribe this medicine would make the other Indians give them very good horses as presents.

Or, if one wishes to buy a certain horse whose owner does not want to sell, this medicine will make him change his mind and sell cheap. Sometimes people rub their hands with this medicine just before shaking hands with the person they wish to influence.

Also in the same red pouch was a little calico packet (C) containing fine light-colored roots called Ne the tcī gun pa ma dji tcī gun, or "cure for poison," an important medicine chewed and rubbed on the body after using "Mī ca' dus-kwe," to prevent that powerful mixture from injuring the user, for if a person uses such things without taking proper precautions, he is likely to go insane.

A few bits of root, an empty buckskin packet, some white down and a wampum bead were found in the bottom of the pouch, and are shown immediately above it in the illustration.

Woven sack (M), 3″ × 2½″, made of buffalo wool yarn and ravelings in dark blue, red and yellow. It contained a string 5″ long of large black beads (E), at the end of which is a brass thimble in which is hidden a tiny packet of the same magic red paint found in (B). The whole outfit, which is called Kā' pi a, is worn at the back of the woman's neck, attached to her necklace, to make people "think well of her." There was also in the sack a little dark-brown rounded lump (D), about ½″ in diameter, called simply A' 'ki (earth), which is used as a paint while fasting, being put on the face at night to ward off evil influences and give good dreams.

Another woven sack (L), 4½″ × 3¾″, made largely of buffalo wool yarn and native fibre (Indian hemp?), in yellowish red, yellow and blue, held five little packages, two of them (F and G) of parchment-like skin, the remainder (H, I, J) of paper.

F is of oblong form, tied with a string of bark fibre, and contains six hemispherical wooden dice and one ordinary flat bone die, packed in a mixture of white down and down dyed red. It was noticed that the wooden dice, which are of unusual form, showed a decided tendency to fall with the flat side, which is colored black, down.   Still further examination revealed that the whole six had been ingeniously "loaded" by the insertion of small pieces of lead on the black side, craftily covered with the black paint. Mrs. Carter would give no explanation of these, but I think they were perhaps kept as charms to influence the dice of everyday use by sympathetic magic. They seem to me to be a little too "raw" for practical use, for they will invariably all fall white side up at every throw, which would cause instant suspicion on the part of the opponent. Of course, I may be mistaken.

The contents of packages G, H, I and J comprise roots used in gambling, as follows:

1. Thē ko wa tho.   Fine hair-like roots.   A few small pieces left.
2. Mes kwī jä bi hī.   Red root.
3. We na nī.   Yellow root, woody texture.
4. Tcī ka wī.   A big black root.

For racing, the roots 1 and 2 are chewed and rubbed on the rider's quirt in four places, and the horse is struck four times with this quirt during the race.   The rider rubs his thighs with the medicine where they touch the horse, and a foot racer rubs his legs with it.

The women when they gamble with the bowl and dice put a little between their teeth and blow on dice and bowl for good luck when opportunity offers; while in cards the players spit on the cards they plan to use, holding the medicine in the mouth.

Roots 3 and 4 are chewed and swallowed to counteract the effect of using the other medicines, which might prove harmful to the user.

This fetish may not be used for two different purposes— as courting and gambling—at the same time.   It is necessary to use the poison-curing medicine and allow four days to elapse after it has been used one way before attempting another. Menstruating women must not approach or touch the image, for if they incautiously do this they are likely to bleed to death.

Mrs. Carter was urged to explain further, to tell all she knew of the bundle, its origin, uses and the ceremonies connected with it. Finally she agreed.

It was started, she said, by her husband's great-grandmother, who at the time was mourning the death of her man. Six days she fasted, and on the night of the sixth it seemed as if somebody, some supernatural being, had taken pity upon her, for she was granted a vision in which she was told to go to a certain place at a certain time if she wished to find something that would help her. Going to that place as appointed, she saw what seemed to be a crow flying toward her carrying some object in its claws which it dropped near where she stood. When she ran to pick it up she found it to be this little figure of a man.

She took it home, but never told how she had obtained it, except to the person who afterward became its owner; and thus it was handed down, no one knowing its history but the owner.

During her lifetime she treasured the little figure, and bestowed great care upon it, for which, in return, the Indians say, it gave her good health, helped her in getting a second husband, gave her luck in games of chance—in fact, helped her in anything she wished to do.

Every year, when the grass comes up green in the spring a feast must be held for the image, the date of which must be appointed several days ahead, and new clothes made to put on it as soon as the bundle is open. The specimen bought by the Expedition has been neglected in this respect for a number of years. Anyone the owner wishes may be invited to the gathering, and often quite a crowd assembles. It is said that besides those bidden to the feast one uninvited guest will surely appear, and that this will be someone who is especially "proud of himself." He may not know that he is proud of himself, but the spirit of the doll will call him just the same, and he will come without knowing why, even from a long distance.

When the day arrives a dog is killed or other meat provided and set to cook. Then after the company is assembled and the uninvited guest appears, they open the bundle, sprinkling it with native tobacco as they untie the cords and expose the image to view. At this point a man known as the Speaker, who customarily makes prayers and speeches at various ceremonies, addresses the fetish as "Ne' nī wa (man) who owns the medicine," and prays, sprinkling tobacco upon it, "We have now begun. We want you to help us and give us good health and long life. Take care of us while we live. If any of us fall sick, care for them." This finished, the feasting begins. The best piece of meat is set aside in a bowl for the uninvited guest, and as many others are called upon as there are pieces of meat in the kettle, to help eat the rest. If there are eight pieces they set out one, and call up seven persons to finish the others, but the owner of the fetish is not included —she does not eat of the feast she has prepared.

After the feast comes the singing, four songs sung sitting, to the accompaniment of gourd rattles; then four dance songs are given for the guests to dance. The image is not carried in the dance as among the Delaware, but lies upon its wrappings throughout the ceremony, after which it is carefully tied up again.

In case of sickness the owner of the fetish, arriving on the scene, opens the bundle and speaks to it, sprinkling tobacco the while, and begs it to help the ailing one. A piece of broadcloth or a good blanket or some other expensive piece of goods is then folded and placed on the rack above the sick person or else near his head, and the image laid upon it to remain all night. When the owner comes for her fetish in the morning, she takes the goods upon which it has rested as her fee.

The bundle containing the image should always be kept

in the best buffalo-hide trunk and taken along when the owner goes away for any length of time, as when the family starts out on a hunting trip. But woe if the owner does not properly care for her fetish! It will not only refuse to help her, but will cause some accident or other harm to come to her or her family.

If the owner wishes to be relieved of it, she must pick out some kinswoman or best friend who will treat it well and not misuse it, and give it to her with instructions as to its use. There is no rule against selling part of each of the medicines in the bundle.

Another account of this same variety of fetish, which shows that the image could be kept and used by a man as well as a woman, was obtained from Pem wä" ta, a Sac and Fox man.

It seems that his grandfather, a long time ago, went out to fast, and remained away ten days. On the tenth a great power (man' i to) spoke to him, and the figure of a little man appeared. "Make one like this," said the Manito, "and stop grieving. Take good care of it, and you will live a long life. If you ever feel badly or full of grief about anything, open the bundle within which the image lies, and you will receive help." Hearing this, the faster dried his tears, and washed from his face the black paint, symbol of his fasting. Then, having partaken of food, he carved from wood the little image according to instructions, and prepared some love medicine and other herbs to go with it, and wrapped them up together in the form of a bundle. Such was the origin of one Mi thi' - ni ni, and in similar ways, according to tradition, most of those in use were obtained; the stories of origin and rules for using and caring for the fetish differing but slightly in different cases.

Pem wä" ta said that the love medicine kept with the image is the same as was found with the preceding, called "kä' pi a," which is worn by the women in a little package concealed in a thimble, attached to the bead necklace at the nape of the neck, when they dress in their best for some special occasion, and which is said to make people "think well" of them. If a woman wants to make a man love her, she talks to the medicine, mentioning the man's name, and when she wants to see him, then paints her face with a little of the medicine itself. At the appointed time, it is said, the man is sure to appear. He will stay with her, too, for a long time if she treats him well, but she is obliged to confess to him that she has used the medicine.

If a man sees or hears about some girl he thinks he would like to marry on account of her wealth or other desirable qualities, he can get her by the use of this same medicine kept with the Mi thi' ni ni. Even though she has never seen or heard of him before, she will believe him and do what he tells her. He can get this power by saying to the image, "I beg you to make this girl (naming her) believe anything I say and do anything I want." Then he paints the medicine on his face and goes to see her. No matter if he is a total stranger, the girl will take a liking to him at once.

But a man must actually marry a girl he wins in this way or the medicine will do him a serious injury. He must not deceive her. Besides, if a man tries to leave a woman after winning her with this love medicine, he cannot get away—she will not let him alone.

If a man's wife begins to go wrong and lead a fast life there is usually a medicine with the Mi thi' ni ni by which he can bring her back. A man owning such an image is likely to have trouble of this sort with his wife, as the presence of the image in the lodge is said to often make the women wild.

With many of these fetishes is kept a preparation which might be called a "witch medicine," for by its use the owner may kill anyone. To accomplish this the medicine is chewed and placed at the tip of a little pointed stick, with which the owner touches the image on whichever part of the body he wishes to injure, naming the proposed victim as he does so. Immediately the person named begins to have pains in the corresponding part of the body. There is no escape for him—the owner of the Mi thi' ni ni can reach him anywhere, and can even specify the number of days he will be sick before death relieves him. Men are often killed this way by a vengeful friend or relative of some woman they have wronged. Sometimes, it is said, if the owner becomes really angry at anyone, the Mi thi' ni ni is seen to move, showing that he is eager and willing to seek out his master's enemy and kill him.

When anyone is sick the owner of the image opens the bundle and lays it on a new blanket somewhere within the sick person's house, where it remains exposed four days. As he opens it, he says, "Grandfather, we beg of you to drive out this disease," and sprinkles Indian tobacco upon its face. Later a feast is held in its honor which is also supposed to induce it to help the sick.

Persons owning these fetishes keep the bundle in a sack, hidden away where no one can see it; but they always take it along whenever they travel. In many cases the only time they give it offerings is when they want it to do something, but some images have a yearly feast when new clothing is put upon them.

The Mi thi' ni ni will not help an owner who does not give him proper treatment, but neglect in some cases at least will not result in serious harm. Because the whole matter partakes of the nature of witchcraft, owners of these fetishes are likely to be secretive and dislike to have their connection with such objects generally known. Secret feasts are held for some images in some quiet place in the woods where no one will know what is going on. At some of these feasts the owner or owners of the fetish eat from a wooden bowl kept for the purpose, it is said, instead of letting the guests eat all the food, as is the usual custom at gatherings of this kind.

No one but the owner can use a Mi thi' ni ni; all others desiring the aid of the fetish must give the owner a gift, such as a piece of cloth or something of the sort. No white man can use a Mi thi' ni ni, even if he owned one, because the customs of his people permit him to eat with a menstruating woman, or to partake of food prepared by a woman in this condition, which spoils any chance he might have of acquiring power. Indian women live apart while menstruating, and are never allowed to approach a Mi thi' ni ni until their period is passed. For the same reason a white man can use none of the Indian fetishes, amulets and charms.

Pem wä^n ta claims that he has heard the following song used with an image:

Ne ni wē cē ko tha' ta wa w'
(Man,   weasel I am using) (repeat four times)

BUNDLE 2/7161.

About the time the preceding information was recorded, Pem wä^n ta offered us an image and outfit, which I finally bought, after some hesitation. The fetish seems to be fairly new, at least much newer than the "Rigid Man" obtained from Laura Carter. Some of the outfit seems quite old, however. Both are kept in a calico bag, wrapped in a piece of red calico.

The image is the figure of a man, a little less than $9\frac{1}{4}"$ high, made of hard wood, apparently oak, and dressed in a red calico shirt, red breech clout and buckskin leggings and moccasins. Across the left shoulder was a broad bead work sash, and from the ears hung long white glass beads. Directly about the fetish was a piece of blue woolen cloth. In the bundle also were a small wooden feast bowl and spoon, an old tattered mink skin painted red on the flesh side, a small blue cloth wallet decorated with ribbon appliqué containing four red mescal beans, a lot of bits of roots and herbs, and two shoulder blades of some small animal; and an old beaded cloth pouch enclosing the tail of a small weasel and a yellow feather. Pem wä^n ta did not explain these things, and I do not see what bearing they have upon the image, but I give the list for what it is worth.

BUNDLE 2/8601.

A curious bundle that seems to belong to this same class, although different in detail, was obtained from Jim Scott, a Fox Indian of the Tama band in Iowa, who said it had belonged to Mo we jä kwa, his wife's grandmother, from whom it had descended to her mother. He said that the exact use and ritual have been forgotten, but that he knew it was supposed to be "medicine." The entire contents are shown in Pl. XXXIX.

The outer cover (A) is a comparatively new sack of basswood fibre, $7\frac{3}{4}'' \times 12\frac{1}{4}''$. Within this, wrapped in a square of figured calico, and ensconced in a little calico sack, was the image (B), a terra cotta figure of a naked man, $5\frac{3}{4}''$ high, and showing signs of considerable age. The organ of generation is plainly shown, and the whole body is rubbed with yellow paint, upon which, in the neighborhood of the neck and chest, nearly obliterated spots of red can be distinguished. Upon the head is a bunch of white down feathers, about the neck a triple string of alternating white and blue beads and in the right ear a loop of similar beads at the lowest part of which is a large round white bead.

The owner claimed that it was made by the grandmother, Mo we jä kwa, but I think from its appearance that it has probably been made by some southwestern tribe, perhaps the Pima. How it came into the hands of the Fox is a mystery. I have since seen a similar image, only female, in the hands of a curio dealer, but he had no data as to its origin. In the bundle were the following articles:

An old brass thimble (C) containing a tiny packet, apparently the love medicine "Kä′ pi a;" a modern-appearing strip of woven bead work (D) $\frac{3}{8}''$ wide and $32''$ long, terminating in a red woolen tassel; a little old sack of red ribbon trimmed with green (E), containing a few bits of herbs and roots; a small leather purse (F), empty; a tin can (G) containing a finely divided brown herb mixture; a red cloth package (H) enclosing a white one with a coarser mixture; two white cloth packages (I, J) of fine herb mixture, some calamus roots tied in a bit of smoke-stained rag (K) and a paper (L) containing medicine.

BUNDLE 2/8602.

Among the Foxes also was found a bundle containing a wooden fetish something like that in Bundle 2/6507, heretofore described. It is the figure of a man of unusual and striking appearance (Pl. XL, A), due largely to the boldness with which the carving has been executed. It seems to be made of walnut, in one solid piece, and measures $13\frac{3}{4}''$ in height. The arms are at the sides, the head represented as shaved, except for the warrior's roach or crest on the crown. Navel and genitals are roughly shown, and the back looks almost unfinished. The lines of the face and the cavity representing the left eye show signs of red paint, and a buckskin thong about the neck bears a packet containing herb medicine. About the waist is a loose girdle of heavy green cloth, beneath which is thrust a flint knife painted red, nearly $5''$ in length, a fire-blackened wooden whistle $7''$ long, bearing an encircling fringe of deer hair just above and partly covering the air-hole, and a $9''$ eagle(?) feather dyed red, the quill of which has been wrapped in beads by way of decoration.

The figure, together with the tail of a deer which serves it for a pillow, was wrapped in the little black flannel blanket shown in the picture, and the whole rolled in a strip of dark red fabric made by the whites.

But little information could be collected, concerning the specimen, except that it was used as a health protector, a helper in war, love and other projects, and also for bewitching enemies. The details of the ritual are forgotten, it is said, but it was customary to hold a feast for the image, every two years, at which ceremonies are performed similar to those given in connection with the war bundles; and, like them, it is said to have originated in a dream or vision.

Kīana, the Fox Indian from whom I bought the fetish, aroused my suspicions concerning its genuineness by offering me later two more fetishes, one of which at least proved on inspection to be newly carved and "aged" with considerable art, but a further examination of the present specimen renewed my faith in its authenticity.

One of the supposedly new fetishes, the turtle figure shown in Pl. XL, B, is so good that I am not really sure yet whether it is new or not. Several Fox Indians told me that if it is not an old one, it is at least a good model of a class of "powerful things" still existing in the tribe and supposed to be protectors of the health. But the other, a very large human figure, is clearly new, and was bought as such, the maker realizing that he could not keep up his pretense of antiquity for the specimen.

The bundles whose descriptions follow are said to have been used each for a single purpose only, but examination of the contents shows that medicines for other uses sometimes occur. The first is:

GOOD-WILL BUNDLE.

BUNDLE 2/6379.

The name Mī ca' dus kwe, which the interpreters render as "High-toned medicine," seems to be applied to bundles quite different in general contents, but alike in containing a compound intended to obtain for the user or users the good will of others. One of these, obtained from Kī ma wa tă pă, a Sac and Fox, was used in promoting friendship between the Sac and Fox and other tribes. This is not as altruistic as it appears, for one of the principal reasons advanced for cultivating the good will of other tribes was that valuable gifts might be obtained from them.

When about to visit another tribe for a "pony smoke"

or other friendly gathering, the party would stop the night before they were due to arrive, and the members of the society owning the bundle would hold a dance at the camp, at which the bundle was opened. After the bundle had been asked to help the visitors to get good friendly treatment and fine presents, sticks were prepared, one for each person, to represent the number of the visiting party; these were divided in two bundles, representing the number belonging to each of the two divisions of the Sac and Fox—Ac kac'ᵃ, and Kic' koˑ.

After painting these sticks with green paint in which some herbs from the bundle had been mixed, a pipe was similarly painted. Next morning two messengers were delegated to take the sticks and the pipe to the chief of the tribe they were about to visit, but these two men and every one in the party were required to paint their faces with the herb mixture from the bundle before approaching the camp of their hosts.

When the chief of the tribe visited, has accepted the pipe and smoked it, and has taken the sticks, the medicine upon them affects him so strongly that he will give the visitors things he would never think of parting with otherwise—even a fine horse.

Kī ma wa tä pä told me that he did not remember how the bundle was said to have originated, or any further detail, except that every spring it was taken out of the trunk or parfleche in which it was customarily kept, and a feast given by the society. At these feasts the members of the society did not partake of the food provided, which was given to the invited guests, while the members, sitting, sang the songs of the ritual. Although the bundle was the property of a society (details concerning which were lacking) the whole tribe enjoyed its benefits.

The outer cover of the bundle was a woven sack, 12½″ × 9½″, made of a black yarn resembling buffalo wool and ravelings of three colors, red, green and yellow.

Contents.—An unusually fine woven bead work sack with patterns in nine different colors and shades, size $6\frac{3}{4}'' \times 4\frac{3}{8}''$. It enclosed: An imitation bear claw made of horn, with two perforations; a woven sack of blanket ravelings, pale green and red, $4\frac{1}{2}'' \times 4''$, in which were three pieces of some rough root and three others recognized as calamus, a double package containing in one side some small roots and brownish flat seeds, in the other a few very small seeds, black and lustrous, a brass thimble containing a buckskin packet of friendship or love medicine, and a package of roots. A smaller woven sack seemingly of buffalo wool, ravelings and fibre (Indian hemp?), was also found in the bead-work pouch, and yielded a tiny packet of red magic paint, a package of finely divided mineral substance with glistening specks resembling mica, another of slender black roots, and a slim bead of shell resembling wampum, but twice the length. All the preceding were stored in the bead sack.

Woven sack, $3\frac{1}{2}'' \times 4\frac{3}{4}''$, mainly of buffalo wool and (Indian hemp?), contains a cloth package of pieces of root and a mixture of pounded herbs wrapped in a fragment of a Washington newspaper of the year 1860; five little packets of cloth and paper enclosing herbs and roots, one of them yielding also a packet of magic paint; a pouch of red trade cloth, itself containing two spherical objects, one gray, one white, resembling marbles; a long purple shell bead of the variety known as "Dutch wampum;" a red mescal bean; a package of herb mixture; a wad of light hair from some animal, perhaps a white buffalo; a package of mica-like substance wrapped in a strip of red and a strip of blue calico; some whitish earthy substance done up in calico; three cloth and paper packages herbs and roots; and three loose pieces of root.

Cloth sack containing two buckskin packets herb medicine, an empty thimble and fourteen oval glass beads.

Two cloth packages containing vegetable medicines—roots, barks, and seeds.

GAMBLING BUNDLE.

BUNDLE 2/6374.

This bundle, known as Ta nē dī′ wa skwē, was also obtained from Kī ma wa tä pä, a man of the Sac division. Informing me that bundles of this class had at one time been abundant among his people, he confessed that he was unable to tell me anything concerning its origin. As to its use, he told me the following:

When there is "big gambling" and the owner decides to take part, he addresses the bundle, praying for success, and then, taking out a little of the paint that has been mixed with herbs of supposed mystic potence, paints the figure of a cross upon each cheek. Some of the herbs are then reduced to pulp by chewing and blown upon the body and hands of the gambler, and upon his cards and money, if these are used. This is supposed to charm the cards and to bewilder one's opponent and "draw" his money or other stakes away from him. But the gambler using this medicine must keep his "heart good" throughout the game, for if he allows himself to become angry the charm will be reversed and luck turn against him. It is said that a gambler who is known to use this medicine is often teased and insulted by his opponents, in the hopes of arousing his temper and spoiling his luck.

The outer cover is a much worn oval cloth bag 13″ long by 7¼″ at its widest part. Its attractive decoration was made by cutting cotton cloth of different colors into rhombus and triangle forms, which were then stitched together to form patterns, the technique but not the materials being similar to the more common forms of ribbon appliqué. Within this was a rough sack made of squares of different patterns of calico sewed together after the fashion of a "crazy quilt," which in its turn contained the magic paraphernalia, as follows:

Tail of black-tail deer, with string for attachment to the hair.

Metal box with engraved top and bottom, containing a bottle wrapped in a rag, labeled, "Red Oxide of Mercury. W. H. Schieffelin & Co., New York."

Package of finely divided mineral substance of yellow color.

Leather dice box (white man's manufacture), containing in the bottom a buckskin package of red paint mixed with herbs—the magic paint mentioned above—in which was a pair of trade earrings. Being imbued with the magic of the paint, these were probably worn as amulets by gamblers. Then came a package of ash-like powder in a red calico sack covered with a rag of blue calico; an herb mixture done up in two white rags—the stuff that is chewed and blown upon the body, hands and paraphernalia of the gambler; and finally, in the top of the dice. box, a yellow powder wrapped in a Baptist tract against Sabbath breaking. This completes the outfit.

HUNTING BUNDLES.

BUNDLE 2/8446.

From Pīä mic kwī, a woman of the Fox band at Tama, Iowa, was obtained a bundle that had belonged to her husband, now dead. She said she knew no details concerning it—only that he had used it to help him in his hunting, and that it is called Cī cä wus kw'. Examination of the contents, however, shows at least one additional use of which she was perhaps ignorant.

The outer cover is a very well made but dilapidated woven sack of native fibre strings, apparently Indian hemp, interwoven with dark brown buffalo wool yarn in geometric patterns. Red yarn was introduced at the ends, but it is difficult to see whether this is light-colored buffalo wool dyed red, or ravelings from some woolen fabric.

Contents.—Strip of red trade cloth enclosing two weasel skins, one brown, one white. The brown one held a little paper package of fine black roots and two gun flints, apparently of English material and make, wrapped in cloth; while the white skin enclosed a package of parchment-like skin containing a bit of fossil bone about 1″ long, resting in a bed of dried flowers and roots.

Printed cloth sack, containing three little packages of birch bark, two of roots, one empty; some cedar leaves wrapped in two layers of buckskin; a cloth package of herb mixture, bits of fossil bone and mica; buckskin package containing roots; another, red paint mixed with herbs; three pieces of fossil wood and a cloth package of ground herbs. A very old bit of paper enfolding a mixture of herbs bore the line, "Manny man of manny mind," written fourteen times, the writing growing smaller with every repetition. A buckskin package of mixed herbs and mica wrapped in the red-crested skin of a young ivory-bill woodpecker's head completed the contents of the cloth sack. All the objects within it were imbedded in down dyed red.

A little sack of red cloth bearing a roughly embroidered wolf figure in green yarn, containing a buckskin package in which were a package of roots and another of ground herbs.

Triangular piece of very old and very coarse red trade cloth wrapped about a faded calico bundle of porcupine quills and roots, imbedded in finely pounded herbs and mica.

Rounded bundle of plaid cotton fabric, containing a large brass thimble, wrapped in three bits of cloth, one red, one blue, one figured. In it was concealed a little magic red paint in a packet of buckskin, tied first with human hair which was concealed by another tie, a long buckskin string, wound about over it. The whole was folded in faded purple ribbon. Another similar but smaller packet was also in the thimble, filled with ground herbs and mica, but this had no human hair, being merely tied to the end of an 8″ buckskin string. In one corner of the outer cloth wrapping were knotted a few roots.

Three packages tied together, one covered with soft tanned

buffalo hide, one of parchment-like material, and one of cloth, each containing a mixture of herbs and roots.

Six pieces of gypsum.

Nine bits of roots.

One straight and three bent twigs from some shrub.

A little packet of the magic mixture of herbs and paint was attached to the edge of the woven sack forming the outer cover.

While most of the medicines in this bundle are probably for hunting, as stated by the widow of its former owner, there seems to be at least one other kind also, as was before remarked. Weasels and woodpeckers (see pp. 218, 226) are frequently used in hunting bundles, both creatures being notably successful in that line, and therefore imparting desirable powers to the bundle owner. The gun flints were undoubtedly tied up with herbs to make them lucky.

As for the fossil bones and mica, they probably represent the bones and scales of mythic animals, but as I have never seen them before in a hunting bundle, I cannot even guess at their use.

Porcupine quills, imbedded in medicine can be only used for two purposes, according to any information I can find— witchcraft and hunting. In witchcraft the sorcerer takes a quill from the medicine, names the man he wishes to injure, and the part—head, heart, stomach or whatever is to be affected—then flips it away with his fingers.

The victim, wherever he may be, immediately feels pain in the place indicated, so the Indians believe, and his sufferings may be made greater or less at the will of the sorcerer. In hunting, an animal instead of a person is named before "shooting" the quill, with the result that the hunter will soon find an animal of the sort named, lagging and crippled as if with pain and consequently easy to kill.

The preceding may all be hunting medicines, but the contents of the brass thimble constitute a love medicine, pure and simple: the hair tied round the packet was secretly taken from the head of the maiden the man wished to win, and the magic paint was to put on his face when he went courting her. Very likely the hair had been taken from the head of the very woman from whom we bought the bundle, and had been kept there by her husband unknown to her, for many years.

BUNDLE 2/8597.

This hunting bundle, a somewhat different variety from the last, was bought from the same Fox woman. It is called Ca we thi tcī gun, and was used to spoil the luck of rival hunting parties; but the exact modus operandi was unfortunately not given. Enough was said or hinted, however, to show that this "medicine" involved practices even nearer witchcraft than the last bundle, for the supposed powers of this one were actually turned against human beings with malevolent intent.

The cover consists of two sacks woven of cords of some native fibre, perhaps "Indian hemp," with patterns worked out in buffalo wool yarn and blanket ravelings, the outside sack, which is in bad shape, measuring $10\frac{1}{2}'' \times 7\frac{1}{2}''$; the inner, nearly perfect, $9\frac{1}{4}'' \times 6\frac{1}{8}''$.

Contents.—Two pieces of gypsum, each deeply grooved on one side.

Two cloth packages containing gypsum crystals.

Piece of gypsum, wrapped with herbs in a piece of bladder-like skin.

Piece petrified wood.

Piece fossil bone, rolled in cloth.

Cloth package of bits of fossil bone mixed with red down, herbs and roots.

Cloth package containing bits of soft and chalky bone.

Package of bladder-like skin, containing bit of bone, much scraped.

Two cloth packages containing bits of dried entrails or umbilical cords.

Piece of dried membrane wrapped in two layers of buckskin.

Package of bladder containing scales of mica-like substance and red paint.

Package of skin, containing dark red paint and herbs.

Package of skin, containing red paint.

Package herbs.

Five packages herb mixture.

Two packages roots.

Four bits of root.

Three metal jinglers, with red deer-hair tassels.

Red cloth sack containing four white and one purple wampum beads, some roots and a piece of fungus tinder or punk.

Small woven sack, $3\frac{7}{8}'' \times 3''$, made mainly of ravelings, and containing a piece of leather, some fine black roots, some loose, some in a package, a few larger light-colored round roots and a package root mixture.

Cloth package, containing a paper package enclosing a piece of root and an herb mixture; another with a scale resembling mica wrapped in red-dyed down; another, red paint and herb medicine, these last two wrapped in an old bit of paper upon which is written "C Cumdsy;" and another paper package of red paint mixed with ground herbs.

Cloth package, containing a number of shafts from the feathers of small birds and several bits of root, all imbedded in fine ground herbs containing sparkling mica-like particles; also a skin package enclosing a bit of bark, a paper package of roots and another of herbs. This seems to be a "witching" preparation, the feather shafts being the mystic arrows shot by magic into the body of the person or animal selected as a victim.

MEDICINE AGAINST WITCHCRAFT.

BUNDLE 2/8599.

From the same Fox woman who sold us the two preceding bundles, a third was obtained, called No thǎ tci gun, which was used mainly to counteract the magic of rival hunting parties, but which could also be used to combat witchcraft of any kind. This bundle, she said, would offset the use of such a bundle as the last one in the hands of another party, and dispel the "hoodoo." But when it came to details Pī ä - mic kwī could not (or would not) give any information.

A rather new woven sack of yarn, $6\frac{3}{4}'' \times 4\frac{1}{4}''$, bearing a panther figure, contained the outfit.

Contents.—Woven sack, $3'' \times 5\frac{1}{2}''$, in yellow and dark brown, made from a loosely spun yarn the nature of which is hard to determine, as the fibres are too coarse and straight for ordinary sheep's wool, and yet not like most buffalo hair or wool. This sack enclosed two thimbles containing tiny sacks of medicine, a bead of the large purple wampum usually called "Dutch," two pebbles of some soft yellowish mineral, a bit of bone, a metal jingler with red dyed deer hair tassel, a paper package of ground herb medicine, three packages of bits of the yellow mineral and a package of gypsum crystals.

A brown weasel skin containing a baby's moccasin, in the toe of which were tied two red mescal beans.

Buckskin bag, the inside colored yellow, containing seeds.

Five packages of herbs, roots and mixtures, one of the latter including red down as an ingredient.

WITCH BUNDLE.

BUNDLE 2/6378.

The belief in witchcraft, is practically universal among the Sac and Fox, being shared by the educated and progressive element, as well as the conservative portion of the tribe.

One of my interpreters, an educated man, often tells in perfect good faith how, traveling along a lonely road one night he encountered what appeared to be a stray dog, but which suddenly changed before his eyes to a tall Indian, naked but for a breech clout, across whose shoulder was dimly seen the strap and pouch used by the "night travelers," or witches, who, it is believed, customarily go about in this guise.[1] To the Indian, a "witch" may be either a man or a woman, a member of the society of sorcerers.

Few will acknowledge membership in such a society, and fewer still will give up any of its paraphernalia to a collector. One small bundle of witch medicine was secured, however, with its little carrying pouch and shoulder strap (Pl. XXXVII, A), from an Indian who asked me as a special favor not to use his name in connection with it. It had formerly belonged, he said, to old Ma' wa ci, now dead.

If a "witch" has an enemy he wishes to get out of the way, he tells the other members of the society how this man has treated him. After holding a meeting, if they all agree that he shall be killed, the first step is to draw a picture of a man on the ground, which represents the intended victim. A little stick or similar instrument is thrust into the figure in whatever part of the body they wish affected in the victim, and a little of the mixture from the bundle sprinkled on the place; this is supposed to cause pain in the corresponding part of his body. Then they set the time when the victim is to die.

It is believed, that witches can assume the forms of four different animals—the bear, dog, owl and mole in succession. Some claim that the raccoon should be placed in this list instead of the mole, and opinions seem to differ as to the exact list. When in the form of a mole, they can approach their enemy unseen, underground, the Indians say.

---

[1] Such a pouch is mentioned in Jones' "Fox Texts." Publications Am. Eth. Soc., Vol. 1, p. 157.

The membership and activities of the society are kept secret. The bundle is known as ma ni to wä thi wä ni'.

Our specimen shown in Pl. XXXVII was wrapped in three layers of calico of different patterns; then a woven sack (B), 4″ × 5″, made mainly of ravelings from woolen fabrics, on one side of which are two deer-like figures in black on a gray ground, flanked by zigzag patterns in red, green, gray and yellow. On the reverse side between similar zigzags are four smaller deer standing separately, above a herd of four deer, the number of animals determined by the number of heads— a rare pattern. On this side the deer are gray and the background black. Within this is a little buckskin pouch (A), 2½″ × 2¼″, provided with a flap, lined with silk, and solidly beaded with patterns in black, white, blue, red, green, yellow, pink and purple. To the pouch is fastened a carrying strap of blue and pink ribbon 3′ 7¾″ long intended to pass across the shoulder. Inside is a mole skin (the mole is one of the animals whose form can be assumed by a witch) in which is a paper package of Indian tobacco for incense, and another containing two little buckskin packets of red paint mixed with magic herbs together with a little wooden paddle for applying it. The mole skin may be seen projecting from the pouch in the illustration.

SEPARATE AMULETS.

Besides the preceding, a few single amulets not connected with any bundle were secured, all of them from the Fox band living near Tama, Iowa.

2/7925. Only one of these was for war—a peculiar necklace bought from Pucitan'ikwe, the Fox chief, who said it had the power to make a man "not afraid to die." It consists of a buckskin thong 4' 3" long, much blackened by age and smoke, and bearing one eagle feather and fourteen bunches of woodpecker (sp?) tail feathers, together with a little brass bell. The thong has been wrapped with long strips of bird quill, some of which are dyed green.

2/7848. A love amulet of an unusual sort was the magic arm band bought from the woman Kickoikwä". The band for encircling the arm or wrist is made of fur, apparently otter, to which is fastened a bead-bordered strip of finer brown fur, 11¼" long by 1⅝" wide, bearing at its lower end a packet of love medicine paint, another of herb medicine of some kind and a small brass bell.

2/8021. This small amulet, for general good luck, consists of three red "mescal" beans in a tight buckskin packet, with a round hole cut over each bean so that it can "look out." Such amulets, I was told, could be worn attached to the hair or clothing, but nowadays are usually carried in the pocket. The Fox name is Mes kwī na da' wī non, or Red medicine.

This concludes the list of "powerful" objects from the Sac and Fox. The next paper will be devoted to such matters among the Pottawattomi, and perhaps also the Kickapoo, Delaware and Shawnee.

APPENDIX.

After the preceding paper was in proof Mr. Alanson Skinner of the American Museum of Natural History kindly sent me an account of the Sac and Fox sacred bundles, dating from the first half of the nineteenth century, which he found in the "Wisconsin Historical Collections." He says: "These excerpts are taken from 'Documents relating to the Stockbridge Mission,' 1825–48. Rev. Cutting Marsh is responsible for these reports, which were sent to Scotland."

The first excerpt, dated 1834, gives part of a conversation between the missionary and the chief "Pow-we-sheak" regarding the "Me-shaum" (mī cam^i) or sacred bundle.[1]

Pow-we-sheak.—The Great Spirit has given us our Me-shaum. How do you know this? Ans.—It is made known to us by dreams when we fast. But cannot the bad spirit speak in this way as well as the good? Ans.—But we know when the good and when the bad spirit speaks. A great while ago, says he, all of the nations leagued against us and we were almost all cut off, only a few lodges remained (referring to the wars they had when in the region of Green Bay) and our Me-shaum was all that saved us.

The second excerpt[2] comprises quite a pretentious account of Sac and Fox religion, including their belief in sacred bundles. Mr. Skinner states that most of the data refer to the Sac (Sauk) at that time on the Mississippi. The account runs as follows:

Religious Rites and Ceremonies.

They are very scrupulous with regard to their religious rites and ceremonies. I have as yet seen no Indians as much so as they be. In the first place I shall commence with giving

---

[1] Wisconsin Historical Collections, 1834. Vol. XV, p. 120.

[2] *Ibid.*, pp. 128–138.

(253)

an account of their Me-shaum, which is sometimes called Grand Medicine-bag.

The Me-shaum is a parcel or bundle in which are recorded by knots in strings, stones, etc., and also by hieroglyphical figures the names and wars of their gods in ancient times; and their religious belief also or revelation which they suppose was at first delivered to their ancestors by We-sah-kah their tutelary god.[1]

We-sah-kah is regarded in their mythology as the creator of the new world after it had been destroyed by a flood. The Me-shaum is held in high veneration; none are permitted to open or inspect it, except the one having the particular charge of it. It is opened only in case of invocations to the Great Spirit, in which dogs are often slain and offered in sacrifice.[2]

ORDINANCES OF THE ME-SHAUM.

To fast every morning in the winter season.

To fast ten days in order to obtain signal revenge upon an enemy.

To invoke and sacrifice every time a man has killed a bear or some choice game.

That a woman shall not come into the lodge at certain seasons (during her monthly courses) nor eat anything cooked at the same fire in the lodge.[3]

To give away property to the poor for the good of departed relatives to the land of shades.

It teaches that the Great Spirit gave them the wild beasts for their sustenance; and required them to be forgiving towards those belonging to their own family or nation if they have received any injury, but that revenge must be taken upon an enemy. These are some of the most important things required

---

[1] We-sah-kah is very probably Noah.

[2] The dog feast is one of the most sacred feasts—no Indian not belonging to the Me-shaum, or white person can witness it.

[3] This superstitious custom has been observed by Indians from time immemorial and the only reason they give for it is "their ancestors did so."

by the Me-shaum. It was formerly considered so sacred, that it was hung upon the limbs of a tree outside of the lodge lest it should be polluted by an unclean woman. It was formerly death for a white man to open and examine it. Some years ago a white man near the De Bukes mines on the Mississippi seeing one hung upon a tree, was led by curiosity to take it down and examine it in the absence of the Indians. As soon as he took it down and opened it the children began to cry to see their fathers' Me-shaum profaned in such a manner. When the Indians returned and found out what had been done, they pursued after the man and he was obliged to leave the country in order to save his life.

NAMES OF THEIR GODS.

We-sah-kah—god of the earth.

Nah-pat-tay—brother of W. who being slain by the gods of the sea, W. sent him to the land of shades or Che-pah-munk, where he still exists as chief of the shades.

Mah-she-ken-a-peck and Nah-me-pa-she—gods who inhabit both land and water; and the

Ai-yam-woy—men of terrible size or giants.

Besides these inferior deities they recognize a Supreme Being whom they call Kâ-shuh-mah-nu-too—Great Spirit.

The Ai-yam-woy were a race of supernatural beings, descendants of the gods of the sea and inhabited the ancient world.

TRADITIONS OF THE ME-SHAUM.

In process of time the Great Spirit addressed the spirits on earth in the following manner: "Spirits of my breath I have created you all to enjoy the earth and wide-spreading waters, and with you I shall now make a division of them. We-sah-kah shall possess the dry land and Nah-me-pa-she and Mah-she-ken-a-peck the waters. But We-sah-kah shall be chief and you shall obey him in all things, for to him I have

given my terrestrial sphere to make war and peace with whom-
soever he will.   At length he will become elated and say within
himself, I am the Great Spirit.   Moreover, in memory of this
eventful day I shall create a race of beings after his own like-
ness."   Accordingly mankind were created in the image of
We-sah-kah.   After this the legions of spirits flew from the
presence of the Great Spirit and inhabited their destined
places.   To mankind was given knowledge and fire as a com-
pensation for their nakedness.   To the beasts of the forest,
hair and fur and to the birds of the air, feathers.

Such were the times of old when mankind were under the
protection of We-sah-kah.

At length the Ai-yam-woy became very numerous and
overran both elements at their pleasure, so that the children
of We-sah-kah were in danger of being totally destroyed by
those terrible demi-gods.

We-sah-kah seeing this sent his brother to the gods of
the sea to remonstrate against the depredations committed
by their children amongst the race of the chief god of the
earth.   But instead of listening they slew Nah-pat-tay; his
blood, however, ran out of the gulf and reached the dry land.
Immediately a drop formed itself into a body and the shade of
Nah-pat-tay being present entered it and he became as before.

He then sought safety by flight, but was met by the Ai-
yam-woy who devoured him, leaving only one drop of blood.
We-sah-kah upon hearing of the death of his brother fasted
ten days[1] and vowed destruction to the gods of the sea.   At
the end of the tenth day We-sah-kah heard the voice of his
brother's shade at the Door of Life crying for entrance.   But
he answered, "Go to the land of shades and there be chief of
men that shall die like yourself."   (Nah-pat-tay, they suppose,
was the first who died and so was constituted chief of the shades
of mortals.)

---

[1] This it is said is the reason why the Indians fast ten days, in order that, as We-sah-
kah did, they may obtain signal revenge upon their enemies.

THE FLOOD.

After the departure of Nah-pat-tay's shade, We-sah-kah prepared himself with the great spear, and went with the speed of an eagle to fight the Ai-yam-woy, the murderers of his brother. He met and slew them; this occasioned a war with the gods which lasted for a long time. The gods of the sea having the great deep at their disposal resolved upon destroying We-sah-kah and his race even at the loss of their own lives. A great council was therefore called for the purpose, and all the chiefs were assembled and agreed upon the destruction of the world by flood. We-sah-kah hearing of this fasted again for ten days. At the end of the tenth day his voice reached the Great Spirit, his prayer was heard and answered and mankind, the beasts and birds, etc. were preserved. Then the waters began to overflow the plains and We-sah-kah fled before them with his family, etc., until he reached a high mountain. But the water soon overtook them and he built a great raft upon which he put all kinds of creatures and then let it loose, so it floated upon the surface of the great waters. After a long time We-sah-kah began to be sorry and fasted ten days. At the end of the tenth day he dreamed he saw the dry land. Awaking out of sleep he sent down the tortoise, but he returned without any clay; he then sent down the muskrat, and he brought up clay between his claws, out of which W. formed the dry land. Then mankind and all the creatures which had been preserved were spread abroad upon the face of it. They now lived in peace and happiness because there were no Ai-yam-woy or any spirits of destruction to trouble them, having all been exterminated by the flood.

THE END OF WE-SAH-KAH.

We-sah-kah was now sole chief of earth and mankind were his children. At length the people became very numerous and unable to remain together. They then separated under their fathers San-ke, Mash-qua-ke (Red Fox) and Ash-e-kan. There was also one other but his name was blotted out from amongst men on account of his offending We-sah-kah, because not contented with long life, he asked not to suffer him to die but live forever on the earth. This so incensed W. that he immediately transformed him and his children into stones and they remain so until the present, and their names are forgotten by all the tribes of the earth.

The place was called Mixed Water, the dwelling of We-sah-kah, from which these three fathers commenced their journey towards the South, each tribe under his particular father.[1]

Before the division took place We-sah-kah gave to each father a Me-shaum, in which this narration is recorded by songs.

Afterwards the Great Spirit met W. and forgetting that he was a creature of the Great Spirit, told him that he had destroyed the infernal spirits from off the earth and rebuilt this new world by his own power. But the Great Spirit opened his Me-shaum and showed W. the beginning of his existence; at this he was ashamed and sorry and humbled himself for ten days. Notwithstanding the Great Spirit disregarded his invocations, and took him by the heel and cast him to the ends of the earth, and put Po-po-na-te-se, god of winter, betwixt him and the world to prevent his ever coming amongst mankind again.

BELIEF RESPECTING THE FUTURE STATE.

If an Indian fulfils during his lifetime the requirements of the Me-shaum, he believes that at death he shall go to Che-pah-munk or the happy land; but if bad he will not be able to cross the bridge, which is no wider than a man's foot and leads over the Mah-na-sa-no-ah or river of death. This is a bottomless river and if the man has been wicked he is

---

[1] They can give no account where the place of the Mixed Water is.

attracted by it and plunges in, but if good it has no power over him, and he passes in safety and joins the legion of Nah-pat-tay, where he enjoys everlasting happiness. * * * * *

Che-pah-munk or the happy land is situated far at the west and abounds in game of all kinds and whatsoever is pleasing to the sight or taste.

MANNER OF TREATING THE DEAD.

When a person dies, his face is painted red, his best clothes are put on, and all is prepared the same as for a journey. With the corpse is buried the implements of hunting, etc., as they suppose that all of these things are needed in that world from "whose bourne no traveler returns."

About two years ago Ke-o-kuck, the head chief, lost his nephew. A paling of stakes was made around the place where the remains were to be deposited. The corpse was then placed in a sitting posture after having been dressed in the usual style (but was not buried), with his rifle, knife, etc., all by his side. Ke-o-kuck then led up one of his best horses, put the reins into the hands of the dead, and shot the horse. A white man being present asked him why he did that. "Because," says he, "I do not want to have him go on foot"— meaning to the west.

They have no idea of the judgment after death or of a future resurrection. Their dead are buried with the head towards the west.

SACRED FEASTS OR INVOCATIONS.

These are numerous whilst they remain at their villages and have anything with which to make them.

When a man makes a feast for the Great Spirit, he partakes of no part of it himself, although he may have fasted for two days previous, but leaves his place or portion for the Great Spirit and is engaged whilst it lasts in chanting the sacred songs. If a dog gets so much as a bone of the meat which has been eaten it pollutes the feast, everything therefore which is left is either burned or buried.

These feasts they call invocations (Mah-neh-tah-moan) or worship of the Great Spirit.

When a man wishes to make a feast or have an invocation, he sends for the Mam-e-she-may-kah (cooks) belonging to the Me-shaum of which he is a member and they are told to make the necessary preparations. If it is a dog-feast (which is the most sacred) they kill the dog, etc., or if he has not sufficient with which to make a feast they go round and beg until enough is obtained. As soon as the kettles are put over the fire an appointed number commence singing, keeping time by shaking a gourd-shell which has something in it which rattles. The place is previously enclosed with curtains if the lodge is large and no one is permitted to enter it except such as belong to the Me-shaum or have a special invitation.

These sacred songs consist of only a few words, which are repeated in a very devout manner, over and over, for a considerable length of time; which forcibly reminds one of the Saviour's injunction, "use not vain repetitions," etc.

A few of the aged women generally attend, and sometimes respond to the sacred songs, emitting the sound through the nose, which sounds more like persons in distress or deranged than like devotion.

Returning one morning from a season of retirement to Ap-pen-oore's (a Fox chief) lodge, where I stayed, I found a party engaged in a sacred feast, and singing the sacred songs.

Ap-pen-oore then mentioned the design of them, etc.— "Only a few words," says he, "of the songs are mentioned which bring to mind the traditions delivered to our ancestors by the gods and a speech is made at the close (of the feast) which shows the meaning of them." The following is a translation of one which they were then singing, as given to me by my interpreter. "Go and you shall have two horns upon your forehead; and when you return your horns shall be blue like the sky." The meaning of which seemed to be, go and be masters of the beasts of the field, the fowls of the air, etc. "At first," says A., "the Great Spirit made eight persons and promised them *two* horns, but some time after he saw them and they had only one. Our Me-shaum is the same to us when we open it as the Book (the Bible) is to the white people, for by it we learn what the gods delivered to our ancestors to be handed down from generation to generation."

ATTENDANCE UPON A FEAST OR INVOCATION, AUGUST 11TH.

This morn an invitation was sent to me by Ap-pen-oore to attend; considering it as a mere matter of civility and not as giving countenance to their superstitions I accepted of the invitation. Considerable of preparation had been previously made, the apartment carefully enclosed and was one of the most sacred and ceremonious which I witnessed. At the appointed time I went in. The sacred songs had all been sung and all was silence for a few minutes. A. then made a speech occupying some fifteen or twenty minutes, repeating, as I was informed, the requisitions of the Me-shaum. All listened very attentively and occasionally responded by a loud grunt. At the close he ordered the cooks to serve the company, which they did, dealing out to each individual his portion in a dish or wooden bowl. When they took the kettles from the fire a ladle full of the broth contained in them was taken out and one went round the fire pouring a little of it into the fire very carefully as he went round. And each portion was also carried once round the fire before it was given to the individual. No one began to eat until all were served, but each was engaged in taking off the things with which the pieces of venison were tied together, or else in stripping them to pieces as no knives or forks were permitted to be used. These, as well as the use of salt, are strictly forbidden by the rules of the Me-shaum, and nothing except a spoon may be used. When all were in readiness to eat, the kettles having been with much care turned over at each end of the fire, each one, beginning at the head, uttered a few words, which were thanks to the Mam-e-she-mah-k̇ah, and then began to eat. The same expression of thanks was given at the close. Some, I observed, were unable to eat their portion; such sent out and invited a friend to come to their assistance, as nothing must be left which could be eaten, and the remainder, viz., the strings and bones, were all collected and burned in the fire, together with some stuff taken from the Me-shaum, which was considered as a kind of incense. Then followed a long speech or prayer by the chief speaker and he was followed by the chief with another. These speeches were said over in a solemn but hurried manner and are used at every sacred feast. After all these and other ceremonies also were performed, it was announced that the feast was closed, and as each went out he went once round the fire, the whole occupying an hour and a half or two hours.

These feasts are attended with great formality and serious-ness and are considered as religious worship offered to the Great Spirit, still they exert no moral influence whatever that I could observe, either to restrain from doing wrong, or as leading to that which is right in the sight of God.

One Indian who attended this feast was remarkably scrupulous in observing every ceremony and in requiring others also to do the same, and exceedingly troubled because my inter-preter carried in a little salt for his own use. He told him that he was a very bad man because he did it, worse than white man, etc. This Indian only the day before I saw intoxicated, but now he enters and partakes of the sacred feast as welcome a guest as any other. However base their conduct or vile their character may be, it does not disqualify for the enjoyment of their most sacred privileges. So soon as an Indian rises to the rank of a *brave*, and this he does whenever he has killed or wounded an enemy in battle, he then can belong to the Me-shaum and partake of the sacred feasts.

The religion of the Me-shaum is therefore peculiarly adapted to their habits and manner of life.

SAC AND FOX INDIANS

PLATE XXI

A Ceremonial Bark-house of the Sac and Fox Bear clan, also winter mat lodge.

B Sac and Fox Bark-house where Sacred Bundles are kept, with cooking arbor in front. The bark walls of the house have been removed on account of warm weather.

A

B

CEREMONIAL HOUSES

PLATE XXII

Sac and Fox "Dance to the Medicine of the Brave."
From Catlin.

PLATE XXII

SAC AND FOX "DANCE TO THE MEDICINE OF THE BRAVE." FROM CATLIN.

PLATE XXIII

Sac and Fox Indians emerging from sweat-house
   before Sacred Bundle Ceremony.   From painting by Ernest Spybuck, a Shawnee.
Preparing dogs for cooking, to be used in the feast
   at a Sac and Fox Sacred Bundle Ceremony.

A

B

INDIAN DRAWINGS

PLATE XXIV

Ceremonial House of the Fox clan, of the Sac and Fox Indians, showing Sacred Bundle Dance in progress. From a painting by Ernest Spybuck, a Shawnee.

PLATE XXIV

INDIAN DRAWING

PLATE XXV

War Bundle, closed, showing war whistles—Sac and
Fox Indians (2/8591).

PLATE XXV

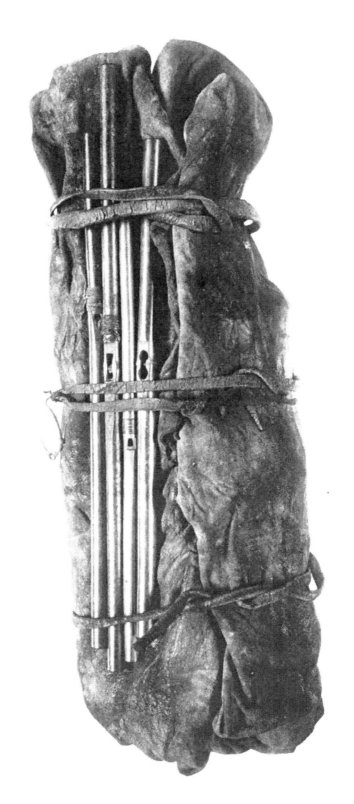

WAR BUNDLE, CLOSED, SHOWING WAR WHISTLES · SAC AND FOX INDIANS

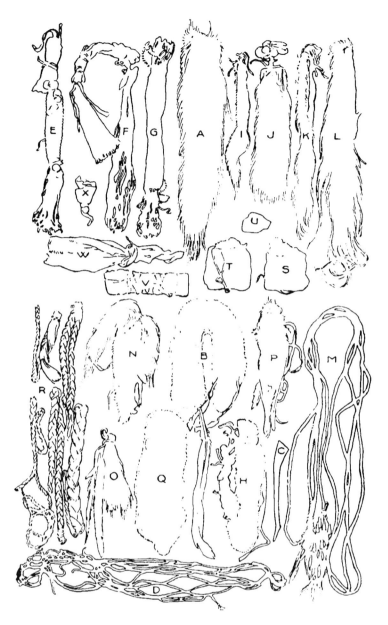

KEY TO PLATE XXVI

A Wolf tail amulet.

B Magic arm band of swan's down.

C Miniature war club, an amulet.

D Part of net-work sash.

E ⎫

F ⎬ Magic woven arm bands.

G ⎭

H Magic arm band of fabric and swan's down.

I ⎫

J ⎬ Magic arm bands of buffalo skin.

K ⎭

L Buffalo tail amulet.

M Captive-leading rope, with quill decoration.

N ⎫

O ⎬ Scalp-lock amulets of bird skins, feathers

P ⎭ and buffalo hair.

Q Scalp-lock amulet of swan's down.

R Sweetgrass used as incense.

S ⎫

T ⎬ Woven sacks containing medicine, etc., packed in down.

U Piece of lava from woven sack.

V Medicine package of birch bark.

W Medicine package of fawn skin.

X Medicine package of buckskin.

PLATE XXVI

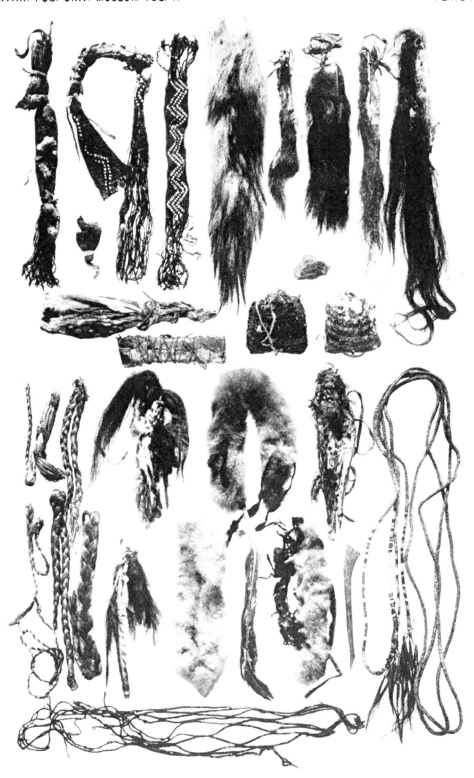

CONTENTS OF SAC AND FOX WAR BUNDLE

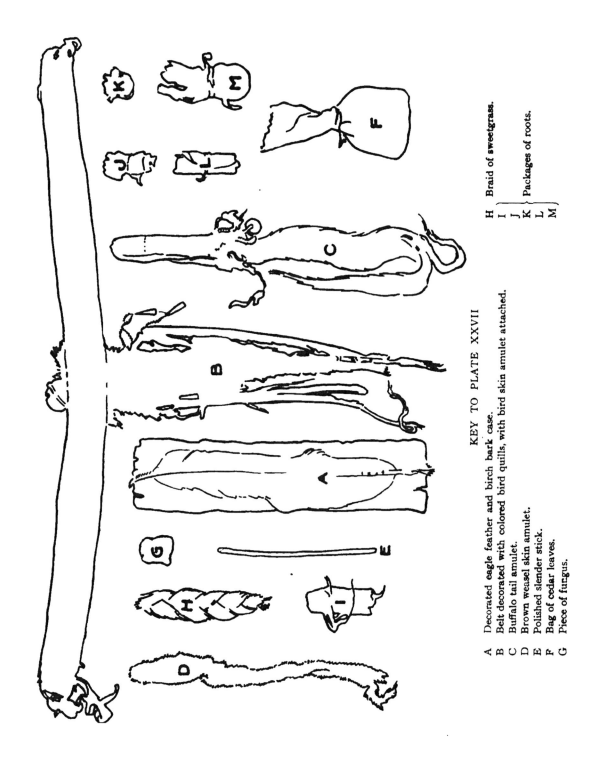

KEY TO PLATE XXVII

A   Decorated eagle feather and birch bark case.
B   Belt decorated with colored bird quills, with bird skin amulet attached.
C   Buffalo tail amulet.
D   Brown weasel skin amulet.
E   Polished slender stick.
F   Bag of cedar leaves.
G   Piece of fungus.

H   Braid of sweetgrass.
I
J
K   Packages of roots.
L
M

PLATE XXVII

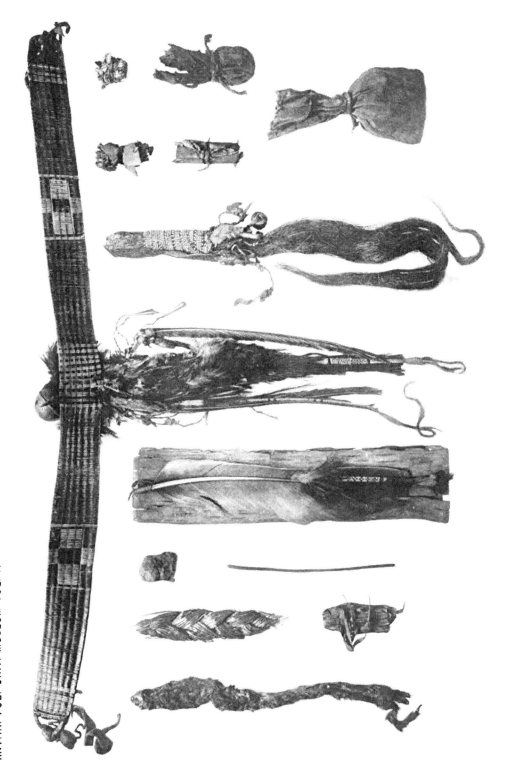

CONTENTS OF SAC AND FOX WAR BUNDLE

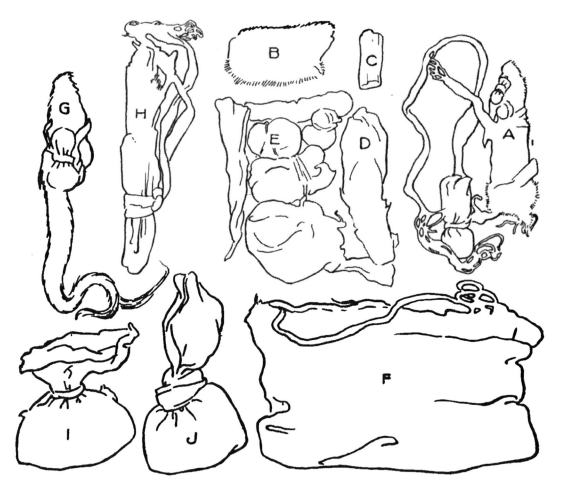

KEY TO PLATE XXVIII

A   Weasel skin amulet on woven neck band.
B   Piece beaver skin with fur.
C   Piece dried meat. (?)
D   Piece buffalo bladder.
E   Packages of cedar leaves and herbs.
F   Woven sack in which above were kept.
G   Buffalo tail amulet.
H   Squirrel skin package of magic red paint.
I
J   } Calico bags of cedar leaves.

PLATE XXVIII

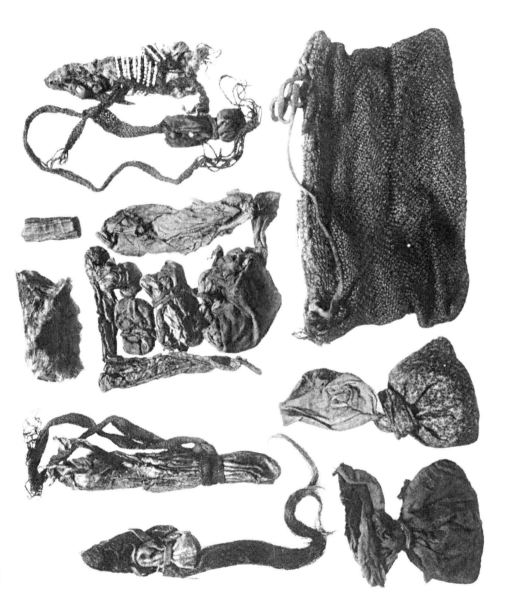

CONTENTS OF SAC AND FOX WAR BUNDLE

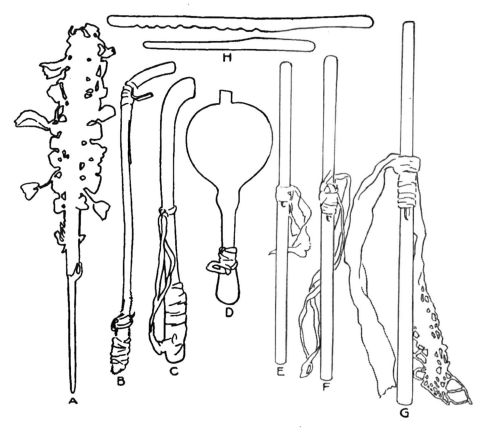

KEY TO PLATE XXIX

A Deer hoof rattle, from Bundle 2/6371.
B Drumstick, from Bundle 2/8452.
C Drumstick, from Bundle 2/8591.
D Gourd rattle, from Bundle 2/5311.
E War whistle, from Bundle 2/6376.
F War whistle, with buckskin neck band, from Bundle 2/8561.
G War whistle, with woven neck band, from Bundle 2/8593.
H Rattle sticks, used in Wolf Bundle ceremonies 2/7869.

PLATE XXIX

MUSICAL INSTRUMENTS FROM SAC AND FOX WAR BUNDLES

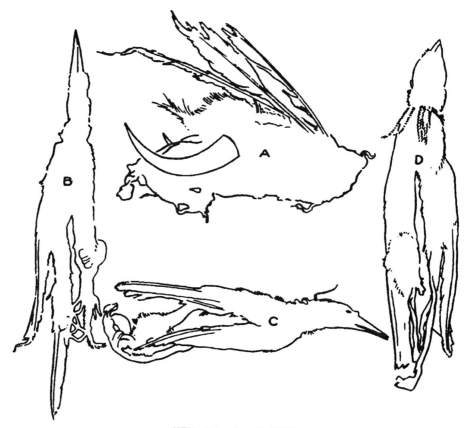

KEY TO PLATE XXX

A   Buffalo hide head band with horns, from Bundle 2/8452.

B ⎫
C ⎬ Split woodpecker skin head bands, from Bundles 2/5317, 2/8561.

D   Split hawk skin head band, from Bundle 2/8591.

· PLATE XXX

AMULETS FROM SAC AND FOX WAR BUNDLES.

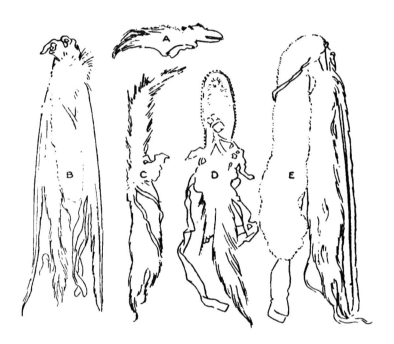

KEY TO PLATE XXXI

A   Part of deer hair head-dress, from Bundle 2/8738.

B   Amulet of swan's down, buffalo hair, feathers and ribbon, from Bundle 2/6376.

C   Amulet of buffalo hair, feathers and ribbon, from Bundle 2/8591.

D   Amulet of buffalo hair, feathers and ribbon, decorated with ribbon and beadwork, from Bundle 2/8591.

E   Amulet of swan's down, buffalo hair, feathers and ribbon, from Bundle 2/6371.

PLATE XXXI

AMULETS FROM SAC AND FOX WAR BUNDLES.

PLATE XXXII

Amulets from Sac and Fox War Bundles.
A   Beaver skin head band, from Bundle 2/8593.
B   Arm band, quill decoration, from Bundle 2/8591.

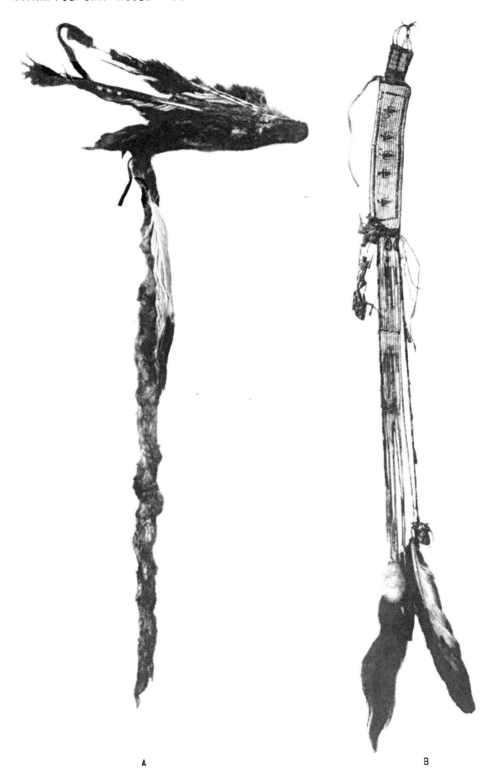

A   B

AMULETS FROM SAC AND FOX WAR BUNDLES

KEY TO PLATE XXXIII

A   Woven necklace, showing attachment of medicine packets and feathers, from Bundle 2/8738.

B   Necklace, showing medicine packets and deer hair fringe, from Bundle 2/5311.

C   Small bird skin wrapped in woven necklace, to which it was doubtless once attached, from Bundle 2/6506.

D   Woven necklace, showing medicine packets, from Bundle 2/6371.

E   Fawn skin cover for D.

PLATE XXXIII

AMULETS FROM SAC AND FOX WAR BUNDLES.

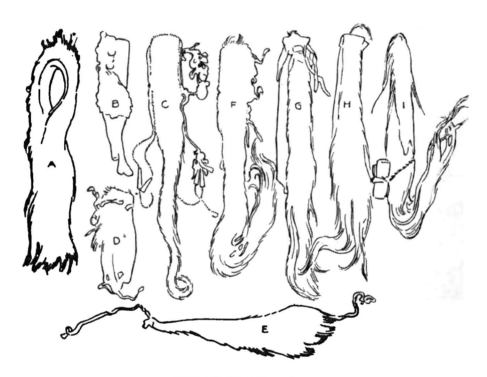

KEY TO PLATE XXXIV

A   Buffalo hide arm band, from Bundle 2/8591.
B   Buffalo tail arm band with medicine packets and quill decorations, from Bundle 2/8739.
C   Buffalo tail, possibly arm band, with medicine packet and quill decoration, from Bundle 2/6373.
D   Buffalo hide arm band with medicine packets, from Bundle 2/8591.
E   Buffalo hide arm band, from Bundle 2/6371.
F   Buffalo tail amulet, with medicine packets, from Bundle 2/8561.
G   Buffalo tail belt amulet, with medicine packet, from Bundle 2/8591.
H   Buffalo tail belt amulet, with medicine packet, from Bundle 2/8591.
I   White buffalo or steer tail belt amulet, with toggle for attachment, from Bundle 2/8534.

PLATE XXIV

AMULETS FROM SAC AND FOX WAR BUNDLES.

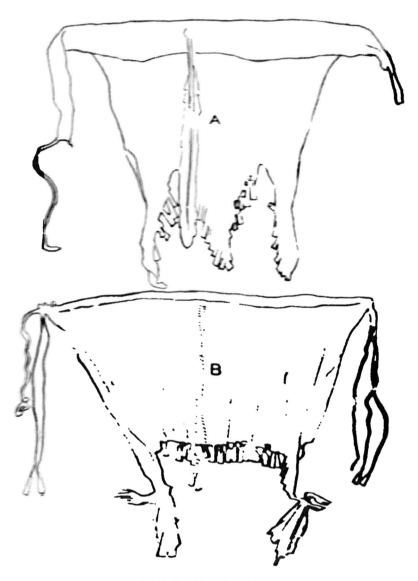

KEY TO PLATE XXXIV

A Apron showing chain work from Bundle 2 637a.
B Apron from Bundle 2 634b.

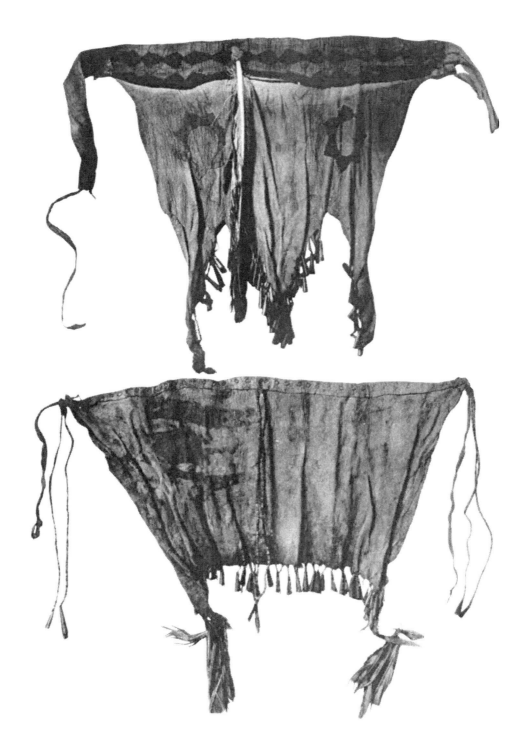

AMULETS FROM SAC AND FOX WAR BUNDLES

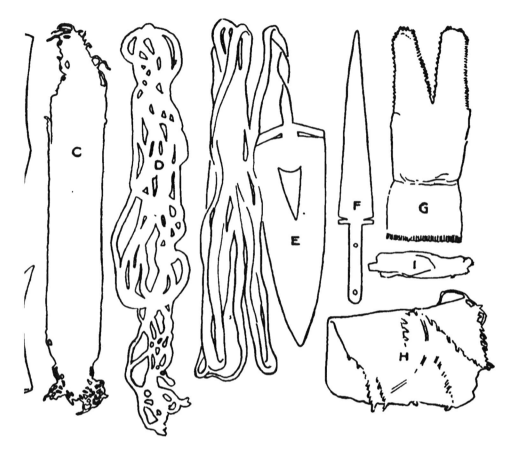

KEY TO PLATE XXXVI

A   Wooden charm in form of a deer's foot, from Bundle 2/8593.
B   Buffalo horn used as medicine cup, from Bundle 2/8591.
C   Woven bead garter, from Bundle 2/8738.
D   Captive leader of fibre, from Bundle 2/8591.
E   Captive leader of rawhide, end cut to resemble spear head, from Bundle 2/6506.
F   Spear head of iron, from Bundle 2/8738.
G
H } Quilled pouches, from Bundle 2/8452.
I   Fossil bone in wrapping, from Pouch H.

PLATE XXXVI

OBJECTS FROM SAC AND FOX WAR BUNDLES

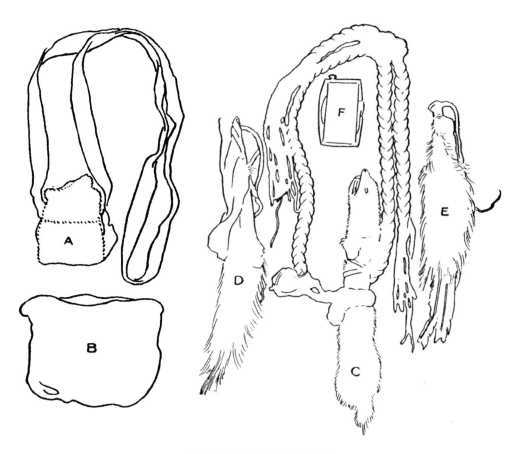

KEY TO PLATE XXXVII

A Witch medicine in beaded pouch, from Bundle 2/6378.
B Woven sack, cover for witch medicine.
C Weasel skin amulet, from General Bundle 2/5327.
D ⎫
E ⎭ Magic plumes.
F Snuff box, containing herbs.

PLATE XXXVII

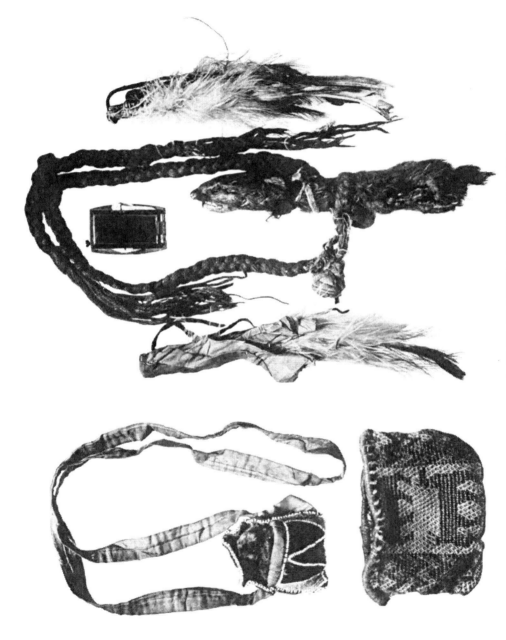

WITCH MEDICINE AND CONTENTS OF GENERAL BUNDLE, SAC AND FOX

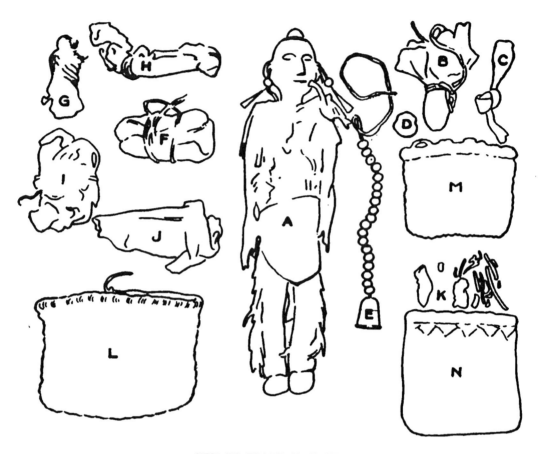

KEY TO PLATE XXXVIII

A   Fetish, of wood.

B
C
F
G   }   Packets containing medicine.
H
I
J

D   Ball of earth.

E   Amulet, consisting of thimble containing love medicine, attached to string of beads.

K   Bits of root and wampum bead, from Sack N.

L
M   }   Woven sacks, } in which medicine and amulet were kept.

N   Cloth sack, }

PLATE XXXVIII

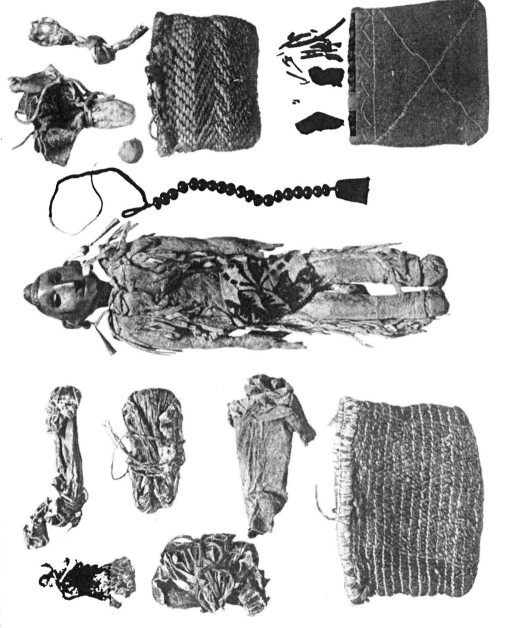

CONTENTS OF SAC AND FOX FETISH BUNDLE

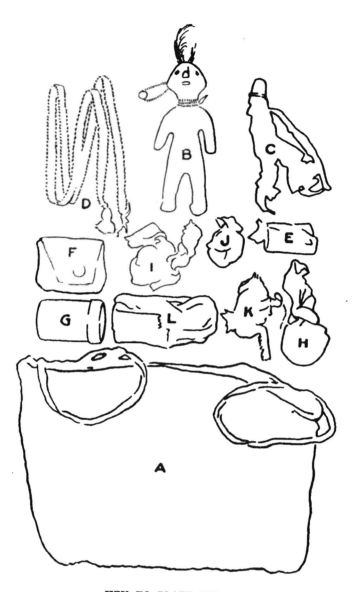

KEY TO PLATE XXXIX

A   Woven sack of basswood fibre.
B   Fetish of baked clay.
C   Thimble containing love medicine.
D   Strip of beadwork.
F   Leather purse, empty.
G   Can containing herb mixture.

E
H
I
J   Medicine packages.
K
L

CONTENTS OF FOX FETISH BUNDLE

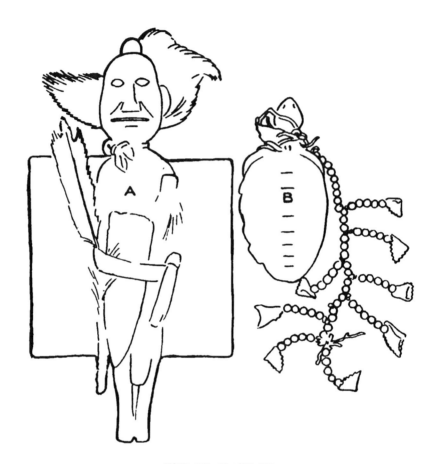

KEY TO PLATE XL

A   Wooden fetish, representing warrior, with stone knife, plume, whistle, blanket
    and deer hair pillow, from Bundle 2/8602.
B   Reproduction (?) of fetish, representing the turtle, from Bundle 2/8603.

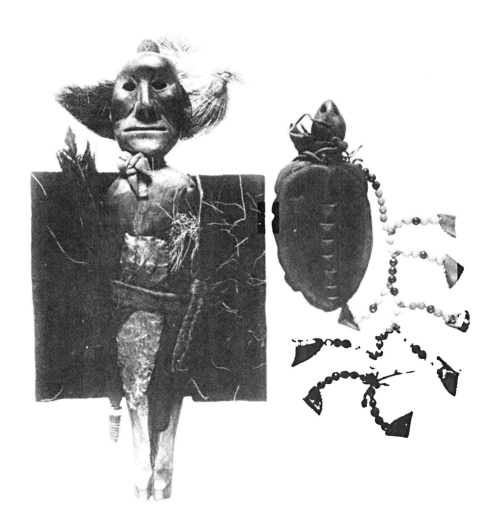

FOX FETISHES

UNIVERSITY OF PENNSYLVANIA
THE MUSEUM
ANTHROPOLOGICAL PUBLICATIONS
VOL. IV   NO. 1

THE TAHLTAN INDIANS

BY

G. T. EMMONS

ILLUSTRATED BY SPECIMENS IN THE
GEORGE G. HEYE COLLECTION

PHILADELPHIA
PUBLISHED BY THE UNIVERSITY MUSEUM
1911

UNIVERSITY OF PENNSYLVANIA
THE UNIVERSITY MUSEUM
ANTHROPOLOGICAL PUBLICATIONS
VOL. IV   NO. 2

SACRED BUNDLES OF THE SAC
AND FOX INDIANS

BY

M. R. HARRINGTON

ILLUSTRATED BY SPECIMENS IN THE
GEORGE G. HEYE COLLECTION

PHILADELPHIA
PUBLISHED BY THE UNIVERSITY MUSEUM
1914

DATE DUE

JUN '(1998			

LaVergne, TN USA
10 October 2010

200318LV00003B/43/P

9 781142 866518